The Gift of Holy Spirit
The Power To Be Like Christ

By
Mark H. Graeser
John A. Lynn
John W. Schoenheit

Fourth Edition
Revised by: John A. Lynn
© ℗ 2011 The Living Truth Fellowship

978-0-9848374-3-4

ISBN: 978-0-9848374-3-4
Fourth Edition
Revised by: John A. Lynn
© ℗ 2011 The Living Truth Fellowship

This book was originally written by Mark Graeser, John Schoenheit, and John Lynn while they all worked together in ministry. They are now working in separate ministries, and the one with which John Lynn is now affiliated is The Living Truth Fellowship, Ltd., by whom this book is now being re-published.

The few revisions and additions in this edition were authored by John A. Lynn, as assisted by Bob Maffit and Ken Schleimer, who worked tirelessly to prepare this edition for publication. The beautiful new cover design was done by Franco Bottley.

God bless you as you take this step in your journey of coming unto a knowledge of the truth.

To receive our monthly newsletter, *FRUIT OF D'VINE*, and to be put on our mailing list, contact us at:

The Living Truth Fellowship
7399 N. Shadeland Ave., Suite 252
Indianapolis IN 46250
Phone: (317) 721-4046
Email: admin@tltf.org
Website: www.tltf.org
YouTube Channel: www.youtube.com/justtruthit

Country of origin the United States of America.

Table of Contents

Acknowledgments

First and foremost we would like to acknowledge God, the ultimate Giver, and the One who through the centuries has given His wonderful gift of holy spirit to people so that they may work hand-in-hand with Him. We would also like to acknowledge the Lord Jesus Christ, who poured out the gift of holy spirit to the Christian Church on the Day of Pentecost and who continues to pour it out to every person when he is saved.

Many people have contributed to this book. Some of them have long passed away, such as E. W. Bullinger, who in 1905 wrote *The Giver and His Gifts*, and whose insights have been extremely helpful. Truth on a subject rarely, if ever, comes to only one person, and we are grateful to many men and women who have studied the subject of holy spirit, written about it, and tried to walk out on what they knew from Scripture. This book is a rewrite of our earlier book on the gift of holy spirit, and we continue to be grateful to those who helped us write that book; Jim Landmark, Pat Lynn, Ivan Maddox, Scott Pfeiffer, Greg Pharis, Wayne Harms, Joe Ramon, and Suzanne Snyder.

Dan Gallagher made a number of helpful suggestions, especially in the area of the manifestations of holy spirit. Karen Graeser added helpful information in regard to discerning of spirits. Tom and Susan Resner contributed valuable information about prophecy, and exposure to their powerful prophetic ministries, as well as the ministries of other prophets, showed us from a practical perspective that prophecy did indeed belong in the "power" category of the manifestations. Eddie DeBruhl had helpful insights about speaking in tongues. Steve Keil was very helpful in sorting through some of the more technical aspects of the Greek text, and made helpful suggestions on our translation from the Greek. James and Joshua Anderson had helpful suggestions in several areas. John VanDerAue spent hours proofreading the manuscript, as did Dave and Carol DeMars and Bob Maffit, who edited this book, checked every Scripture, built the Scripture, Topical, Hebrew and Greek indices, and more. Shawn Mercer also proofread the manuscript and made helpful suggestions, and along with Franco Bottley, did the cover design. Matthew Johnson worked hard on the layout of the book, and did the wonderful charts. Christians are both fellow-laborers with God and fellow-laborers with each other, and if this book is a blessing, it is because the family of God came together to make it so. Ken Schleimer is the man who got this book set up for electronic publication and is responsible for doing every chart, the layout, and formatting for this book. Franco Bottley did the new cover design for our 2011 edition.

Mark H. Graeser
John A. Lynn
John W. Schoenheit

Preface

God is love, and He has shown His love for Christians by giving us a most magnificent gift—the gift of His very nature, the gift of holy spirit. God has made this wonderful gift available to anyone who chooses to become a Christian. The gift of holy spirit is the very nature of God, and is permanently sealed inside each and every Christian (Eph. 1:13), so it is vital that each follower of Christ understand this powerful gift from God and how to utilize it in his life. Doing so will contribute significantly to the spiritual fulfillment of each Christian, and will facilitate the harmonious functioning of the Body of Christ as a whole.

Our intention in this book is to set forth the pertinent scriptural truths about the gift of holy spirit for your consideration. What you read may differ from what you hear about "the Holy Spirit" in most churches. Our goal is not to be contentious, but to present sound doctrine, supported by Scripture, so that Christians can better understand what God has done for them and how they can more effectively function in the Body of Christ.

When it comes to any spiritual matter, the written Word of God is our only rule of faith and practice. God works with each of us as individuals, so the individual spiritual experience God gives one Christian may not be the same as the experience of another. Therefore, if we focus on our experiences, there may be contradictions and confusion. We need to learn that when it comes to spiritual things, experience is no guarantee for truth. Rather, we must go to the written Word of God as our ultimate standard for truth. As Jesus once said in a prayer to God, "…your word is truth" (John 17:17b).

We do our best to document what we teach with "chapter and verse" because we believe the Bible, the Word of God, is **truth**. This is not a book about people's experiences, because, as we noted above, experiences are not a guarantee of truth. For example, God may speak audibly to one person, speaking slowly and in a deep voice. Does that mean that if another Christian heard the voice of God speaking quickly and in a high voice, his experience was counterfeit? Certainly not. However, when something is stated clearly in Scripture, we can be sure it is true for all people, which is why Jesus called the Word of God the "**truth**."

For many Christians, "spiritual experiences" and "sincerity" are given priority over the written Word of God as the criterion to determine doctrinal truth and the practical application of it. Too often, Christians use their experiences to validate the Word of God, rather than allowing the written Word to be the ultimate "judge" (Heb. 4:12-NRSV) of "...everything needed for life and godliness..." (2 Pet. 1:3-NRSV). This leaves them open to counterfeit spiritual experiences.

As children of God, Christians need to revere the Word of God just as Jesus Christ did. He expressed his basis for life with the words, "**It is written**." When we live our lives with the Word of God as our standard of truth, then we will have a wonderful relationship with our heavenly Father and the Lord Jesus and truly be able to serve others the Bread of Life. We will also have the tools to discern genuine, godly experiences from those that are not.

God's Word reaches out to people in a way that is primarily rational, because God gives **evidence** for what He wants us to believe. The conflict between the truths of Scripture (which may or may not have specific emotional appeal) and experiences (which are by nature exciting and impressive) has been going on for centuries. When Jesus sent out his disciples, they "...returned with joy..." because of what they had experienced, and said, "...Lord, even the demons submit to us..." (Luke 10:17). Jesus had to remind them, "...do not rejoice that the spirits submit to you, but rejoice that your names are written in heaven" (Luke 10:20). The same tension exists today. We all need to learn to rejoice at the powerful and elemental truths of God's Word as much as we do when we see or experience miracles and healings. The psalmist got to that point. He wrote, "I rejoice at thy word, as one that findeth great spoil [treasure]" (Ps. 119:162-KJV).

Certainly, genuine spiritual phenomena are to be expected in the life of a Christian, but we must be discerning in our examination of such phenomena. The Bible gives many examples of false prophets who deceived people by demonstrations of spiritual power. The magicians of Egypt turned sticks into snakes, but their power was not from the true God. Thank God that He gave us His Word so that we can know what He will and will not do. Only by examining one's experiences in light of the Word of God can we determine the power or force behind the experiences.

When it comes to spiritual things beyond the realm of man's five senses, the Word of God is the **only** credible witness. God, the Author of life, presents clear, straightforward answers to the most profound questions of the human heart. Thus we must look into God's Word, the literature of eternity, and let Him speak for Himself about the deep issues of life. The Bible is the standard of all literature, and God the Author of all authors. As literature, it contains a rich variety of linguistic thoughts, expressions and usages. Like any author, God has the right to use language as He deems appropriate to His purposes. That means the person who wants to learn about God from Scripture must become well versed in the medium through which God chose to communicate—words.

Satan's attack on God's Word, and on mankind's ability to understand and use language, began with his first recorded words: "Did God really say…?" (Gen. 3:1). His assault has never relented, and today if a person uses a "big" word, he is usually subject to mocking and ridicule by his peers. As a result, the average American cannot

> **God, the Author of life, presents clear, straightforward answers to the most profound questions of the human heart.**

define important parts of grammar such as a "participle," "adverb," or "predicate nominative," even though the Bible is full of them. No wonder there is so much disagreement among Christians as to what the words in a verse mean. The field of figures of speech, critical to biblical study, is almost totally lost to the average Bible reader. Yet E. W. Bullinger, an eminent British Bible scholar (1837–1913), identified the use of more than 200 figures of speech in the Bible. These figures greatly enrich its literary value and at the same time entrust its readers with great responsibility.

Those who endeavor to study, understand, and interpret the Bible must become very sensitive to the literary devices it employs, because its study is not merely for cultural amusement. Our very lives, both now and in the future, depend on an accurate understanding of God's words, which are the very "**words of life.**" It is our firm conviction that when properly translated and understood, the Bible will integrally fit together without contradictions. Like the pieces of a jigsaw puzzle depicting a stunningly beautiful scene, every single verse in the Word of God will (and must) fit into a unified picture. This is certainly true when it comes to verses about holy spirit.

We do not consider ourselves the fount of all spiritual wisdom, and we do not present this book as the last word on the subject. We do believe, however, that what we set forth in this book about the gift of holy spirit will deepen each reader's appreciation of the gift God has given us. Furthermore, it can better equip each Christian to be like Jesus Christ and do the work he did. We ask you to consider the biblical and logical validity of our thesis and decide its merit for yourself.

Introduction

The gift of holy spirit is one of the greatest gifts that God has ever given, and we will show from Scripture that each and every Christian has this precious gift sealed within himself. We will also show that because of the indwelling of holy spirit, each and every Christian can manifest the power of God. As we study the verses that, in the Greek text, contain the words *pneuma* (spirit) and *hagion* (holy), it will become apparent that these words are used to refer to God, who is both "holy" and "spirit," and therefore called "the Holy Spirit," and also to God's gift to mankind, which is both "holy" and "spirit," and therefore referred to as "holy spirit." Not distinguishing between God the Giver and the gift He gives has caused great error and confusion in Christianity. In this book we will attempt to clearly set forth that distinction.

As we understand what "the holy spirit" is and how we receive it, we can manifest the power of holy spirit in our lives and receive great blessings. After all, God, by way of the Lord Jesus, gave the gift of holy spirit to equip and enable each Christian to bless the Body of Christ and mankind in general. This gift gives each Christian real spiritual power that he can use day by day. As Jesus said, "But you will receive power when the Holy Spirit [holy spirit] comes on you…" (Acts 1:8a). The power that each Christian has is very real, and very helpful. Scripture declares that the power of holy spirit is "for the common good" (1 Cor. 12:7b). It is good for the individual, good for the Body of Christ, and even good for all mankind, because all those in your world are blessed when you walk in God's power.

We are aware that there are many Christians who do not manifest spiritual power. Some believe the power of holy spirit was available only in the first century, and is not for today. Others believe that the power is available, but is not for them. Others simply have not been taught how to use it or have not been convinced of the value of it. We trust that we can set forth the truth and logic of Scripture clearly enough so that anyone searching for truth will see that every Christian not only has holy spirit, but can also manifest the power of God. As with every spiritual matter,

1

our unwavering standard to distinguish truth from error is the written Word of God.

In setting forth the truth about the gift of holy spirit, we will clarify from Scripture key terms such as "baptized in holy spirit," "anointed," and "filled with" holy spirit. We believe that if Christians correctly understand and properly apply the truths conveyed by these terms, their walk with the Lord will be greatly enhanced. Furthermore, if each Christian knows and uses biblical terminology, it will help to generate more unity among Christians. The central thesis of this study is that **all Christians have been given the same power of God, holy spirit, and each has avenues to utilize that power.**

Scripture teaches that the Body of Christ is like the human body; no part is unimportant; each part has been placed specifically by God and the Lord Jesus; and each part is essential to the fluid working of the whole body. In the Body of Christ, which is the Church, we do not all have the same function, but we can each function with the same power of holy spirit. As we will see, God's Word states that a person is filled with holy spirit at the moment he is born again. It is empowering for each Christian to know he can manifest the power of the spirit, and the experience of walking daily with the Lord in one's own calling makes life meaningful and exciting.

We realize there is a lot of confusion about the gift of holy spirit among Christians today, and again we must emphasize that the written Word of God takes precedence over sincere Christian opinion. At stake is not only the integrity of God's Word, but also our practical application of it to the end of true Christian unity. We will see Scripture shows clearly that the way God becomes our Father is by birthing us, and in birth we receive the fullness of His divine nature, which, being both "holy" and "spirit," is referred to as "holy spirit." The Bible also teaches that at the moment one is born again, he receives all the spiritual power or ability he will ever receive from the Lord. Over time he may learn to manifest more of the power he has, but he was "filled" with holy spirit when he was born again, and he can never get more than "filled." We will also see there is a sign by which each Christian can know for sure he has received God's gift and is filled with His spirit, and that sign is speaking in tongues.

If you have been confused about holy spirit, it will bless you immensely to learn that when you confessed Jesus as Lord and believed God raised him from the dead (Rom. 10:9), you received a magnificent gift from the Lord Jesus—the gift of holy spirit, containing all you will ever need to manifest the love and power of God. When you were saved, you were once and for all born again, anointed, baptized with holy spirit, and forever filled (to capacity) with holy spirit, which is the divine nature of God.

The gift of holy spirit is every Christian's divine deposit. One of the dictionary definitions of the word "deposit" is "anything given as security or in partial payment." The divine deposit that God has already given to each Christian is only a token of what He will one day do for us. The word "deposit" is also defined as "anything laid away or entrusted to another for safekeeping." God has placed this gift in us and entrusted us to use it to His glory.

In examining God's divine deposit, we will see why being "born again" is a must for every human being who desires true life. Then we will look at what it means to be born again, and what one receives in his New Birth. We will examine the vital difference between the Giver (God, the Holy Spirit) and the gift of His divine nature (holy spirit). Next we will consider the subject of water in Scripture, and then set forth what God's Word says about each of the pertinent "liquid" terms used in Scripture.

After that, we will see that the one gift of holy spirit has a number of manifestations that are readily available to every Christian. In closing, we will set forth from Scripture our completeness in Christ, and upon that basis, exhort all of us to walk boldly in him. God's giving us the gift of holy spirit is similar to His giving a carpenter a toolbox full of precision tools—we are well positioned to do great things, but we must learn how to use what we have. We pray your heart will burn within you as the simplicity of God's Word (His heart to us) is set before you that you will rejoice in all you have been freely given, and you will walk your personal path of righteousness in the power of God's gift of holy spirit.

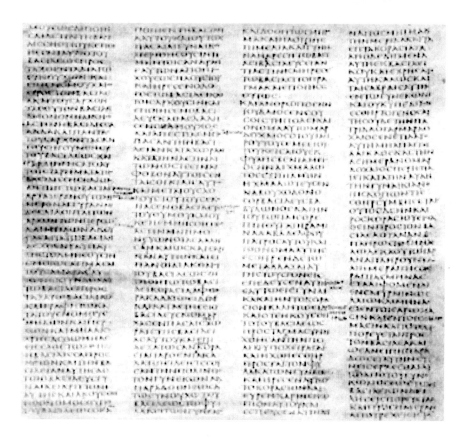

Greek uncial manuscript.
All the letters are upper case, there is no punctuation,
and there are no spaces between the words.
The early Greek texts of the Bible were written this way.

Chapter 1

It's Greek to Me
(Why we use both Holy Spirit and holy spirit)

Understanding the Greek Text

As we begin to study the subject of holy spirit, it is important to understand why we sometimes write "Holy Spirit," and sometimes "holy spirit." The student of Scripture needs to know that the Bible was originally written in "uncial" text, that is, in only capital letters with no spaces between the words.[1] This is true for all three biblical languages—Hebrew, Aramaic, and Greek. Had the Bible been written in English during Paul's lifetime, this is how John 3:16 and 17 (KJV) would look:

FORGODSOLOVEDTHEWORLDTHATHEGAVEHISONLY
BEGOTTENSONTHATWHOSOEVERBELIEVETHINHIM
SHOULDNOTPERISHBUTHAVEEVERLASTINGLIFEFOR
GODSENTNOTHISSONINTOTHEWORLDTOCONDEMN
THEWORLDBUTTHATTHEWORLDTHROUGHHIM
MIGHTBESAVED

Is that hard for you to read? It is for us. Thankfully, scholars have now separated the modern Greek and Hebrew texts into individual words and, of course, all English translations are in standard English, using both capital and lower case letters. For most words it makes no difference whether the letters are capital (upper case) or lower case. For example, what is the difference between "Dog" and "dog"? Nothing.

---

1. Uncial writing was a development of the lapidary capitals used for inscription in stone. The early manuscripts of the New Testament were written in uncial script. Beginning in the 800's, a style of writing called "miniscule" was used. The individual letters were all lower case, the font was smaller, and all the letters ran together, similar to our cursive writing today. Miniscule writing caught on quickly because it saved space and production costs. F. F. Bruce, *The Books and the Parchments*, (Flemming H. Revel Company, Westwood, New Jersey, 1963), p. 182; Bruce Metzger, *The Text of the New Testament: Its Transmission, Corruption, and Restoration* (Oxford University Press, New York, 1992), pp. 8–12.

However, there are some words that, if the first letter is capitalized (upper case), mean something completely different than if the first letter is lower case. A "bill" is something you pay, while "Bill" is a man's name. Other words that change meanings when capitalized are "Mark" and "mark," "Frank" and "frank," "Sue" and "sue," "Joy" and "joy," and the list goes on. Every Bible reader has been taught to pay attention to capital letters and what they mean. For example, "God" is the true God (Gen. 1:1), while "god" is a false god (Judg. 16:24). If a Bible student did not pay attention to capital letters and know what they indicated, the Bible would be a confusing book indeed.

Just as there is a huge difference between "God" and "god," so there is a huge difference between "Holy Spirit" and "holy spirit." "Holy Spirit" is a name or designation for God, and is most often used when He is exercising His power, while "holy spirit" refers to the gift of God.

"Spirit"—One Word, Many Meanings

In this section, we are going to introduce the Greek words for "spirit" and "holy." We do this because it is impossible to write the words "holy spirit" in English without making them either God (if the "H" and "S" are upper case) or God's gift (if the "h" and "s" are lower case). By using the Greek, we can write about holy spirit without assigning a specific meaning to the words. There is great value in learning these two Greek words, and it is easy to do.

The word "spirit" has many definitions in both English and Greek. In English we call God a "Spirit," that is, an invisible being. We also call both good and evil invisible beings "spirits." Also, we use "spirit" as a disposition of the mind, an attitude, as in the sentence, "She was in good spirits today." We also use "spirit" to refer to the general intention or real meaning of something, as in "the spirit of the law." We even call alcoholic beverages "spirits."

The Greek word for "spirit" is *pneuma*, and just as English has many definitions of "spirit," Greek has many definitions of *pneuma*. The Greek noun *pneuma* comes from the verb *pneo*, "to blow or breathe." Thus, to the ancient Greeks, *pneuma* was "breath," and it came to be associated with invisible things that exerted a force or power. A good Greek Lexicon will show that besides breath, *pneuma* also was the Greek word for wind.[2] Our English word "pneumatic" ("air powered") comes from the Greek word *pneuma*, and so does our word "pneumonia," a disease of the lungs.

Pneuma may be invisible, but it has power. Breathe on your hand. Can you feel it? Sure you can. You can feel the breath, but you cannot see it. *Pneuma* is used in the Greek language, and thus in the Bible, of an invisible force or substance, as when the Bible says, "God is spirit [*pneuma*]" (John 4:24a). Many things are called *pneuma* in the Greek New Testament.[3] A partial list includes:

- God (the "Spirit" in John 3:8b).
- The gift of God known as holy spirit (Acts 2:38).
- Angels, who are "ministering spirits" (Heb. 1:14).
- Demons (Matt. 8:16; Luke 9:39).
- "Breath" or "life." The girl's *pneuma*, (breath or life) returned when Jesus raised her from the dead (Luke 8:55a).
- "Wind." John 3:8a says, "The wind blows wherever it pleases...."
- "Attitude" or thoughts. "...The spirit is willing, but the body is weak" (Matt. 26:41b).

Holy Spirit or holy spirit—
The Context is the Key

Since *pneuma* can refer to so many different things, how do we know which of them is referred to in any specific verse? We know the same way we know in English—by reading the context. The context must be used to determine whether *pneuma* means "Spirit" or "spirit," and there are times when the translators do not agree about what the context is saying, which is why versions sometimes differ. For example, in Matthew 12:18, the KJV reads "spirit" but the NIV reads "Spirit." Matthew 22:43 is another verse

---

2. Just as the Greek word *pneuma* means "breath," "wind," "spirit," etc., the Hebrew word *ruach* is an almost exact linguistic parallel and means "breath," "wind," "spirit." As "spirit," it is used not only of the spirit of God, but also of angels, demonic spirits, attitudes of the mind, etc.

3. A more complete list with more examples can be found in Appendix B, "Usages of 'Spirit' in the New Testament."

where the KJV reads "spirit" and the NIV reads "Spirit." The difference is
due to the fact that the translators cannot tell from the Greek text whether
or not "spirit" should be capitalized, so they make a judgment call based
on their understanding of the context.

There are times in the Bible when the word "spirit" refers to God,
and thus should be capitalized. There are times when "spirit" refers to
an angel, a demon, the gift that is given by God, etc., and should not be
capitalized. For example:

> **John 3:6 (KJV)**
> That which is born of the flesh is flesh; and that which is
> born of the **Spirit** is **spirit**.

Translators realize from the context of this chapter that the one who
gives birth is the Spirit with a capital "S"—God, and that the thing that
is born is also the spirit, but should have a lower case "s." As we said, the
early Greek texts of John 3:6 had the word for "spirit" in all capital letters
both times, *PNEUMA*. Thus, whether the New Testament says "Spirit"
with a capital "S" (such as Matt. 4:1 or Luke 2:27), or "spirit" with a lower
case "s" (such as Matt. 26:41 or Luke 1:80), the Greek text reads *PNEUMA*.

Translators must pay very careful attention to the context to determine
whether "Spirit" or "spirit" is correct, and this is not always an easy task. John
Nelson Darby, who in the late 1800's translated his own version of the Bible,
wrote in the preface of his 1871 translation: "The use of a large or small 's'
is of extreme difficulty in the case of the word Spirit;…."[4] Armed with the
knowledge that we must be sensitive to the context to see what is meant
by *pneuma* (spirit), we are ready to discuss "Holy Spirit" and "holy spirit."

God, "the Holy Spirit"

God is holy (Isa. 6:3; John 17:11), and He is spirit (John 4:24), so it is only
logical that He would be referred to as "*the* Holy Spirit." It is not unusual

---

4. John Nelson Darby (DHB), Revised Preface to the Second Edition of the New
Testament, 1871 (The Holy Scriptures: A New Translation from the Original Languages,
Uit het Woord der Waarheid, Netherlands), p. xxiii.

that God would be called "the Holy Spirit,"[5] because He has many names and titles that describe His various attributes, and it is very appropriate that "holy" would be one of them. "Holiness is such an essential attribute of God that 'holy' becomes a descriptive name."[6] In fact, holiness is such a fundamental attribute of God, and there are so many names associated with His character, that it would be strange if "holy" were left off the list.

Hebrew words translated "God," "Lord," "LORD" or "Almighty," include: Yahweh,[7] *Elohim, El, Elyon, Adonai,* and *Shaddai.* The attributes of God that are used as designations for Him include:

- Almighty (2 Cor. 6:18; Rev. 1:8)[8]
- Ancient of Days (Dan. 7:9, 13, 22)
- The Blessed [One]" (Mark 14:61)[9]
- Father (Ps. 68:5; Eph. 1:2)
- Jealous (Exod. 34:14)
- Judge (Judg. 11:27)
- The King (Ps. 5:2, 47:6; 1 Tim. 1:17)
- King of kings (1 Tim. 6:15)
- Lord (Matt. 1:20, 22)[10]
- LORD of hosts (1 Sam. 1:11-KJV, 17:45-KJV)
- Lord of lords (1 Tim. 6:15)

---

5. See Appendix D, "Reasons 'Holy Spirit' is one of the names of God or the Gift of God."

6. Geoffrey Bromiley, editor, *The International Standard Bible Encyclopedia* (William B. Eerdmans Publishing Company, Grand Rapids, 1982), Vol. 2, p. 508.

7. Yahweh is the personal name of God, and as such we do not put it in *italics*. The name "Jehovah" was an early and still accepted way to represent this name of God, but Yahweh more accurately represents the Hebrew text. Most versions of the Bible translate Yahweh as "LORD" following the Jewish custom that the name of God is not to be pronounced. However, we believe that Yahweh should be spoken. For much more on this subject, see our book, *One God & One Lord: Reconsidering the Cornerstone of the Christian Faith* by Mark Graeser, John A. Lynn, & John Schoenheit (The Living Truth Fellowship, Indianapolis, IN, 2011), Appendix L. Also, Joseph B. Rotherham, Rotherham's Emphasized Bible (RHM) (Kregel Publications, Grand Rapids, MI, reprinted 1994), pp. 22–29.

8. This is not the same "Almighty" as the Hebrew word *Shaddai*, which is a term referring to strength. The Greek word here is *pantokrator*, which means "ruler of everything."

9. Just as some of the names and titles of God were used for pagan gods or human rulers, some are also used of Jesus, who is called "King of kings," etc. For more on the names of God and Jesus, see our book, *op. cit., One God & One Lord*, look at Chapter 6, "The Name of Jesus Christ," Chapter 12, and Appendix E.

10. Thus God is called "Lord" in the Old Testament in Hebrew, and also called "Lord" in the New Testament in Greek.

- The Mighty (Gen. 49:24; Ps. 132:2; Isa. 1:24)[11]
- The Most High (Luke 1:32, 35, 76)
- The Name (Lev. 24:11)
- Potentate (1 Tim. 6:15-KJV)[12]
- The Righteous (Prov. 21:12; Isa. 24:16)[13]
- The Rock (Deut. 32:18; Isa. 30:29)
- Shepherd (Gen. 49:24; Ps. 80:1)[14]

God was also known as "the Holy," which usually gets translated as "the Holy One."[15]

2 Kings 19:22 (KJV)
Whom hast thou reproached and blasphemed? and against whom hast thou exalted *thy* voice, and lifted up thine eyes on high? *even* against the Holy *One* of Israel."

Note that God is called "the Holy *One*" and that the word "one" is in *italics*. When the translators of the King James Version added a word to the Bible for the sake of clarity, they often put it in *italics* to let the reader know that it was not in the original text.[16] Most of the time, the translators of the King James Version did not put the above word "one" in *italics*,

---

11. Most versions read "the Mighty One," but the "One" is not in the Hebrew text.

12. The Greek is literally, "powerful one," and it was used in Greek literature of rulers among the gods (such as Zeus) and rulers among men.

13. Many versions read "the Righteous One" but the "One" is not in the Hebrew text. This has caused a debate among scholars about whether or not the verse is actually referring to God or to righteous men, and the versions differ. The context, however, favors the verse referring to God, and reading similarly to the NIV, NRSV, or ESV.

14. Many of these names are used of Jesus as well, which has caused some people to assume that Jesus is therefore God. However, some are used of other people besides Jesus as well. These cases are treated individually in our book, *op. cit., One God & One Lord*, throughout Appendix A.

15. In the New Testament, Jesus Christ is also known as the "Holy One" (Mark 1:24; Luke 4:34; Acts 3:14; 1 John 2:20). Furthermore, all those who believe in Christ are also called "holy ones," which has been translated as "saints" in many versions of the Bible (Rom. 1:7; 2 Cor. 1:1; Eph. 1:1).

16. The fact that the King James Version, American Standard Version, and New American Standard Version put many added words in *italics* is helpful to the English reader, because he can see what was in the original text and what was not. We quoted 2 Kings 19:22 from the KJV because it had the word "one" in *italics*, showing the English reader that it was not in the Hebrew text.

even though it is not in the Hebrew text. Some other references in the Old Testament where God is called "the Holy" are Job 6:10; Psalms 71:22, 78:41, 89:18 and Isaiah 1:4. God continued to be known as "Holy" in the New Testament (Luke 1:49; John 17:11). Also, God is called "...the Holy One of Jacob..." in Isaiah 29:23, and "your Holy" in Isaiah 43:15, which is usually translated "your Holy One." He has many names and titles, so it is easy to see why God, who is holy and who is spirit, would be known as "the Holy Spirit."

We have already seen that the Greek word for "spirit" is *pneuma*. The Greek word for "holy" is *hagios* (we use *hagion* in this book because it is the neuter form of the word and needs to agree with the neuter noun *pneuma*). When the words *pneuma hagion* refer to God, translating them as "the Holy Spirit" is correct, because we capitalize proper nouns and personal titles.[17] When "the Holy Spirit" is used as a designation for God, it emphasizes His power at work. That is why, though the Bible often calls God the father of Jesus Christ (e.g., Rom. 15:6), in the Four Gospels it is not "God" who impregnates Mary, but rather His power in operation, "the Holy Spirit."

> **Matthew 1:18**
> This is how the birth of Jesus Christ came about: His mother Mary was pledged to be married to Joseph, but before they came together, she was found to be with child through **the Holy Spirit**.

> **Luke 1:35**
> The angel answered, "**The Holy Spirit** will come upon you, and the power of the Most High will overshadow you. So the holy one to be born will be called the Son of God.

Luke 1:35 is very helpful in showing that "the Holy Spirit" (capital "H," capital "S") is a name used for God when His power is in operation. In a very Hebraic way, this verse equates the Holy Spirit with "...the power of the

---

17. *Pneuma hagion* is actually, "SPIRIT HOLY," which is the usual word order in the Greek text. Greek usually places the adjective after the noun, as some other languages do also. Therefore, when it is translated into English it should read, as it does in every English version, "HOLY SPIRIT."

Most High...." The angel was speaking to Mary, a young Hebrew woman, in terms she could understand. It was common in the Hebrew language to say something and then repeat it in different words so the meaning would be clear. This occurs throughout the Hebrew Old Testament.[18] In this case, the Holy Spirit is shown to be the "power" of God. Mary understood that even though the angel had said "the Holy Spirit" would overshadow her, she was pregnant by God, and so she announced to her cousin Elizabeth: "...my spirit rejoices in God my Savior, for he has been mindful of the humble state of his servant...for the Mighty One has done great things for me..." (Luke 1:47–49).[19]

What we have seen in this chapter is the foundation for understanding the subject of holy spirit in the Bible. It is imperative the English reader realize any time he reads "Spirit" or "spirit" in the Bible, whether the "S" is upper or lower case, is due to the translators' judgment based on his theology and understanding of the context. We know that *pneuma* may refer to God, or to other spiritual realities such as angels, demons, the attitude of the mind, or God's gift of holy spirit. We have also seen "the Holy Spirit" is another designation for God, just as "the Most High" or "the Almighty" are designations for Him.

---

18. Saying something two different ways for clarity was common in the Bible. This can be seen in the speech of Balaam the prophet (Num. 23:8–10), in God's talking with Job (Job 39:2–7), in Psalms (Ps. 2:2–9), and in many other places in the Old Testament (Eccles. 8:1; Isa. 1:23 and 24; Jer. 1:5; Lam. 1:1; etc.)

19. We, the authors, do not believe "the Holy Spirit" is a separate entity from God. We do not believe in the "Trinity," at least as it is defined by orthodox theologians, that the Father is God, the Son is God, the Holy Spirit is God, and together they make one God. Neither do we believe, as "Oneness" theologians do, that there is one divine person who is expressed in three modes. We believe there is God the Father, Jesus Christ His Son, and holy spirit. We believe "the Holy Spirit" is a name of God the Father, particularly referring to His power in action. It concerns us that some Christians would, because of our disagreement concerning the doctrine of the Trinity, discard everything we write in this book. We would ask them to prayerfully consider reading what we have written. E. W. Bullinger was an orthodox Trinitarian, and a linguist, and he saw clearly the difference between Holy Spirit and holy spirit, and presented his conclusions in his book, *The Giver and His Gifts* (Eyre & Spottiswoode, London, 1905). Bullinger's work was reprinted by Kregel, and is now being printed with a new title, *Word Studies on the Holy Spirit* (Kregel Publications, Grand Rapids, MI, 1979). For an in-depth study of our perspective on who Jesus Christ is and the "Trinity," see our book, *op. cit., One God & One Lord.*

Chapter 2

The Giver and The Gift

God is the ultimate Giver. From the time He created man in His own image (Gen. 1:27) until this very day, God has been giving gifts to mankind. James 1:17 tells us: "Every good and perfect gift is from above, coming down from the Father…." Ephesians 1:3 says God has blessed us with "every spiritual blessing" in Christ. We have already seen that because God is holy and God is spirit, He is referred to as "the Holy Spirit." However, we must be aware that there is another use of holy spirit that does not refer to God, but to the gift of God. God loves us so much that when we choose to make Jesus Christ our Lord, we are born again, and receive God's very nature as a gift. The nature of God is, like God, both holy and spirit, and so it is referred to as "holy spirit."

It is important to capitalize "Holy Spirit" when it refers to God, and it is just as important to use lower case letters ("holy spirit") when referring to the gift God has given to those who are saved. God the Giver, who is "the Holy Spirit," gives His gift, holy spirit, to those who believe in the Lord Jesus Christ. This is a tremendous truth, and shows how much our heavenly Father loves us. Through the years God has given many gifts to mankind, but what could be a greater gift than the very nature of God Himself? It behooves us as God's children to learn as much as we can about this wonderful gift of holy spirit.

Three things have contributed greatly to people's misunderstanding and ignorance concerning God's gift of holy spirit. First, the translators capitalize the "H" and "S" and translate *pneuma hagion* as "Holy Spirit" when there is no reason in the Greek text to do so, and even when the context indicates the gift of God, holy spirit, is the subject being discussed. Second, the translators, not being aware *pneuma hagion* can refer to the gift of God, added the definite article "the," making the Bible read "the Holy Spirit" when there is no word "the" in the Greek text. When the article "the" is absent in the text, it is usually an indication the text is referring to the gift of holy spirit, and not "the Holy Spirit." Third the translators translated pronouns associated with *pneuma hagion* as masculine, "he" instead of "it," a subject we cover in Chapter 4.

The reason the translators have been so insensitive to the subject of the gift of holy spirit is that most have believed the doctrine of the Trinity, which says "the Holy Spirit" is the "Third Person" in the Trinity, and for the most part fails to recognize that *pneuma hagion* can refer to the gift of God. It is due to the doctrine of the Trinity that translators capitalize the "H" and "S" when the context is clearly referring to the gift God gives, add a "the" when none is in the Greek text, and translate the pronouns associated with *pneuma hagion* as masculine, even when the context is clearly referring to the gift of God and neuter pronouns are called for. However, there have been Trinitarian scholars who have recognized God's gift of holy spirit.

E. W. Bullinger (1837–1913) was a linguist, author (of more than a dozen major books and numerous tracts and pamphlets, as well as The Companion Bible), editor (of the Portuguese Reference Bible for the Trinitarian Bible Society), and musician. Concerning the fact English Bibles almost always translate *pneuma hagion* as "the Holy Spirit," he wrote:

> …the great mistake has been made of concluding, without sufficient thought or care, that the word *pneuma* must nearly always refer to Him [the Holy Spirit], wherever it may be used.
>
> This mistake is so general that, even where there is no article in the Greek, the definite article ["the"] is often introduced and imported into the English; and where there is nothing to indicate capital letter is the original, they have been used without any Textual authority in the English and other translations.
>
> This practice has been the fruitful source of many very popular errors. The English reader has been helpless in this matter. He sees the definite article, and the capital letters in the English, and naturally concludes that "the Holy Spirit" is meant. He does not know that he is reading an interpretation, or comment, instead of what ought to be a simple translation.[1]

Bullinger is quite correct. In many places where *pneuma hagion* refers to the gift of God, translating it as "the Holy Spirit" instead of simply "holy

---

1. Bullinger, *op. cit., Word Studies on the Holy Spirit*, p. 15.

spirit" misleads the English reader. We need to recognize *pneuma hagion* can refer to the gift of God, and when it appears in the Bible ask ourselves if it refers to God or His gift. When *pneuma hagion* appears in the Greek text without the article "the" (about 50 times in the New Testament) it usually refers to the gift of God.[2] However, when *pneuma hagion* has the definite article "the," it can be referring to either the Giver or the gift. When the definite article "the" is used with the gift, as in Acts 2:38, Scripture is simply making the point that holy spirit is "the" gift, i.e., the one being referred to in the context or in the scope of Scripture. Thus, in the case of Acts 2:38, because Peter was referring to the gift people would receive and what the Apostles had just received, the gift of holy spirit was "the" gift that had been poured out that day.

> *Pneuma hagion* **can refer to the gift of God, and when it appears in the Bible we need to ask ourselves if it refers to God or His gift.**

Many verses of Scripture reveal holy spirit is a gift given by God to man. The Greek word translated "gift" in Acts 2:38 (and many other verses that refer to holy spirit) is *dorea,* which is defined in *Vine's Expository Dictionary of the New Testament* as "'a free gift,' stressing its gratuitous character."[3]

Acts 2:38
Peter replied, "Repent and be baptized, every one of you, in the name of Jesus Christ for the forgiveness of your sins. And you will receive the gift [*dorea*] of the Holy Spirit ["holy spirit"].[4]

---

2. Bullinger makes the following observation: "*Pneuma hagion* (without Articles) is never used of the Giver (the Holy Spirit), but only and always of His gift" (E. W. Bullinger, The Companion Bible, (Zondervan Bible Publishers, Grand Rapids, MI, reprinted 1974), Appendix 101, p. 147). We feel Bullinger's statement is too strong, because we have seen some places where *pneuma hagion* does not have the article and yet refers to the Giver, such as Matthew 1:18 and 20. However, Bullinger is generally correct, and if there is no article the gift of holy spirit is usually being referred to.

3. W. E. Vine, *The Expanded Vine's Expository Dictionary of New Testament Words,* (Bethany House Publishers, Minneapolis MN, 1984), "gift," pp. 476 and 477.

4. The words *pneuma hagion* are clearly referring to God's gift, which is holy spirit. Because most translators are not aware of this, their versions read, the "Holy Spirit." When we encounter a verse that reads "Holy Spirit" when it should read "holy spirit," we

Acts 2:38 is a verse from Peter's sermon on the Day of Pentecost, the day that holy spirit was first poured out in New Birth, and thus the day the Christian Church started.[5] Thousands upon thousands of Jews had gathered at the Temple in Jerusalem to celebrate the Old Testament feast of Pentecost, and Peter made an impassioned appeal to them, saying that if they repented and made Christ their Lord, they would receive the gift of holy spirit.

Peter's sermon was effective, and about 3,000 people were saved that day (Acts 2:41). What should not be lost on us, however, is the distinct difference Peter made between God, the Giver, and holy spirit, the gift. Peter made the point that God had promised He would "pour out my Spirit [spirit] on all people" (Acts 2:17). It is God who made the promise, and who, through His Son Jesus, pours out on people not Himself, but His nature, holy spirit. God is the Giver; holy spirit is His gift to mankind. The context, specifically Acts 2:4, makes it clear that *pneuma hagion* in verse 38 refers to the gift of God.

Besides using "holy spirit" instead of "Holy Spirit," there is another very important thing we need to be aware of in Acts 2:4; something easily seen in the Greek text but ignored by almost all translators. As we pointed out earlier, when *pneuma hagion* refers to the **gift** from God, usually there is no article "the" in the Greek text. That is the case in Acts 2:4a, which should be translated as "And they were all filled with holy spirit,…," instead of, "And they were all filled with **the** holy spirit,…."[6]

---

will add [holy spirit] to indicate that God's gift of holy spirit is being referred to. When the translators add the word "the," such that their translation reads "the Holy Spirit," we will add [No "the." Read "holy spirit"].

5. We cover more about the New Birth and how one becomes a Christian in Appendix A, "The Administration of the Sacred Secret."

6. Thankfully, Bible study tools are readily available and generally quite easy to use today, so that even a non-Greek reader can see this for himself. There are many Greek Interlinear Bibles available. An interlinear has the Greek text with the English word right above (or sometimes below) the corresponding Greek word. If you want to see this point for yourself, go to a Christian bookstore and open a Greek Interlinear to Acts 2:4 (then purchase it if you do not own one, as it is a wonderful tool for Bible Study). If you do look in a good interlinear, it will say that they were "filled of spirit holy." The Greeks say "filled of" (using the genitive case), while we English speakers say "filled with."

Acts 2:4a (Author's translation)
And they were all filled with holy spirit…

It would be much easier to see that Acts 2:4a refers to the gift of God had the translators followed the Greek text and not added the definite article "the" to the English Bible. The Apostles were not filled with God, they were filled with the gift of God, holy spirit. Another verse referring to holy spirit as a free gift, *dorea*, occurs in Acts 10.

Acts 10:45
The circumcised believers who had come with Peter were astonished that the **gift** [*dorea*] of the Holy Spirit [No "the." Read "holy spirit"] had been poured out even on the Gentiles.

These verses make it clear that holy spirit is a gift from God. Thus, as we said, God who is holy and spirit, gives "holy spirit," His very nature, to believers. This is why Scripture says Christians are "partakers of the divine nature."

2 Peter 1:4 (KJV)
Whereby are given unto us exceeding great and precious promises: that by these ye might be **partakers of the divine nature**, having escaped the corruption that is in the world through lust.

The phrase, "partakers of the divine nature" is a good translation, and occurs in many versions, including the ASV, ESV, NASB, and RSV. The rendering "participants of" or "participate in" as per the NRSV or NIV, is not as good. We do not "participate" in the divine nature born inside us any more than we participate in our fleshly nature. It is a part of us.

Putting together the above three verses, we learn that believers are filled with the gift of God, holy spirit, which is the nature of God. In his teaching on Pentecost, Peter made it clear that God raised Jesus from the dead and then gave him the gift of holy spirit that had been promised in the Old Testament, after which Jesus did the actual pouring out of the spirit on the people (Acts 2:32 and 33).

Jesus had taught that God would give holy spirit to those who ask Him.

Luke 11:13

If you then, though you are evil, know how to give good gifts to your children, how much more will your Father in heaven give the Holy Spirit [No "the." Read, "holy spirit"] to those who ask him!"[7]

This verse, like Acts 2:38, makes it clear that holy spirit is something given by God, our heavenly Father. Although almost all English versions are like the NIV above and read, "the Holy Spirit," the Greek does not have the definite article "the." The verse should read, "...how much more will your Father in heaven give holy spirit to those who ask him!" How simple, and how beautiful. Sadly, many people today are in the same position as the disciples in Ephesus when Paul first came to their city. They do not know God's gift of holy spirit is even available.

Acts 19:1 and 2

(1) While Apollos was at Corinth, Paul took the road through the interior and arrived at Ephesus. There he found some disciples

(2) and asked them, "Did you receive[8] the Holy Spirit [No "the." Read, "holy spirit"] when you believed?" They answered, "No, we have not even heard that there is a[9] Holy Spirit [holy spirit]."

---

7. The Greek word for "gifts" in this verse is *doma*, which is the Greek word for "gift" that places more emphasis on the concrete character of the gift than on its beneficent nature. Vine, *op. cit., Expository Dictionary*, "gift," p. 477. Jesus was not referring to the gift in the Administration of the Sacred Secret (see Appendix A) but as it will be available in his future kingdom.

8. The Greek word "receive" is important, and points to the manifesting of holy spirit. This will be covered later in Chapter 6 when we explain Acts 8:14–17.

9. The New International Version and other versions have the phrase "a Holy Spirit." Someone looking at a Greek Interlinear or a Greek text may wonder why there is no "a" in the Greek. The answer is that the Greek language has no indefinite article, which is "a." In Greek, when there is a noun, such as "horse," it is assumed that it is "a" horse. If it is "the" horse, then a "the" will be in the Greek text.

How could that have been the case? Well, Acts 19 informs us that the one who had discipled these people in Ephesus taught only John's water baptism, so they did not know about the gift of holy spirit they received when they were saved.

Other verses than these refer to the gift of holy spirit. For example:

> **Acts 10:45**
> The circumcised believers who had come with Peter were astonished that the **gift** of the Holy Spirit [holy spirit] had been poured out even on the Gentiles.

> **1 Thessalonians 4:8**
> Therefore, he who rejects this instruction does not reject man but God, who gives you his Holy Spirit ["holy spirit"].

The above verse in 1 Thessalonians is especially helpful, because in it we have both God, the Giver, and the gift of holy spirit, which is specifically stated to be something given by God.[10]

In Acts 8 there is a record of a man named Simon offering money for the power to give the gift of holy spirit, and being rebuffed by Peter.

> **Acts 8:15–20 (RSV)[11]**
> (15) who came down and prayed for them that they might receive the Holy Spirit [No "the." Read, "holy spirit"];
> (16) for it had not yet fallen on any of them, but they had only been baptized in the name of the Lord Jesus.
> (17) Then they laid their hands on them and they received the Holy Spirit [No "the." Read, "holy spirit"].

---

10. This is also a good verse to show that translating *pneuma hagion* as "Holy Spirit," as most versions do, cannot be right. If the Holy Spirit is a person of the Trinity distinct from the Father, we would expect the verse to read that the "Father" sent the Holy Spirit, not that "God" gives "His" Holy Spirit, since in Trinitarian doctrine the Holy Spirit is "God," and thus certainly does not belong to God. However, if the verse is referring to holy spirit, the gift of God, then it makes perfect sense that God gives it and it is called "His" holy spirit.

11. We use the RSV here because it properly refers to the spirit as an "it" in verse 16. The subject of the pronouns associated with holy spirit is covered in Chapter 4.

(18) Now when Simon saw that the Spirit [spirit] was given through the laying on of the apostles' hands, he offered them money,

(19) saying, "Give me also this power, that any one on whom I lay my hands may receive the Holy Spirit [No "the." Read, "holy spirit"]."

(20) But Peter said to him, "Your silver perish with you, because you thought you could obtain the gift of God with money!

These wonderful verses teach us a lot about the gift of holy spirit. First, three times the gift of God is called "holy spirit," without the article "the." Also, Peter clearly calls holy spirit "the gift of God" (verse 20), which is correct. God is "the Holy Spirit," but God's gift to mankind is "holy spirit," and what a gift it is—His very nature given to Christians!

Since it is the context that ultimately determines whether *pneuma hagion* refers to "the Holy Spirit" (God) or "holy spirit" (the gift), it is a good rule of thumb to remember that whenever *pneuma hagion* is referred to as "given," "filling," "falling upon" or as the element of baptism, it is the **gift.** In contrast, if the *pneuma hagion* is referred to as if it were a person, it is referring to **the Giver**, God.

For example, Acts 1:5 records Jesus telling the Apostles they will "... be baptized in holy spirit..." (Author's translation). The Apostles were about to be baptized, fully immersed, in God's gift of holy spirit. Although almost all translations read "the Holy Spirit," there is no article "the" in the Greek text, and there is no reason in the context to capitalize *pneuma hagion*. The Apostles were not baptized in God, but in His gift.

However, Acts 5:3a properly capitalizes Holy Spirit.

Acts 5:3a
Then Peter said, "Ananias, how is it that Satan has so filled your heart that you have lied to the Holy Spirit....

The article "the" is in the Greek text, because Ananias did not lie to the gift of God, but to God. Here is another example:

Acts 28:25
They disagreed among themselves and began to leave after Paul had made this final statement: "The Holy Spirit spoke the truth to your forefathers when he said through Isaiah the prophet:

Here, the article "the" is in the Greek text, and "Holy Spirit" is properly capitalized, because it was God who spoke through Isaiah the prophet.

We have now seen that the Greek words *pneuma hagion* can refer to either God, the Giver, who is the "Holy Spirit," or to the gift of God's nature, which is also holy and spirit, but should be referred to as "holy spirit." We are now in a much better position to understand the great thing God did for us in giving us His very nature and thereby filling us with His power.

Chapter 3

Power From On High

No one knows exactly what "holy spirit" is, because it is intangible, but we do know what it does and why God gave it. When a person has the gift of holy spirit upon him, as in the Old Testament, or sealed in him, as in the Church Age, he is equipped with spiritual power.[1] Jesus made it clear when one has the gift of holy spirit, he has the power of God. He was talking with his disciples just before his ascension, and he told them they would receive power when holy spirit came on them.

> **Acts 1:8a**
> But you will receive **power** when the Holy Spirit [No "the." Read, "holy spirit"] comes on you;…

This verse should catch our attention immediately. Every serious Christian wants spiritual power, and according to this verse, we get it when we receive the gift of holy spirit. This was not the only time Jesus told his disciples they would receive power when they received holy spirit. Between his resurrection and his ascension, Jesus spent forty days instructing them, and much of what he said to them was regarding the gift of holy spirit he was going to give to them soon after his ascension. As recorded in the gospel of Luke, he gave them some very specific instructions:

> **Luke 24:49**
> I am going to send you what my Father has promised; but stay in the city until you have been **clothed with power from on high**."

God had promised something, and that something was power from on high. Later on during those forty days, Jesus referred back to his above statement about the impending blessing coming upon his disciples. The

---

1. The way God gives the gift of holy spirit to Christians differs from the way He gave it before the Church Age, which started on the Day of Pentecost in Acts 2. We will cover this in Chapter 6, "The Gift of Holy Spirit Today."

following verses from the book of Acts shed more light on the promise of the Father: power from on high.

> **Acts 1:4**
> On one occasion, while he was eating with them, he gave them this command: "Do not leave Jerusalem, but wait for **the gift my Father promised**, which you have heard me speak about.

When Jesus had spoken of "...the gift my Father promised..." a few days before, as recorded in Luke 24, he had told them the gift was power from on high. Jesus continued teaching his disciples, and clarified what the promised gift was, and what he was referring to when he spoke of power from on high. As we are about to read, it is receiving holy spirit.

> **Acts 1:5**
> For John baptized with water, but in a few days you will be **baptized with the Holy Spirit** [No "the." Read, "holy spirit"].

The context, and the lack of the article "the" in Acts 1:5, make it clear that *pneuma hagion* refers to the gift of God, holy spirit. Thus, Acts 1:4 and 5 reveal that the gift promised by the Father is to be baptized (fully immersed) in holy spirit. Putting together the verses in Luke and Acts gives a very clear picture. In Luke, the promise of the Father was power from on high. In Acts, the gift promised by the Father was to be baptized in holy spirit. Thus, when a person receives holy spirit, he receives power from on high, the power of God. This is what Jesus said in Acts 1:8a, when he said, "But you will receive power, when the holy spirit has come upon you..." (Author's translation). Every Christian should be thankful for the gift of holy spirit, and should desire to operate the power of God.

When God gives His gift of holy spirit to people, they have spiritual power. This is clear from examining both the Old Testament and New Testament Scriptures. Joseph had the spirit of God, and the power he manifested in his life was so clearly discernible that even the pagan Pharaoh recognized it and made Joseph a ruler because of it. Pharaoh said, "…Can we find anyone like this man, one in whom is the spirit of God?" (Gen. 41:38b).[2]

God put His spirit on Bezalel, who did a lot of the work on the Tent of Meeting (Tabernacle).

Exodus 31:1–5
(1) Then the LORD said to Moses,
(2) "See, I have chosen Bezalel son of Uri, the son of Hur, of the tribe of Judah,
(3) and I have filled him with the Spirit of God [spirit of God], with skill, ability and knowledge in all kinds of crafts—
(4) to make artistic designs for work in gold, silver and bronze,
(5) to cut and set stones, to work in wood, and to engage in all kinds of craftsmanship.

These verses are very informative. First, we see God's gift of holy spirit being called "the Spirit [spirit] of God."[3] This is important to recognize, because, as with many things in the Bible, God's gift of holy spirit is referred to in a number of ways. Some are: "holy spirit" (Acts 2:38), "the spirit of God" (1 Cor. 3:16; or "God's spirit"), "the spirit of the Lord" (Luke 4:18), "the spirit of truth" (John 15:26), "the spirit of knowledge" (Isa. 11:2), "the spirit of Christ" (1 Pet. 1:11)[4] and often simply "spirit" (Mark 1:10). In each case, the context makes it clear that what is being referred to is given by God (or now by Jesus) to a person. In this case in Exodus, Scripture is clear that God put his gift of spirit on Bezalel, and thereby Bezalel was empowered to do wonderful things in the area of the crafts.

A second thing that becomes clear by studying these verses in Exodus is that the presence of the spirit of God empowered people in a variety of areas. The gift of holy spirit, which is invisible and within the person,

---

2. In this verse, "spirit" with a lower case "s" is accurate, because it is the gift of God.
3. This is one of the places where Bible versions differ as to whether it should read "spirit" or "Spirit." Versions such as the KJV, NJB, NRSV, DHB, and DRB have spirit with a lower case "s," while versions such as the ASV, ESV, NIV, and RSV have "Spirit" with an upper case "S." The reference is to the gift of God, so the "s" should be lower case.
4. In 1 Peter 1:11, holy spirit is called "the spirit of Christ" because it reveals the Christ.

becomes evident as it is manifested. God's gift of holy spirit gave people spiritual ability, including the ability to get guidance from God and to prophesy. Moses had holy spirit upon him, and was leading the people, but he needed help. He told God: "I cannot carry all these people by myself; the burden is too heavy for me" (Num. 11:14). God's solution to Moses' problem was to put holy spirit on 70 others so they could help him rule the people.

> **Numbers 11:17 (KJV)**[5]
> And I [God] will come down and talk with thee [Moses] there: and I will take of the spirit which *is* upon thee, and will put *it* upon them; and they shall bear the burden of the people with thee, that thou bear *it* not thyself alone.

God put His gift of holy spirit upon others besides Moses. Once the elders had holy spirit on them, they had the power to rule. They also had the power to prophesy, as the following verse shows.

> **Numbers 11:25 (KJV)**
> And the LORD came down in a cloud, and spake unto him, and took of the spirit that *was* upon him, and gave *it* unto the seventy elders: and it came to pass, *that*, when the spirit rested upon them, they prophesied, and did not cease.

When a person has holy spirit, he has spiritual power. No wonder Christ reminded his disciples just before he ascended, "But you will receive power, when the holy spirit has come upon you..." (Acts 1:8a- Author's translation). We need to be aware of the use of the word "upon" in the verse above, because throughout the Old Testament, holy spirit was said to be usually **upon** people, but Christians have holy spirit born **in** them. Before the Day of Pentecost God gave holy spirit conditionally and in a limited way. The Bible represents this fact by saying holy spirit was "upon" people. This is something we will cover in much more detail in upcoming chapters.

---

5. We use the KJV here because it properly uses a lower case "s" in "spirit."

Many Scriptures in both the Old Testament and the Gospels testify to the fact that the spirit was "upon" people (some versions have "on" instead of "upon").[6] The gift of holy spirit spiritually empowered people, as we have seen. Other examples are Othniel (Judg. 3:10), Gideon (Judg. 6:34), Jephthah (Judg. 11:29), and Samson (Judg. 14:19), Judges of Israel who Scripture specifically states had the spirit of God to help them rule and fight. King Saul had the spirit, and prophesied (1 Sam. 10:6), but Saul lost the spirit of God because of his sinful life (1 Sam. 16:14). When the spirit of God came on Amasai, he prophesied (1 Chron. 12:18). So did Azariah (2 Chron. 15:1 and 2), Jahaziel (2 Chron. 20:14), Zechariah (2 Chron. 24:20), and others. It was holy spirit that gave David the power to hear from God and get the plans for the Temple (1 Chron. 28:12).

God continued to empower people with holy spirit in the New Testament. This was true of John the Baptist.

Luke 1:15b

"...and he will be filled with the Holy Spirit [No "the." Read, "holy spirit"] even from birth."[7]

Elizabeth, John's mother, had holy spirit and prophesied (Luke 1:41) as did John's father, Zachariah (Luke 1:67). Since the Christian Church started on the Day of Pentecost, when people are saved and receive holy spirit they have the power to speak in tongues (Acts 2:4, 10:45 and 46, 19:6) and prophesy (Acts 2:17, 11:28, 19:6), as well as operate other manifestations of holy spirit, which we will study in an upcoming chapter. Wisdom and power have always come via the gift of holy spirit. Romans 5:5b even testifies that we Christians have come to know God's love through holy spirit.

---

6. Supporting Scriptures include: Numbers 11:25, 29, 24:2; Judges 3:10, 6:34, 11:29; 1 Samuel 10:6, 10, 16:13; 2 Kings 2:9; 1 Chronicles 12:18; 2 Chronicles 20:14; Matthew 3:16; and Luke 2:25.

7. This is another instance, like Acts 2:4, where the Greek text reads that John would be "filled of holy spirit," because the Greeks said "filled of," while we say "filled with."

Romans 5:5b (RSV)[8]
...God's love has been poured into our hearts through the
Holy Spirit [No "the." Read "holy spirit"] which has been
given to us.

This is an important verse if we are truly going to understand the
fullness of what God's gift of holy spirit within us does. Christians have and
understand God's love "through" His gift of holy spirit. It is through this gift
that God can empower us, speak to us, and give us spiritual understanding.

It is very important to understand that God does not give us holy spirit
for the sole reason of empowering us to speak in tongues, prophesy, do
healings or miracles, or otherwise manifest His power. He also gives it so
we can have a relationship with Him and His Son Jesus. God also wants
each and every Christian to have a spiritual understanding of life, and
His holy spirit helps us understand His love, His mercy, His thoughts, and
ways. It is God's gift of holy spirit in us that allows us to really understand
spiritual things, as the following verse shows:

1 Corinthians 2:12 (KJV)
Now we have received, not the spirit of the world, but the
spirit which is of God; that we might know the things that
are freely given to us of God.[9]

What value should we put on having a spiritual relationship with God,
being empowered to have a spiritual understanding of life, and knowing
the things that are freely given to us by God? God's gift of holy spirit is
priceless, and only via that holy spirit can Christians gain the spiritual
understanding that so many seek. In contrast, Scripture teaches us the
man without the spirit of God cannot know the things of God.

---

8. We quote the Revised Standard Version because it accurately uses the words "through"
and "which." That *pneuma hagion* in this verse refers to holy spirit, the gift of God, is
clear both from the context and because the Greek text has no article "the" (even though
almost every version includes it). It is the gift of God "which has been given to us," not,
as some versions have, "who has been given to us."

9. We use the KJV here because it properly uses a lower case "s" on spirit, and properly
refers to spirit, which is the gift of God, as a "which" and not a "who." Some other versions
that use "which" or "that" are: YLT, ASV, RSV, NRSV, DRB, and DHB.

1 Corinthians 2:14 (KJV)
But the natural man receiveth not the things of the Spirit
[spirit] of God: for they are foolishness unto him: neither
can he know *them*, because they are spiritually discerned.

We should be profoundly thankful we have holy spirit from God and
can understand spiritual matters. Furthermore, we need to work very
hard to help non-Christians come to the point of being saved so they too
can have everlasting life and spiritual understanding.

In this chapter we have seen that when a person has holy spirit, he
has spiritual power. This was as true in the Old Testament as it is today.
The power that comes with the presence of holy spirit was one of the last
things that Christ spoke about with his disciples before he ascended into
heaven. Surely if Jesus thought it was so important to cover this with his
disciples at that critical time, then holy spirit is something we should
desire to learn more about so we can tap into the power we have in God's
wonderful gift of holy spirit.

Chapter 4

God's Gift of Holy Spirit— a "He" or an "It"?

One of the major reasons why holy spirit has not been recognized by Christians to be a gift from God is that personal and masculine pronouns such as "he" or "whom" have been used with *pneuma hagion*. If we are to be confident that holy spirit is indeed a gift, and not a person, then the question about the pronouns associated with it has to be answered. The pronouns associated with the gift of holy spirit can, and should, be translated as pronouns such as "it," "which," and "that."[1]

We saw in Chapter 2, "The Giver and the Gift," that *pneuma hagion* often refers to the gift of God, the divine nature born inside us. This divine nature is a "thing," not a person. Thus it should be referred to with pronouns such as "it," "that," or "which," and not "who," or "whom." For example, Ephesians 1:14 is referring to the gift of holy spirit that is sealed inside us, so the verse should not be translated, "[the promised holy spirit] **who** is a deposit guaranteeing our inheritance…." Instead, the translation should read as the KJV has, "[the holy spirit] **Which** is the earnest of our inheritance…."[2]

There are three primary reasons why people think *pneuma hagion* is a person. First, it is translated "**the** Holy Spirit" instead of "holy spirit" even when the Greek text has no article "the." Second, the "H" and "S" get capitalized, indicating a proper noun, even when there is no reason in the Greek text or the context of the verse to capitalize them. Third, personal pronouns such as "he," or "who," are used with it.[3] We have covered the

---

1. A pronoun is a word that takes the place of a noun so that the noun need not to be repeated; "he," "she," "it," "that," "those," etc. are all pronouns.

2. Even more proper English grammar today would be, "[the holy spirit] that is the earnest of our inheritance."

3. Personal pronouns such as "he," "she," "who," and "whom" indicate that a person is being referred to, while relative pronouns such as "it," "which," or "that" are not usually or properly used in regard to people.

addition of "the" to *pneuma hagion* even when there is no "the" in the Greek texts, and we have also shown that when the gift of God is being referred to, holy spirit, and not "Holy Spirit," is proper. Now we need to examine how pronouns in languages such as Greek should be translated.

Unlike English, but like many languages, including Spanish, French, German, Latin, and Hebrew, the Greek language assigns a gender to all nouns. This gender assignment happened in ancient antiquity, and often there seems to be no reason why a particular noun has a particular gender assigned to it. When a language such as Greek, which assigns genders to nouns, is spoken or written, proper grammar dictates that the gender of any pronoun relating to that noun must agree with the gender of the noun.

In French, for example, a table is feminine, *la table,* while a desk is masculine, *le bureau.* Thus a literal translation of a French novel might contain the line, "I like the table, **she** is just right for the room, but I do not like the desk, **he** is too big." In translating from French to English, however, we would never translate "the table, she," or "the desk, he." Not only is it improper English, it misses the point. Even the French people do not think of tables and desks as being masculine or feminine. It is simply a part of the language that has come down to them. And just as we would not say, "the desk, he," we would **never** insist that a table or desk was somehow a person just because it had a masculine or feminine pronoun. Furthermore, good English translators recognize that even though a noun is assigned a gender in another language and the pronoun follows the noun, their job is to bring the meaning of the original into English, not introduce confusion as they translate. Hence, someone translating from French to English would use the English designation "it" for the table and the desk, in spite of the fact that in the original language the table and desk have a masculine or feminine gender.

What is true in the examples from the French language is true in any language that assigns a gender to nouns. In Spanish, a car is masculine, *el carro*, while a bicycle is feminine, *la bicicleta*. Again, no English translator would translate "the car, he," or "the bicycle, she." People translating Spanish into English use the word "it" when referring to a car or bicycle.

Let's examine some examples in the Bible. The Greek word for "lamp" is *luchnos*, a masculine noun, and therefore proper grammar dictates that any pronoun associated with it is masculine. Thus, if the Greek text of Matthew 5:15 were translated literally, it would read, "Nor do they light a lamp and place **him** under the bushel...." However, every version we checked said, "it" and not "him," as proper English dictates. The Greek word for wine is *oinos*, a masculine noun, so it takes a masculine pronoun. Christ taught that no one puts new wine in old wineskins, because the wineskins would burst and the wine, "**he** will be poured out." Of course, English versions say "it" will be poured out.

The same grammatical rule, that the pronoun must agree with the noun, is followed when the noun is feminine. According to the literal Greek text, Christ told his disciples that when they entered into a "city" (*polin*; feminine) or "village" (*kome*; feminine), to "...find out who in **her** is worthy..." (Matt. 10:11; literal). The English versions correctly read, "it" instead of "her." Similarly, the Greek word for fig tree is *suke*, a feminine noun. When Jesus was entering Jerusalem, he saw a fig tree, but when he came to "her" he found nothing but leaves (Mark 11:13). Again, all the English versions say "it," not "her."[4] When translating from another language into English, we have to use the English language properly. Students of Greek, Hebrew, Spanish, French, German, etc., quickly discover that one of the difficult things about learning the language is memorizing the gender of each noun—something we do not have in the English language.

Once we clearly understand that the gender of a pronoun is determined by the gender of the noun, we can see why one cannot build a doctrine on the gender of a noun and its agreeing pronouns. Only confusion would result from that kind of erroneous exegesis. For example, the noun *pneuma* (spirit) is neuter in gender and thus is naturally translated "it." However, referring to the exact same reality, the *parakletos*, (John 14:16, etc., "Counselor"[5]), is masculine. Theologians agree that the counselor is "the Holy Spirit" (or to us, holy spirit), which was to come. Since *parakletos* is masculine, and spirit (*pneuma*) is neuter, are we to believe the gender

---

4. An interesting cultural observation is that generally in English, if a landscaper, gardener, or plant lover refers to a special tree or bush in an intimate way, masculine pronouns are used. "Oh my little fern, he isn't doing so well, but this guy over here, my aloe vera, he is doing great."

5. The Greek word *parakletos* can mean counselor, helper, comforter, etc., and so the translations differ as to how this word should be translated.

of holy spirit changes somehow? Of course not, that would be ridiculous. Worse, since "spirit" in Greek is neuter, but "spirit" in Hebrew, also a biblical language, is feminine, are we to believe the sex of the holy spirit changed after the time of Jesus when the believers started to speak and write in Greek? Of course not.

Here is another good example of how confusing a theology would be if one tried to build it from the gender of nouns. Sometimes the Greek word *logos* is used to refer to the Word of God (Luke 5:1), and *logos* is a masculine noun. Sometimes the Greek word *rhema* is used of the Word of God (Matt. 4:4), and *rhema* is a neuter noun. Are we to believe that, first, the Word of God even has gender, and second, that it somehow changes gender? No.

Our point is this: no translator should ever use the gender of the nouns in a language to build a theology. Only error could result from that kind of exegesis. The way to properly translate the Scripture from a language that assigns gender to nouns is to study the subject matter and understand the subject being discussed, and then translate accordingly. Does *pneuma hagion* have a gender? We know people come in two genders, masculine and feminine, so references to people should be either "he" or "she." Animals also have a gender. Rocks do not, and should be "it" (by the way, in Greek, "rock" is feminine while in Hebrew it is masculine). In the case of *pneuma hagion*, when it is used as a name for God, and refers to God, it is proper to use the pronoun "He," or other personal pronouns such as "Who."[6] When it is referring to God's gift, it is proper to use pronouns such as "it," "which," "that," etc.[7]

---

6. There has been much scholarly discussion in recent years about the gender of God, and this is not the place for a long discussion about it. Although we believe that God has no actual gender, in Scripture He presents Himself as masculine. He presented himself as a man to Abraham (Gen. 18:1 and 2), and to many others (Exod. 24:10 and Dan. 7:9 are good examples).

7. Trinitarians, of course, see things differently. They view "the Holy Spirit" as the third person of the Trinity, so even though *pneuma*, spirit, is a neuter noun, they use masculine personal pronouns with it. Note the gender of the Greek nouns and pronouns in [brackets] in contrast with the gender that appears in the translation.

John 14:17 (NASB)
"*that is* the **Spirit** [neuter] of truth, **whom** [*auto*, neuter, not masculine] the world cannot receive, because it does not behold **Him** [*auto*, neuter, not masculine]

Once the above information is understood, it becomes clear why some versions of the Bible use personal pronouns such as "who" or "whom" when referring to *pneuma hagion*. If the translators believe *pneuma hagion* refers to the third person of the Trinity, they will believe that it is proper to use masculine pronouns and personal pronouns. Thus, their versions read "the Counselor...he" in the gospel of John, and "he," "who," or "whom" in other places in the New Testament. However, we, believe *pneuma hagion* refers to the gift of God, it must be used with pronouns such as "it," "which," and "that."

One point should be certain from all the above discussion. No one can build a case for the "person" or "non-person" of *pneuma hagion* simply because an English version of the Bible reads "he," or "who" in association with holy spirit, or because the noun "Counselor" is masculine. One must study the context to see how the pronouns should be translated.

Having discussed nouns and their associated pronouns, we should now say something about verbs. Every Bible student should be aware that Greek verbs have no gender, and that the gender associated with any given verb is ascertained from the context. It is vital to understand this because there are quite a few verses referring to spirit in which a masculine personal pronoun has been added because of the theology of

---

or know **Him** [not in Greek], *but* you know **Him** [*autos*, neuter, not masculine] because **He abides** [verb with no gener] with you, and will be in you."

In spite of the neuter noun and pronouns in Greek, almost every English version uses the personal pronoun "whom" and masculine personal pronouns "him" and "he," as the NASB does. This shows that Trinitarian scholars do not use the gender of the pronoun, but the subject being discussed, to determine how the English should read. This reveals an inconsistency in one of the standard arguments for the existence of the Trinity, that many Trinitarians say that the use of masculine pronouns shows that "the Holy Spirit" is the third person of the Trinity. A case in point is the Greek word *parakletos* (helper, "comforter," counselor), which is masculine. It is good Greek grammar to use the masculine pronoun *ekeinos* to describe the "Helper," *parakletos*, which is masculine (John 14:26), but Trinitarians have said that the use of *ekeinos* is evidence that "the Holy Spirit" is masculine (cp. A. T. Robertson, *Word Pictures in the New Testament* (Baker Book House, Grand Rapids, MI, reprinted 1960), Vol. 5, p. 252 and 253). However, when neuter pronouns appear in the Greek text, they simply change them to masculine in their translations. One cannot have it both ways. If the gender of the pronoun is evidence for the actual gender of the noun, then the "helper" is masculine, but the "holy spirit" is neuter—certainly not a person. The proper way to think about the pronoun, as we have seen, is that its gender should never be used as "evidence" for the gender of its related noun.

the translator, although there is no definitive reason for it in the Greek text. This unwarranted addition of the personal pronoun naturally leads people to conclude that "the Holy Spirit" must be a person.

One such verse is John 16:13a: "But when he [referring to the "helper" in verse 7 and following through the context], the Spirit of truth, comes, he will guide you into all truth…." The phrase, "he will guide," is the Greek verb *hodegeo*. It is a third person singular verb, and, as we said, Greek verbs have no gender. Since Trinitarians believe the context of John 16 is the "Person," "the Holy Spirit" they translate *hodegeo* as "he will guide." But since the verb has no gender, it could just as easily be translated "it will guide" or "she will guide," whichever is best supported by the context. When we understand this, then we will scrutinize the context to see whether the subject being referred to is a "he," "she," or "it." In this case, we believe that the context is God's gift of holy spirit, which is not a person, and that the verse should be properly translated, "it will guide."

Greek verbs do not have a gender, so any assigned to them are the interpretation of the translator. This comes up in many areas besides holy spirit. For example, Luke 11:24 speaks of demons, and some versions say that when an unclean spirit comes out of a man, "he goes" through arid places. But are we sure the demon is a "he"? The Greek verb is genderless, and can be masculine, feminine, or neuter. Thus there are versions that say "he" (cp. KJV; RSV) and versions that say "it" (cp. NASB; NRSV), but because of mainstream theology, none say "she," although biblically that is a possibility.[8]

Another example regarding "spirit" is in the gospel of John. In this verse, Jesus is talking with his disciples about the spirit of truth, and he says, "…*but* you know Him because He abides with you, and will be in you." (John 14:17b-NASB). The words "He abides" are an interpretation

---

8. Although we usually think of angels and demons as masculine, there are both female good spirits (Zech. 5:9) and female evil spirits. The Hebrew word "*lilith*" (Isa. 34:14) is the name of a female demon. "Lilith" gets translated many ways in the English versions, including "night monster" (ASV, NASB, AMP), "night hag" (RSV), "night spectre" (RHM) and by her name, "Lilith" (TANAKH; The Message). Some translators apparently miss the point that Isaiah is referring to a demon at all, and have "screech owl" (KJV) or "night creature" (NIV). *Lilith* is "a malevolent supernatural being" (Bromiley, *op. cit.*, *Bible Encyclopedia*, Vol. 3, p. 536). Unless the context tells us the gender of a demon, using "it" in Luke 11:24 is our best choice because it allows for either male or female gender.

of the Greek, which is simply, "abides" in the third person singular, and thus could be "he abides," "she abides," or "it abides." In this case, because Jesus is speaking of God's gift of holy spirit, which is a "thing" and not a "Person," it is proper to say, "it abides."

God's holy spirit is a most amazing and valuable gift, and it behooves us as Christians, especially those who translate the Bible, to understand it. Bible students who are not familiar with the original languages can do this only when the Greek and Hebrew texts are properly translated. If the translation is not accurate, then we do not have the Word of God, we have the words of men. Translating Scripture is one of the most important and spiritual of all responsibilities, because millions of people who do not read the original languages trust the translation to accurately represent the original. When it comes to the subject of God's gift of holy spirit, countless Christians have been misled or confused by the improper use of the pronoun "he" or other personal pronouns. When the pronouns associated with *pneuma*, spirit, are translated correctly, it is much easier to see the love and mercy of God expressed to us by His giving to us the wonderful gift of holy spirit

> **God's holy spirit is a most amazing and valuable gift, and it behooves us as Christians, especially those who translate the Bible, to understand it.**

Chapter 5

The Messiah and the Gift of Holy Spirit

We have seen that through the ages God put His gift of holy spirit upon people to give them spiritual power and understanding. It makes sense that if the Messiah were going to walk in the power of God, he too would need holy spirit upon him. This was foretold in the Old Testament, confirmed by Jesus himself, and then spoken of after Jesus' earthly life. Isaiah foretold it in the Old Testament.

> **Isaiah 11:2 (KJV)**[1]
> And the spirit of the LORD shall rest upon him, the spirit of wisdom and understanding, the spirit of counsel and might, the spirit of knowledge and of the fear of the LORD;

This wonderful prophecy, written more than 700 years before Jesus started his ministry, revealed that God would put holy spirit on the Messiah when he came. It also reveals more of the names or attributes of God's gift of holy spirit. It is called "the spirit of the LORD" (Yahweh) in the opening of the verse, but then called "the spirit of wisdom" because through it can come wisdom.[2] Through God's spirit also comes understanding, counsel, might (not only spiritual, but also physical, like Samson's), knowledge, and respect for the true God.

It was when Jesus started his earthly ministry that God put His gift of holy spirit on him.

> **Luke 3:22 (NASB)**
> and the Holy Spirit [holy spirit] descended upon Him in bodily form like a dove, and a voice came out of heaven, "Thou art My beloved Son, in Thee I am well-pleased."

---

1. We use the KJV here because it correctly uses "spirit" with a lower case "s," and also "upon."

2. We say, "can come wisdom" because no one has to pay attention to the wisdom given by God. King Saul certainly did not. However, for anyone with ears to hear, the spirit gives wisdom, knowledge, and much more.

Although the NASB capitalizes "Holy Spirit," which refers to the gift of God and should be rendered "holy spirit," it reads that the spirit came "upon" Jesus. This is in harmony with the Old Testament, which also records that the spirit of God came "upon" people. The Greek preposition translated "upon" is *epi*, of which Thayer writes, "its primary signification is *upon*...." However, it is very flexible, and Thayer takes five pages to expound upon it.[3]

Appropriately, when God gave holy spirit to His Son Jesus, He did it in a very special way, with the normally invisible spirit taking on the form of a dove. Scripture also tells us that when Jesus was given the gift of holy spirit, it was not measured, as God had given it up until that time:

John 3:34 (NASB)[4]
"For He whom God has sent speaks the words of God; for He gives the Spirit [spirit] without measure.

The Word of God makes the special point of saying Jesus had holy spirit "without measure" because God did give it by measure in the Old Testament, something we will say more about in an upcoming chapter. Knowing that he was the Messiah, and that he had holy spirit, Jesus appropriately read the following verses when he was in the synagogue in his home town, Nazareth.

Luke 4:18 and 19 (NASB)[5]
(18) "The Spirit [spirit] of the Lord is upon Me, Because He anointed Me to preach the gospel to the poor. He has sent Me to proclaim release to the captives, And recovery of sight to the blind, To set free those who are downtrodden, (19) To proclaim the favorable year of the Lord."

---

3. Joseph H. Thayer, *Thayer's Greek-English Lexicon of the New Testament* (Hendrickson Publishers, Inc., Peabody, MA, reprinted 2000), p. 231.

4. We like the word "measure" here, as many versions have, because it more literally follows the Greek text and also because we feel it matches the sense of what God did in the Old Testament.

5. The quotation is from Isaiah 61:1 and 2.

It was not well received when Jesus quoted this Messianic prophecy to the people, affirming he had the spirit of God upon him, and confronting them on their not accepting him. In fact, they set about to kill him by throwing him off a cliff, but, empowered by holy spirit and walking in faith, he passed through the midst of them and went away. Jesus did not do any miracle or healing before his baptism. This is evidence that he, like the prophets of old, was spiritually empowered only when he received holy spirit.

Acts confirms that Jesus was given holy spirit by God.

Acts 10:38
how God anointed Jesus of Nazareth with the Holy Spirit [No "the." Read "holy spirit"] and power, and how he went around doing good and healing all who were under the power of the devil, because God was with him.

This verse contains a wealth of information. We do not mean to be contentious about the doctrine of the Trinity, but we assert that if Jesus were God he would not need to receive holy spirit. Furthermore, the above verses say "God" gave the spirit to Jesus, and if Jesus were God, this makes no sense. It is God who gives His very nature, holy spirit, to human beings so they can have spiritual power, and it was God who gave Jesus, His only—begotten human Son, holy spirit without measure so he could be spiritually empowered to fulfill what God had called him to do.

Acts 10:38 also shows that when holy spirit is present, so is spiritual power. God did not anoint Jesus with two things, 1) holy spirit, and 2) power. God anointed Jesus with one thing, holy spirit, which is spiritual power. In the Greek text, the "and" can be understood and translated as "even," so that the verse would read, "…God anointed Jesus of Nazareth with holy spirit, even power…." What did Jesus do with the spiritual power he received from God? He did good and healed all those who were under the power of the Devil. What a great example Jesus set for all of us.

Many people in the Old Testament to whom God gave holy spirit did not continue to live a godly life and obey Him. For example, Gideon made an idol that became a snare to people (Judg. 8:27). King Saul sinned so badly that God took holy spirit from him (1 Sam. 16:14), David committed adultery and had Uriah killed, and then prayed for God not to take holy spirit from him (Ps. 51:11). It is important to realize that having holy spirit does not keep one from sinning. God's gift of holy spirit neither takes away nor supersedes our free will. It is our choice whether or not to obey God's commandments. Many people to whom God gave holy spirit did not take full advantage of what they were given, and did not walk faithfully before Him. We Christians should follow the example of Jesus and stay faithful in our walk, doing good and helping others with the spiritual power we have been given.

Chapter 6

The Gift of Holy Spirit Today

Christians today enjoy the presence and power of holy spirit in a way never experienced before the Church Age. Today, in the "...administration of the grace of God..." (Eph. 3:2-DHB), we Christians have what God has promised to Israel in the future, which is why what we have is called "the promised holy spirit."[1] What we have today is so totally different from what God gave to the believers in the Old Testament that John 7:39 says that before Jesus was glorified there was no holy spirit. Jesus spoke about the gift of holy spirit while he was in the Temple at the Feast of Tabernacles.

> **John 7:39 (NRSV)**
> Now he said this about the Spirit [spirit], which believers in him were to receive; for as yet there was no Spirit [spirit], because Jesus was not yet glorified.

Verse 39 is somewhat hard to understand. Why would the Bible say, "...as yet there was no spirit..."?[2] Why does Scripture say that spirit did not yet exist at the time of Christ? The answer is that the gift of holy spirit that in the Old Testament and Gospels God **promised** to give people in the future was very different from the holy spirit that those people had at the time. Moses, Joshua, Deborah, David, Zachariah, Elizabeth, and other Old Testament and Gospel believers had a holy spirit that was completely different from the gift of holy spirit that has been promised for the Millennial Kingdom and given to us today. So different, in fact, that what we have today did not exist when Jesus was speaking about it to the crowds gathered in the Temple.

---

1. For more on administrations, and the Administration of Grace in which we live, which is also called the "...administration of the sacred secret..." (Eph. 3:9-RHM), see Appendix A, "The Administration of the Sacred Secret."

2. Many Bible versions say the spirit was not yet given, but even if that is the correct reading of the Greek text, which it almost certainly is not, it still means that before Jesus was glorified there was no spirit.

Scholars today believe the original Greek text of John 7:39 should be translated "...for as yet there was no spirit...," as represented in the most modern Greek texts. However, it can be seen why that reading would cause problems for copyists and translators. First, there is the fact that most copyists believed in the doctrine of the Trinity, and if "the Spirit" is the third person of the Trinity, then he always existed. Second, the obvious presence of spirit in the Old Testament caused confusion, because it certainly seemed as if "spirit" did exist. After all, Moses had holy spirit. So did David, Deborah, the prophets, and many others. Third, almost no one knew that after the resurrection from the dead, believers would be given a new holy spirit, one that had not existed before Christ was glorified. Instead, most people believed that when a person died he went immediately to heaven and lived forever in a perfected state with no need for a new and different holy spirit.[3] Wanting the verse to make sense, the men who copied the Greek text modified the verse. Therefore, there are several different later renditions of the verse, including, the spirit "was not yet given," "...was not yet upon them...," and had "not yet come."[4]

John 7:39 also makes the point that the promised gift of holy spirit would not come until **after** Jesus was glorified. We today, looking back, know that this was indeed the case. When Jesus was speaking of the holy spirit that was to come, he spoke of the holy spirit that God promised Israel in the Millennial Kingdom as part of the New Covenant (Jer. 31:31–33; Isa. 32:15; Joel 2:28). However, Christians received holy spirit on the Day of Pentecost as part of the Sacred Secret, receiving the firstfruits of the spirit (Rom. 8:23).[5]

Actually, God has given the Christian Church more than He promised to give Israel. It will help us to appreciate God's gift of holy spirit that we have today if we clearly understand how it differs from what God gave in the Old Testament and Gospel periods, before the Christian Church started.

---

3. For more on holy spirit in the Millennial Kingdom see Appendix C, "The Promised Holy Spirit." For more on the state of the dead and the resurrection, see our book, *Is There Death After Life* by Mark Graeser, John A. Lynn, & John Schoenheit (The Living Truth Fellowship, Indianapolis, IN, 2011).

4. Bruce Metzger, *A Textual Commentary on the Greek New Testament* (United Bible Societies, Germany, 1975), p. 218.

5. For more on the age we live in today, see Appendix A, "The Administration of the Sacred Secret."

In the Old Testament and Gospels:

1. The gift of holy spirit was usually said to be **upon** believers, but today, in the Administration of Grace, holy spirit is born in every Christian, is sealed in him, and becomes part of his very nature. Furthermore, it is born in the believer at the very moment he is saved.[6]
2. Only a **few** believers had holy spirit, but today in the Administration of Grace, holy spirit is in **every** Christian.
3. God gave holy spirit in a **limited** way, by measure, but today, in the Administration of Grace, every believer is filled with holy spirit.
4. God gave holy spirit **conditionally**, and a person could lose it, but today it is permanently sealed inside every Christian, and guarantees them everlasting life.
5. It was not stated that the gift of holy spirit God gave before Pentecost **influenced** a person's life in a transforming way, but today, in the Administration of Grace, holy spirit helps **conform** people into the image of Christ by helping them live godly lives.
6. There were seven manifestations of holy spirit available to believers. Today there are **nine** (1 Cor. 12:8–10). The manifestations of **speaking in tongues** and **interpretation of tongues** did not exist in the Old Testament or Gospel periods, but are now available to all Christians.

The above points are very important, and are certainly one of the reasons why the Bible calls the Church Age the "administration of God's grace" (Eph. 3:2). It is only because of the grace of God that the Christian Church has been blessed with holy spirit the way we have been. Let us elaborate on them.

1) In the Old Testament and Gospels, holy spirit was usually said to be "upon" believers, but today, in the Administration of Grace, holy spirit is born "in" every Christian at the moment he is saved, and is forever sealed in him as he is "sealed" in Christ.[7]

---

6. The Church Age started on the Day of Pentecost in Acts 2 with the outpouring of holy spirit, and will end with the Rapture, when both living and dead Christians will be bodily taken into heaven to be with Christ (1 Thess. 4:16 and 17). The Church Age has many names, including the "administration of God's grace" (Eph. 3:2, usually shortened in our writings to "the Administration of Grace"), and the "Administration of the Sacred Secret" (our translation of Eph. 3:9).

7. Because the gift of holy spirit is intangible, delineating between it being "in" or "on" someone is rather a moot point. The important distinction is that before the Church

We saw in Chapter 3 that in the Old Testament, people who had holy spirit had it "upon" them conditionally. Many verses in the Epistles to the Church make it clear the gift of holy spirit that we have is **in** us, not upon us. In fact, it is born **in** us and is part of our very nature, as we will see in numbers 2–4 below.

2) In the Old Testament and Gospels, only a few believers had holy spirit, but today in the Administration of Grace, holy spirit is in every Christian.

In the Old Testament God gave His gift of holy spirit to only a few believers, who were then empowered to do His work. For example, we know that of the millions of Israelites who left Egypt, not even the leaders had holy spirit.[8] Moses asked God for help, which God gave him by placing holy spirit on the 70 leaders chosen by the congregation (Num. 11:14–17, 24–27). Seventy is not a large number compared to the millions of Israelites. At that time, Moses prayer is significant: "…I wish that all the LORD's people were prophets and that the LORD would put his Spirit [spirit] on them!" (Num. 11:29b). Moses did not know about the Age of Grace in which we live, when each Christian has holy spirit.

Joshua was another leader who received the spirit long after he became a believer. He was called "Moses' aide" when Moses went up Mt. Sinai, only a few months after the Exodus (Exod. 24:13), so he had obviously been a leader while still in Egypt, long before Moses returned there from Midian. However, Joshua received God's gift of holy spirit, and the spiritual power that came with it, only when Moses laid his hands on him. If Joshua received holy spirit when he was with Moses in the wilderness, then he had served God for years in Egypt without the help of holy spirit.

---

began on the Day of Pentecost in Acts 2, holy spirit was conditionally given, while after Pentecost it has been permanently given. In John 14:17 (Author's translation), Jesus uses the preposition "with," as follows: "… the spirit is with you, but shall be in you." Even though when he sent them out, the spirit was 'in' them, but conditionally. Again, the important distinction to be made is born in, or in upon a condition.

8. Exodus 12:37 says there were about 600,000 men who left Egypt, not counting the women and children, and Numbers 1:45 and 46 says there were 603, 550 men who were 20 years old and older. Thus, the total number of Israelites who left Egypt was in the millions.

Deuteronomy 34:9
Now Joshua son of Nun was filled with the spirit of wisdom because Moses had laid his hands on him. So the Israelites listened to him and did what the LORD had commanded Moses.

Another section of Scripture showing that most believers in the Old Testament did not have holy spirit is in Joel. These verses foretold there was a time coming when both old and young people, and even men and women servants would have holy spirit. Joel's prophecy was exciting and encouraging to the Old Testament believers because they did not have holy spirit, unless, like Moses, David, Elijah, etc., they were specifically chosen by God.

Joel 2:28 and 29
(28) "And afterward, I will pour out my Spirit [spirit] **on all people.** Your sons and daughters will prophesy, your old men will dream dreams, your young men will see visions. (29) Even on my servants, both men and women, I will pour out my Spirit [spirit] in those days.

That men, women, sons, and daughters would all receive holy spirit was a huge difference from the way things had been throughout the Old Testament. The word "afterward" in verse 28 refers to after the Tribulation and Armageddon, i.e., in the Millennial Kingdom.[9] It is important to realize that Joel is not referring to the Day of Pentecost and the fact that Christians would have holy spirit. We live in the Administratin of Grace, which was a time period unknown to the people of the Old Testament and, indeed, to Satan himself (1 Cor. 2:7–9).[10] Joel was speaking about Israel, as J. Vernon McGee wrote:

He [Joel] is speaking of the kingdom which is coming on the earth, and the pouring out of the Spirit [spirit] has reference to the Millennium. Of course none of the prophets spoke of the

---

9. For more on the Millennial Kingdom, and the promises made about it, see Appendix C, "The Promised Holy Spirit.

10. See Appendix A, "The Administration of the Sacred Secret."

church age; all of them spoke of the last days in reference to the nation of Israel.[11]

Today, in the Church Age, every Christian is given holy spirit at the time he is saved. This is in contrast to the Old Testament when not many people had holy spirit. In fact, it is the presence of holy spirit, the nature of God, born and sealed inside a believer, that makes him a Christian.[12] Peter made it clear that every Christian gets holy spirit when he believes. We have already seen this verse, but in this new context it helps to see it again.

Acts 2:38
Peter replied, "Repent and be baptized, every one of you, in the name of Jesus Christ for the forgiveness of your sins. And you will receive the gift of the Holy Spirit [holy spirit].

Peter had just finished teaching that the people in his audience had crucified Jesus, whom God had raised from the dead. Then he asked them to "repent," which is to change from their wickedness and denial of Jesus and believe that he was the Messiah and Lord. By doing this, they would be saved and at that moment would receive holy spirit. There is no reason to believe that anyone in Peter's audience took him to mean that one could repent (be saved), but somehow not receive holy spirit until a later time. Ephesians tells us that when a person believes in Christ, he is at that moment forever sealed with holy spirit.

Ephesians 1:13
And you also were included in Christ when you heard the word of truth, the gospel of your salvation. Having believed,

---

11. J. Vernon McGee, *Thru the Bible with J. Vernon McGee*, (Thomas Nelson Publishers, Nashville, TN, 1982), Vol. III, Proverbs–Malachi, p. 673.

12. This is a very important point that we cannot state emphatically enough. A person is not a Christian because he believes a certain way, goes to a church on Sunday, was baptized in water, reads the Bible, or does good works. A Christian is one who is a child of God by New Birth, having the seed and nature of God, holy spirit, sealed within him. The way to get saved and be a Christian, filled with holy spirit, is clearly laid out in the Bible:

Romans 10:9
That if you confess with your mouth, "Jesus is Lord," and believe in your heart that God raised him from the dead, you will be saved.

you were marked in him with a seal, the promised Holy
Spirit [holy spirit],

This verse is very important and very clear. When a non-Christian
believes in Christ, he is saved, and receives and is sealed with holy spirit.
Every single Christian has God's gift of holy spirit.

In 1 Corinthians Paul reproved the Corinthians for their ungodliness,
reminding them they should be careful as to how they build their lives
on Christ, who is the foundation of the Church. He reminded them that
God's gift, holy spirit, was in each of them.

1 Corinthians 3:16 (KJV)[13]
Know ye not that ye are the temple of God, and *that* the
Spirit [spirit] of God dwelleth in you?

Each Christian has holy spirit, which he received at the moment of
his New Birth; the instant he was saved. Paul told the believers in Corinth
they were the Temple of God and that they had holy spirit, that is, that
each of them had holy spirit. If, as some Christians teach, salvation is a
separate experience from receiving holy spirit, sometimes even separated
by years, then how is it that every person in the church at Corinth had holy
spirit? Surely there would have been some new believers in the church
who would have not yet received it. Paul can write to the Corinthians,
and every other Christian congregation, and affirm that every believer
has holy spirit because a person receives this gift of God's divine nature
at the same instant he is born again.

There are two primary reasons why people mistakenly teach that
holy spirit comes "after" salvation. One is that many Christians do not
outwardly manifest any spiritual power after they are saved, and this causes
people to believe that getting saved and receiving holy spirit are separate
experiences. However, just because a person **has** holy spirit does not mean
that he will **use** it. Many sincere Christians never manifest the power of
God. Salvation is not dependent upon manifesting the power of God—it
was not during Old Testament times, and it is not today. Just because a

---

13. We use the KJV here because it uses "Spirit [spirit] of God" (a genitive of origin)
rather than the more confusing, "God's Spirit."

believer does not manifest holy spirit does not mean that he does not have it. Is there any verse that says if you do not manifest the power of God, you do not have the spirit of God? Certainly not. We remind the reader of what we wrote in the preface of this book:

> When it comes to any spiritual matter, the written Word of God is our only rule of faith and practice. God works with each of us as individuals, so the individual spiritual experience God gives one Christian may not be the same as the experience of another. Therefore, if we focus on our experiences, there may be contradictions and confusion. We need to learn that when it comes to spiritual things, experience is no guarantee for truth. Rather, we must go to the written Word of God as our ultimate standard for truth. As Jesus once said in a prayer to God, "…your word is truth" (John 17:17b).

The Bible is clear that when a person is saved, he receives holy spirit. The individual experiences of people may vary, and one person may not outwardly manifest holy spirit for years, or maybe never, but if we believe what the Bible says, we know that each Christian has holy spirit. When a person is "born again," something is actually "born" inside him, and that something is holy spirit, God's nature and God's power. A Christian may never use the spiritual power he has, but the fact remains that God gave it to each of us for our benefit.

The second reason some people do not believe holy spirit comes at the time of salvation is that there are Scriptures that can seem to indicate that receiving holy spirit comes afterward. The first verse we will examine is Acts 1:8. Many people read the King James Version of the Bible, and sometimes the older English it uses can confuse the modern reader. Consider the following verse:

> **Acts 1:8 (KJV)**
> But ye shall receive power, **after that** the Holy Ghost [holy spirit] is come upon you: and ye shall be witnesses unto me both in Jerusalem, and in all Judaea, and in Samaria, and unto the uttermost part of the earth.

Occasionally this verse is used to teach that holy spirit comes after salvation, but this is a misunderstanding of the King James English, in which the phrase "**after that**" sometimes meant "when." The Greek text clearly indicates the power comes "when" holy spirit comes, which is at the time a person is saved via being born again. The modern versions we checked all had "when," including the New King James Version, which has updated the English of the King James Version.

Another section of Scripture that has caused people to think that someone may receive the holy spirit after he is saved is also in Acts.

> ### Acts 8:14–17 (NASB)
> (14) Now when the apostles in Jerusalem heard that Samaria had received [*dechomai*] the word of God, they sent them Peter and John,
> (15) who came down and prayed for them, that they might receive [*lambano*] the Holy Spirit [no article "the." Read "holy spirit"],
> (16) For He [it] had not yet fallen upon any of them; they had simply been baptized in the name of the Lord Jesus.[14]

---

14. Three pertinent verses to be properly understood with regard to the gift of holy spirit are Acts 8:16, 10:44 and 11:15. Most versions translate these verses to say that holy spirit "falls" on people, which makes it seem as though holy spirit came upon them and acted upon them without their consent. While it is true that the word *epipipto* can be understood as someone or something falling on someone, it does not have to be understood that way. Another usage of *epipipto* is when something "falls upon," i.e., happens to, or occurs in the life of someone. For example, Luke 1:12 describes what happened to Zechariah when he saw the angel in the Temple. The KJV says that fear "fell" on him. Fear did not fall on him as if it were coming from the sky. Fear was Zechariah's own response when he unexpectedly saw the angel. Another example is Romans 15:3, which says "For even Christ did not please himself but, as it is written: 'The insults of those who insult you have fallen on me." The insults in this verse did not "fall" on Christ, as if they came from the sky, but rather they happened to him, or occurred in his life.

Such examples help us properly understand the three difficult verses in Acts that are listed above. A careful study of these verses indicates that holy spirit did not "fall" from the sky upon the disciples, but that they experienced in manifestation the gift of holy spirit already within them.

The context of Acts, Chapter Eight makes this very clear. The disciples in Samaria were indeed born again, but had never manifested holy spirit outwardly by speaking in tongues, interpretation, prophecy, etc. Acts 8:16 (KJV) indicates that those believers had not had the holy spirit "fall," i.e., "happen" or "occur" to them, but when Peter and John laid hands on them (verse 17), they all received into evidence (*lambano*) holy spirit they had already received internally (*dechomai*—verse 14).

(17) Then they *began* laying their hands on them, and they were receiving [*lambano*] the Holy Spirit [no article "the." Read "holy spirit"].

These verses seem to say that the disciples in Samaria "received" the Word of God but had not received holy spirit. The reason for the confusion is that in many versions two different Greek words were translated by the same English word, and the meanings of the Greek words are not clearly understood. The two Greek words that need to be properly understood in the context of the gift of holy spirit are *dechomai* and *lambano*. Both words have a wide range of meaning, and both can mean "receive." However, there are some important differences. *Lambano* has an emphasis on the *action* taken by the one receiving. *Vine's Dictionary of New Testament Words* notes:

> "There is a certain distinction between *lambano* and *dechomai* (more pronounced in the earlier, classical use), in that in many instances *lambano* suggests a self-prompted taking, whereas *dechomai* more frequently indicates "a welcoming or an appropriating reception"[15]

"Self-prompted taking" is a key phrase. Too many people do not outwardly manifest holy spirit because they are waiting for God to move them when they should take hold of what God has already given them and use it. *Thayer's Greek-English Lexicon* adds,

> "...the suggestion of self-prompted taking still adheres to *lambano* in many connections ...in distinction from [*dechomai* being] a receiving of what is offered."[16]

Studying the uses of *lambano* in connection with the gift of holy spirit shows us that when someone "receives" or "takes" the holy spirit, there is often a visible manifestation of it. The record in Acts 8 is a case in point. Under the ministry of Philip, many people in the city of Samaria were saved. This is quite clear because Acts 8:14 says they "...had received the word of God...." However, the word "received" ("accepted" NIV) is *dechomai*. The people of Samaria had accepted the Word of God and were saved, but there

---

15. Vine, *op. cit.*, *Vine's Complete Expository Dictionary*, "Receive," p. 511.
16. Thayer, *op. cit.*, *Thayer's Greek-English Lexicon*, p. 131.

was something missing, there was still a "self-prompted taking" that had not occurred. The people were saved, but they had missed *doing* something, that is, receiving the gift of holy spirit into manifestation.

Peter and John came to Samaria and ministered to the people, at which time they "received" [*lambano*] the holy spirit, that is, they actively took the gift of God that was inside them and manifested it outwardly. When the people of Samaria "received" [*lambano*] the holy spirit, something visible in the senses world occurred, because Simon the sorcerer "saw" that the people "received," and you cannot usually see when someone gets saved (Acts 8:18). In fact, Simon offered Peter and John money to buy the power to lay hands on people and have them "receive" [*lambano*], outwardly manifest holy spirit. This record in Acts 8 is similar to what happens in the lives of many Christians today. They are born again under the preaching ministry of one person, but they do not outwardly manifest holy spirit at that time. Then later, after being ministered to by someone else, they go ahead and "receive," actively take and manifest holy spirit, often by speaking in tongues.

Another record in which *lambano* is important occurs in Acts Chapter Ten. Peter was preaching the death and resurrection of Christ to the Roman Centurion, Cornelius, and his household. During Peter's preaching, those Romans got saved and started to speak in tongues (Acts 10:46). Peter exclaimed, "…They have received [*lambano*] the Holy Spirit [holy spirit] just as we have" (Acts 10:47b). Had Peter not seen visible proof of holy spirit within them, he would have been very skeptical as to whether or not Gentiles could have really been saved in the same manner as the Jews. But he saw that proof when the new converts "received" [*lambano*] holy spirit and spoke in tongues.

God's gift of holy spirit is not something a person receives **after** he is saved. We Christians receive it **when** we are saved. No one has to earn holy spirit because, like salvation, it is a free **gift** (Acts 2:38, 10:45), not a reward for good works. We do not earn it, we do not have to pray for it to come into us, and we do not have to be "spiritually qualified" to receive it. It was God's idea to give it to us as a free gift at the moment we are born again. If you are a Christian, you have God's gift of holy spirit sealed permanently inside you.

3) In the Old Testament and Gospels, God gave holy spirit in a limited way, by measure, but today, in the Administration of Grace, every believer is filled with holy spirit.

During the Old Testament and Gospel periods, when God placed holy spirit upon people, He did so by "measure," in other words, in a limited way. God gave people a limited measure of holy spirit according to the amount they needed to accomplish the work that God wanted done. Thus, different people had different measures of it. For example, we have seen earlier that Bezaleel was given a particular measure of holy spirit so he would have the spiritual wisdom to do the work on the Tent of Meeting (Tabernacle). The people in the Old Testament recognized that some people were given more holy spirit than others. That is why Elisha asked for twice as much spirit as Elijah. Elisha knew that more spirit meant more spiritual ability, which is why he wanted a "double portion" of the spirit that was on Elijah.

> **2 Kings 2:9 (KJV)**
> And it came to pass, when they were gone over, that Elijah said unto Elisha, Ask what I shall do for thee, before I be taken away from thee. And Elisha said, I pray thee, let a double portion of thy spirit be upon me.

John the Baptist had a measure of spirit that gave him great spiritual power and understanding, and which was equated with "…the spirit and power of Elijah…" (Luke 1:17). Furthermore, God knew that the job He required of John would take great spiritual ability and training, and so He put holy spirit on John from birth (Luke 1:15). This is unique to John the Baptist, as no other person in the Old Testament or Gospels is said to have holy spirit from birth. It was due to the fact that believers in the Old Testament and Gospel periods did receive the spirit by measure that the Bible makes the specific point that Jesus did not have the gift of holy spirit by measure (John 3:34). Rather, he was given the fullness of the spirit.

Today, in the Administration of Grace, every Christian has all the holy spirit it is possible for God to give. There is no indication in the Church Epistles that anyone can have, or does have, holy spirit by measure, or any less than all God can give. When a person becomes born again, he is born of the very nature of God, holy spirit, which is why the Bible says that Christians are partakers of the divine nature.

> **2 Peter 1:4a (KJV)**
> Whereby are given unto us exceeding great and precious promises: that by these ye might be partakers of the divine nature…

God is holy, and God is spirit, and when holy spirit is born inside us we become partakers of His very nature. In birth, when children get the nature of their parents, they are filled with that nature. It is not just in part of them, it is in every part of them, and so it is with Christians. We are each filled with holy spirit, and have God's divine nature in every part of us.

God uses other ways of telling us that we Christians are filled with His holy spirit. For one thing, He says He has given us "every spiritual blessing" (Eph. 1:3). He is not holding back anything from us, His children. Furthermore, God says each Christian is "complete" in Christ.

> **Colossians 2:10 (NASB)**[17]
> and in Him you have been made complete, and He is the head over all rule and authority;

There is no verse like this in the Old Testament or the Gospels, because at that time holy spirit was given by measure. In contrast, we now have holy spirit as part of our very nature. Thus we are "complete" in Christ, and cannot receive any more holy spirit than we already have. Other ways God has communicated to us that we are filled with holy spirit is that holy spirit has been "poured out" into us, indicating the boundless amount of holy spirit that Christ has now given. Also, we are baptized, or fully immersed in holy spirit.

God says every Christian has "Christ in you" (Col. 1:27b) indicating how much spiritual ability and power that we, as Christians, have. If

---

17. We use the NASB here because we feel that the word "complete" is an accurate representation of the Greek text and the subject matter being discussed, and it is easy to understand.

Christians differed in how much innate spiritual power or ability they had, then God could not say that every Christian had "Christ" in them.

4) In the Old Testament and Gospels, God gave holy spirit conditionally, and a person could lose it, but today it is permanently sealed inside every Christian, and guarantees them everlasting life.

Throughout the Old Testament and Gospel periods, God put holy spirit "upon" people conditionally, and He could therefore take it back if they did not walk uprightly before Him. King Saul was one person who sinned and lost holy spirit (1 Sam. 16:14). David also sinned, but prayed that God would not take it away (Ps. 51:11). It seems certain that Samson lost holy spirit when he told Delilah all his heart and got his hair cut, because he lost his spiritually generated strength. Scripture tells us that the LORD had left him (Judg. 16:20). What left Samson, and thus separated him from God was holy spirit, not God's love for him. It also seems he got it back and was spiritually strengthened again after he prayed for the LORD to remember him (Judg. 16:28–30).

Today, however, in the Church Age, God seals His gift of holy spirit inside believers, and they **cannot** lose it.[18] It is clear in the writings to the Christian Church that we have holy spirit permanently. The vocabulary God uses concerning holy spirit and indeed, salvation, is dramatically different in the Old Testament than in the Epistles to the Church (Acts–Jude). One reason Christians must spend time reading and re-reading the Bible is that the only way to notice the changes in vocabulary and phraseology is to be familiar with the entire Bible. Then and only then will words and phrases that are spoken only of the Christian Church stand out as they ought to. One could write a book on the permanence of salvation, and we cover it in more detail in Appendix A, "The Administration of the Sacred Secret," so we will only summarize the major points at this time, points that are readily evident in Scripture.

We have already seen that when a person becomes a Christian, he receives holy spirit. However, unlike in the Old Testament, in the

---

18. For more information on the permanence of salvation for Christians, see Appendix A, "The Administration of the Sacred Secret" and our booklet: *25 Reasons Why Salvation is Permanent*, available at www.TheLivingTruthFellowship.org under Bible Teachings click on articles.

Administration of Grace the Christian receives holy spirit at the moment he becomes "born" of God. As in any natural birth, the seed of the Father is involved, and in our spiritual New Birth, God contributes imperishable spiritual seed, which becomes part of our nature (1 Pet. 1:23). Why does God use language about birth? The answer is that it is common knowledge that birth cannot be undone. Once something is born, it cannot be unborn. Once holy spirit is born in a person, it cannot be unborn. It stays in the person permanently. Christians are literally children of God by spiritual birth, as the Bible claims so boldly.

> **1 John 3:1a**
> How great is the love the Father has lavished on us, that we should be called children of God! And that is what we are!…

When a child is born, it always has the nature of the parent. This is true of any birth. Kittens have the cat nature of their parents, puppies have the dog nature of their parents, baby boys and girls have the human nature of their parents, and Christians have the holy spirit nature of their Father, God. That is why Peter says that we Christians are "…partakers of the divine nature…" (2 Pet. 1:4-KJV).

It is of paramount importance that each Christian understands the tremendous work God has done for us in this Age of Grace. We do not live in Old Testament times, when holy spirit was given to some people but could be taken from them. We live in a time when God's gift of holy spirit is born inside each of us and becomes part of us, thus changing our very nature.

The new nature created within us when we become Christians is **holy**, and so we become holy by nature. This is why the Bible calls us "holy ones," which is usually translated as "saints."

> **Romans 1:7**
> To all in Rome who are loved by God and called to be **saints**: Grace and peace to you from God our Father and from the Lord Jesus Christ.

The Greek word translated "saints" is *hagios*, the Greek word for "holy," and it has several meanings, including, "worthy of veneration;" "set apart to God;" and "pure."[19] It is used, among other things, of God (John 17:11), Christ (Acts 4:27), angels (Mark 8:38), the Temple (1 Cor. 3:17) and the Law (Rom. 7:12). It is also used of Christians. It is vital to understand that we Christians are not called "holy" because we live perfectly holy lives, but because we have the holy nature of God created in us. Then, since we have God's nature, and are His children by birth as well as the followers of Jesus Christ, we are exhorted to live holy lives.

The holy spirit is born inside us and is our very nature, so the Bible says we are **sealed** with it.

> **Ephesians 1:13**
> And you also were included in Christ when you heard the word of truth, the gospel of your salvation. Having believed, you were marked in him with a seal, the promised Holy Spirit [holy spirit],

You can search the entire Old Testament and the Gospels to find someone sealed with holy spirit, but you will not find a single one. Before the Administration of Grace, God's gift of holy spirit was only "upon" people. No one before Acts 2 was sealed with it.

The gift of holy spirit is imperishable seed born and sealed inside us, becoming part of our very nature and making us new creations, so God calls it a guarantee of our future hope (2 Cor. 1:22, 5:5; Eph. 1:14-RSV). The word "guarantee" (RSV), "guaranteeing" (NIV), "pledge" (NASB), and "earnest" (KJV), are the translations of the Greek word *arrabon*, which originally was a Phoenician word used in their trading. It was a down payment or pledge of the full amount that was to follow. In our case, the gift of holy spirit that we have now is the down payment of all we will get in the future. If a person could lose holy spirit, it would not actually **guarantee** anything. This is why nowhere in the Old Testament or the Gospels is holy spirit called a **"guarantee"** of anyone's future everlasting life, because those who had it then could lose it. Today, however, a Christian cannot lose his salvation. His everlasting life is totally secure, and so the presence of holy spirit can honestly be called a **"guarantee"** of his future hope.

---

19. Thayer, *op. cit. Thayer's Greek-English Lexicon*, p. 6.

In the New Birth, a natural person of body and soul receives the seed of God, holy spirit, and literally becomes a child of God with a new, divine nature. Thus it is very appropriate that the Bible calls each Christian a "new creation."

> **2 Corinthians 5:17**
> Therefore, if anyone is in Christ, he is a new creation; the old has gone, the new has come!

Many people in the Old Testament and Gospels were saved, yet the Bible never says they became new creations. What God has given to us in this Administration of the Sacred Secret is an expansion of what He promised in the Old Testament for the Millennial Kingdom. It was foretold that God would put a new spirit in people, but He never specifically stated they would be new creations. That is a privilege God reserved for Christians.

There is one more point we need to make about the permanence of holy spirit inside us, and hence the permanence of our salvation. Some people believe that a Christian can make the freewill decision to repent of his faith and thus become unsaved, and in doing so would lose the gift of holy spirit within him and his guarantee of our future hope. That is not true. There are some decisions a person makes that change him in a permanent way, and choosing salvation is one of them. When a person becomes a Christian, his very nature is changed permanently, and he cannot reverse that change by another freewill decision. We accept this thinking when it comes to our flesh. If a person makes the freewill decision to blind himself by poking out his eyes, he cannot then make the freewill decision to regain his sight. The change is permanent. Likewise, the New Birth permanently changes us. We have a brand new spiritual nature created within us, and it cannot be undone by a simple freewill decision.

5) In the Old Testament and Gospels, it was not stated that the gift of holy spirit that God gave at that time influenced a person's life in a transforming way, but today, in the Administration of Grace, holy spirit helps conform people into the image of Christ by helping them live godly lives.

In the Administration of Grace, the gift of holy spirit is the very nature of God within a Christian, so it does two things. First, it allows for direct communication between God and the believer. Second, because it is inside the person and becomes part of him, it exerts an influence to become what it is, which is holy. We will look at both these points, starting with the fact that holy spirit does not speak on its own. Jesus made this point very clearly to his followers.

> **John 16:13 (Author's translation)**
> But when it, the spirit of truth, comes, it will guide you in all truth, for it will not speak of itself, but whatever it hears, it will speak, and it will tell to you the things that are to come.[20]

God's gift of holy spirit is not a person, and does not think, speak, or act on its own. In other words, God's spirit inside a person does not have "a mind of its own." It is neither a person nor a personality. It is spirit, the nature of God, and as such it allows us to communicate with God and the Lord Jesus Christ. When we hear from God or Jesus via holy spirit inside us, it is not the spirit that is talking. Rather, the way it "guides" and can "tell you what is to come" is by being the conduit of communication between God or the Lord Jesus and the believer. Jesus made it clear that it would "speak" only what it heard from God.

The use of the word "guides" is very accurate. The voice of the Lord coming via holy spirit is a quiet voice that guides, not "forces." The gift of holy spirit makes intimate communication possible between God and the believer, so it is called such things as the spirit of: "truth" (John 14:17), "wisdom," "understanding," "counsel," and "knowledge" (Isa. 11:2). Throughout the Old Testament, the presence of holy spirit upon someone allowed him to hear from God and thus have knowledge, wisdom, and understanding, but there will be an amplification of that when the holy spirit is poured out within all believers in the Millennial Kingdom, and as it has been born inside Christians today.

---

20. The first "it" is masculine. This is because the subject that the "it" refers to is not "the spirit" (which is neuter), but rather the "helper" (v. 7; which is masculine), and the "helper" is "the spirit of truth." For more on nouns and pronoun agreement, see Chapter 4.

The promised holy spirit so helps people live godly lives that it is actually called "the helper" (our preference). The Greek noun that different versions translate as "Counselor," "Comforter," "Helper," "Advocate," "Friend," etc., is *parakletos*. In the Greek world, a *parakletos* was a legal advisor or advocate who came forward on behalf of, or as a representative of, another. However, the word was also used by the Greeks in the wider sense of a helper, aide, assistant, adviser, counselor, etc.[21]

John 15:26 shows that "the helper" is the spirit of truth, which we have seen from other verses is the gift of God, holy spirit.

> **John 15:26 (Author's translation)**
> But when the helper comes, which I will send to you from the Father, *even* the spirit of truth, which comes from the Father, it will bear witness of me,

The gift of holy spirit is called "the helper" because through it the Lord can bless and help us in many ways, including influencing us toward godliness. We today should look daily for the Lord's help and guidance via holy spirit.[22]

Another thing we learn from John 15:26 is that holy spirit comes from the Father, God.[23] It is God who lovingly gives His very nature to people in order that they can "walk by the spirit" as an alternative to living only according to the dictates of their "flesh" (sin nature). As Peter told his audience on the Day of Pentecost, the Lord Jesus Christ is the intermediary through whom God gave us His holy spirit. Jesus received it from God and now pours it out to all who believe in him as Lord (Acts 2:33). God is spirit, and is the ultimate source of holy spirit.

---

21. Thayer, *op. cit.*, *Thayer's Greek-English Lexicon*, p. 483. Jesus Christ also represents us to God and helps us in our lives, so it is appropriate that he also is called a *parakletos* ("...we have an advocate [*parakletos*] with the Father, Jesus Christ the righteous" 1 John 2:1-KJV).

22. Christ was speaking about the holy spirit that believers would receive in the Millennial Kingdom, and it applies to Christians because we have the "promised" holy spirit. See Appendix C, "The Promised Holy Spirit."

23. We say "comes," although some versions have "proceeds." The Greek word is *ekporeuomai*, and means to go forth, or out; to depart. Figuratively, it means to come forth, to issue, or proceed (Thayer, *op. cit.*, *Thayer's Greek Lexicon*, p. 199).

God and the Lord Jesus direct us by holy spirit inside us, which is why Scripture exhorts us to live by spirit (Gal. 5:16 and 25) i.e., live by the guidance we receive from them through the gift of holy spirit born within us.[24]

Another thing to remember about holy spirit is that when it was born in us it became part of our very nature and influences us like our fleshly nature influences us.

Galatians 5:17
For the sinful nature desires what is contrary to the Spirit [spirit], and the Spirit [spirit] what is contrary to the sinful nature. They are in conflict with each other, so that you do not do what you want. [25]

Neither the "sinful nature" nor the holy spirit are separate personalities. Both are part of us. Our sinful nature is the nature we have as descendants of Adam and Eve, and our "spirit" is our divine nature (2 Pet. 1:4).[26] Yet both natures influence us, and God describes that influence as a "desire." Our sinful nature "desires," or influences us, toward worldliness, and our holy nature "desires," or influences us, toward godliness. Just as no one would insist that our "flesh" is a person with a will of its own, no one should take these verses to mean that "spirit" is a person or has a will of its own.

What a blessing to know that our divine nature, holy spirit, exerts a godly influence in our lives. We should be very thankful to God for providing this "helper" so that we can effectively live godly lives. The gift of holy spirit inside us does not force us to do anything. It can be, and

---

24. Although most versions say, "...walk by the Spirit," there is no article "the" in the Greek, and because the subject is the gift of God, "spirit" should have a lower case "s."

25. The Greek text literally reads "flesh," not "sinful nature." Although in some contexts they are synonyms, there can be a difference. Not all the desires of the flesh are sinful, or come from the sin nature. For example, sleep is a "desire of the flesh," yet sleep is not sin, nor is the desire for it from the "sinful nature." Given that there can be differences between the "flesh" and the "sinful nature," we do not think that "sinful nature" is the best translation, and prefer "flesh."

26. This is a great example of the context helping us to determine what use of "spirit" is proper in the verse. In this case, *pneuma* refers to our new, divine nature, and it is juxtaposed to our sinful nature.

sadly is, often overruled by our own sinful desires. We can easily quench the influence of holy spirit in our lives, so God commands us:

1 Thessalonians 5:19 (NASB)
Do not quench the Spirit [spirit];

We quench the spirit when we refuse to set aside our own desires and sin, and insist on doing things our own way. We need to set aside our own will and listen intently to God out of a pure heart, and with a desire to become like Christ, dealing with things such as hatred, anger, envy, etc. Then our divine nature will shine forth. The Bible calls the outworking of our new nature "...the fruit of the spirit...."

Galatians 5:22 and 23a
(22) But the fruit of the Spirit [spirit] is love, joy, peace, patience, kindness, goodness, faithfulness,
(23) gentleness and self-control....

Many commentators point out the word "fruit" refers to something that grows from a tree or a plant, which began as a seed. Just as a tree is the ultimate source of its fruit, our divine nature, holy spirit, which is the spiritual seed from God, is the source of the "fruit of the spirit." These qualities are not attained purely by human effort, but require the influence of holy spirit if they are to be fully developed in one's life. The fact that there are many Christians who do not evidence these character qualities is a testimony to the fact that we can ignore or negate the influence of our divine nature if we so desire. We need to work hard to have these fruit in our lives, and also we need to be thankful for what we have today, because there is no verse in the Old Testament or the Gospels that is similar to these verses in Galatians. There is no indication in the Old Testament that the gift of holy spirit became part of people's nature.

There are many other verses written to the Church that let us know holy spirit inside us helps us be like Christ. Christians have a wonderful advantage when it comes to living godly lifestyles, because we have been given the divine nature of God, which constantly tugs at us to live a godly life. We owe it to the Lord Jesus, who died for us, and to God, who gave holy spirit to the Church today, to do what it takes to be able to clearly understand what they are communicating to us through holy spirit so we can live godly lives.

6) In the Old Testament and Gospels, there were seven manifestations of holy spirit available. Today there are nine, as enumerated in 1 Corinthians 12:8–10. The manifestations of speaking in tongues and interpretation of tongues did not exist in the Old Testament or Gospel periods, but are now available to all Christians.

Christians have two manifestations of holy spirit that were not available before the Day of Pentecost: speaking in tongues and the interpretation of tongues. Speaking in tongues was first manifested on the Day of Pentecost in Acts 2. We do not know when believers began to manifest interpretation of tongues, but it was known and understood by the time 1 Corinthians was written, probably in 53 or 54 A.D. (1 Cor. 14:5). These two manifestations are more evidence that the gift of holy spirit we have today differs from holy spirit God gave before the Day of Pentecost. For the 4,000 years of the Old Testament and the Gospels, the manifestations of the spirit were the same. However, as we have seen, God has given His gift of holy spirit to the Church in a new and powerful way—by birth. New babies soon develop language skills and, since Christians are God's children by birth, it is appropriate that He would give us a special language that allows us to communicate with Him.

> **1 Corinthians 14:2 (NASB)**
> For one who speaks in a tongue does not speak to men, but to God; for no one understands, but in *his* spirit he speaks mysteries.

We like the NASB translation of this verse because it says, "for no one understands…." Most versions add the word "him," even though it does not exist in the Greek texts. God is telling us that "no one" who speaks in tongues understands what he himself is saying. If he did, it would not be "tongues" to him. For example, no one who speaks English speaks in tongues in English, because that would not be "tongues." For the language to be "speaking in tongues," it has to be a language that the speaker does not understand, which is exactly what the Greek text says; no one understands. This is stated another way in 1 Corinthians 14:14. "For if I pray in a tongue, my spirit prays, but my mind is unfruitful." When a person speaks in tongues, he does not know what he is saying, thus his mind is said to be "unfruitful."

It is generally true, but not always so, that when someone speaks in tongues "no one understands him." Nevertheless, there are times when someone speaks in tongues and someone else understands. This was the case on the Day of Pentecost—the Apostles spoke in tongues and people in the audience understood. Thus, when translators add the word "him," as they do in the NIV, RSV, ESV, etc., they make the verse say something untrue. This verse confirms that when a person is speaking in tongues he is speaking to God. In fact, it says that he is speaking sacred secrets. This communication between God and man is one of the great blessings of holy spirit in the Church Age.

Conclusion

We have now seen that there are significant differences between the gift of holy spirit that God poured out upon Old Testament believers and the holy spirit born in Christians today. Today Moses' wish for Israel has, by the grace of God, been granted to Christians, because each and every one has God's wonderful gift of holy spirit. Better yet, holy spirit is permanently born and sealed inside each Christian, having become part of his very nature, making him a new and holy creation of God and guaranteeing his hope of a wonderful future with the Lord. Furthermore, each Christian is filled with holy spirit, not given just a measure of it. Lastly, we have seen that in this Age of Grace, God has empowered us with two manifestations that did not exist before the Day of Pentecost, speaking in tongues and the interpretation of tongues, manifestations not available before the Church Age.

Chapter 7

Your Liquid Asset

The Gift of Holy Spirit—Spiritual Water

One cannot study the holy spirit field very long before noticing all the parallels in the Bible between spirit and water. There seem to be several reasons for this. Fresh, clean water was vital in the biblical culture, and not always easy to come by, so comparing holy spirit to water emphasizes its importance. More to the point, however, is that spirit acts like water in that it exerts a power, often seems to have a flowing quality, and takes the shape of its container. Consider the following verses:

> **Isaiah 44:3 and 4**
> (3) For I will pour water on the thirsty land, and streams on the dry ground; I will pour out my Spirit [spirit] on your offspring, and my blessing on your descendants.
> (4) They will spring up like grass in a meadow, like poplar trees by flowing streams.

The "water" in the first half of the verse is partly figurative and partly literal. While it is true that in the future God will restore the earth and it will have abundant water, the greater truth captured in the second part of verse 3, and in verse 4, is that "water" also symbolizes the gift of holy spirit that God will pour out upon people.[1] As a result, they will thrive like grass in the meadow or trees by a stream.[2]

There are other places in Scripture where spirit is compared to water. For example, when Jesus was in the Temple at the Feast of Tabernacles, he cried out to the people:

---

1. Some Scriptures that refer to the abundant water on earth once it is restored are Isaiah 35:6 and 7, 41:18–20, 51:3; Ezekiel 47:1–12; Joel 2:21–24; and Zechariah 14:8.

2. **Amphibologia** is the figure of speech when one thing is said but two are referred to. In English we call it "double-entendre." E. W. Bullinger, *Figures of Speech Used in the Bible* (Baker Book House, Grand Rapids, MI, reprinted 1968), pp. 804–806.

John 7:37–39 (Author's translation)

(37) Now on the last day, the great *day* of the feast, Jesus stood and cried out, saying, "If any man thirst, let him come to me and drink.
(38) He who believes in me, as the Scripture has said, out of his belly will flow rivers of living water."[3]
(39) But this he said about the spirit, which those who believed on him were to receive; for as yet there was no spirit,[4] because Jesus was not yet glorified.[5]

In John 4, when Jesus was speaking to the woman at the well, he cryptically referred to the spirit as water, something that we can see from the context, specifically in John 4:23 and 24. He was at Jacob's well in the area of Israel known as Samaria, but he had nothing with which to get the water out of the well. When the woman there pointed out that fact to Jesus, he answered her, saying:

---

3. The word "belly" is *koilia*, and in the Greco-Roman culture it was used metaphorically to refer to the seat of the emotional desires and appetites of man (cp. Rom. 16:18 and Phil. 3:19). Today we often use "heart" as the seat of the emotional life, but the Greco-Roman culture used "heart" more to refer to the seat of the spiritual/mental life (cp. in the Greek text: Matt. 15:19, 24:48; Luke 1:51, 2:19, 9:47; Rom. 10:9; Heb. 4:12). It will help us understand the Bible if we learn what the words meant in the biblical culture, and not change "belly" to "heart" as many versions have done. The believer's connection to the holy spirit within him is not just a mental process, but something deeper, from his very core. It can involve deep emotions and convictions. Verse 38 also contains "his," and scholars have debated to whom the "his" refers. In the Old Testament, God was the fountain of living water, the source of spiritual and physical sustenance, and Christ became the giver of holy spirit after he was glorified. However, the most natural reading of the Greek text makes "his" refer to the believer, not the Messiah (in fact, in the modern punctuation of the Greek text, "his" must refer to the believer). In John 4:14, Jesus speaks of spiritual water, and makes the point that he is the source, although it comes "springing up" (NASB) or "gushing up" (NRSV) from within the believer. Thus it is true that the spirit flows from inside the believer, even though Jesus gives it to people when they are saved, and he energizes it as the believer manifests holy spirit. It seems likely that "his belly" is a "double-entendre," referring to both the believer and the Messiah.

4. For an explanation of why this verse says, "…for as yet there was no spirit…," see Chapter 6, "The Gift of Holy Spirit Today."

5. Although the King James Version reads "Holy Ghost," the textual research that has been done since 1611 shows that the word "Holy" was added. There was a tendency among copyists to make phrases throughout the Bible consistent, a principle known as "harmonization." At some point in history, "spirit" was changed to "holy spirit" in some of the Greek texts, and found its way into the KJV.

John 4:13 and 14
(13) Jesus answered, "Everyone who drinks this water will be thirsty again,
(14) but whoever drinks the water I give him will never thirst. Indeed, the water I give him will become in him a spring of water welling up to eternal life."

One of the ways the gift of holy spirit is compared to water in the Bible is that it is often said to be "poured out" (cp. Prov. 1:23; Joel 2:28 and 29; Zech. 12:10). Quoting from the Old Testament, Peter used this wording in his teaching on the Day of Pentecost.

Acts 2:17
"'In the last days, God says, I will **pour out** my Spirit [spirit] on all people. Your sons and daughters will prophesy, your young men will see visions, your old men will dream dreams.

We have seen that God has chosen water as a fitting analogy for the gift of holy spirit, and that it is poured out from above. We are about to see that God uses other liquid terminology in Scripture.

Anointed with Holy Spirit

In the biblical culture it was common to anoint people, and even things, with oil. Although people were anointed for cosmetic reasons (Ruth 3:3-KJV; Eccles. 9:8; Dan. 10:3-KJV, etc.), we usually associate anointing with consecrating something for a special purpose. The Tent of Meeting (Tabernacle) was anointed (Exod. 40:9) and so was the altar (Exod. 40:10). Anointing with oil was part of the God-prescribed formula for installation and consecration to an office such as priest or king (see Exod. 28:41, 29:7, 40:13 and 15; 1 Sam. 9:16, 10:1, 16:3, 12 and 13; 1 Kings 19:16.) Moses actually prescribed a special oil for anointing (Exod. 30:22–30).

Prophets, priests, and kings were anointed with oil to consecrate them into office, so it is fitting that God would use the term "anoint" with holy spirit to symbolize the high position that He views anyone with holy spirit to have. After all, they have the spiritual enablements to do what God calls them to do. In fact, God apparently sometimes used "oil" as a symbol of the spirit, and poured out holy spirit at the same time that the literal anointing oil was poured out. This occurred in the case of David, who was anointed with oil by Samuel and holy spirit by God at the same time.

> **1 Samuel 16:13**
> So Samuel took the horn of oil and anointed him in the presence of his brothers, and from that day on the Spirit [spirit] of the LORD came upon David in power. Samuel then went to Ramah.

Because the king was anointed, he became known as "the anointed" or "the anointed one" (1 Sam. 26:9, 11, 16, 23; 2 Sam. 1:14, 22:51, 23:1; Ps. 18:50; Isa. 45:1). The Hebrew word "to anoint" is *mashach*, and "anointed" is *mashiach*, from which we get our English word "Messiah," which actually means "the anointed one." The New Testament Greek verb, "to anoint," is *chrio*, which properly means "to touch with the hand" but was used from the time of Homer to mean "to anoint."[6] From the word *chrio* comes the noun *christos*—the "anointed one." Thus, Jesus "Christ" is more literally Jesus the "Anointed One."

Many people in the Bible were anointed, so there were many "Messiahs," or many "Christs." When David said that he would not kill King Saul because he would not "...lay a hand on the LORD's anointed..." (1 Sam. 26:9), the Hebrew text reads "the LORD's *mashiach*." There were many anointed ones (Messiahs), but only one Messiah would save mankind. Thus, "Messiah" is like king, Lord, savior, etc., in that it applies to more people than Jesus Christ. "Christ" is the title that Jesus carries and the office he is fulfilling as the promised Messiah (anointed one), the Savior.[7] We have already seen in Chapter 5, "The Messiah and the Gift of Holy Spirit" that God anointed Jesus with holy spirit to empower him to do the work he was called to do. Jesus' anointing with holy spirit was foretold in the Old Testament (Isa. 11:2, 61:1), announced by Christ himself (Luke 4:18), and then stated after the fact by Peter (Acts 10:38).

---

6. Thayer, *op. cit.*, *Thayer's Greek-English Lexicon*, p. 673.

7. For more on "savior," see Appendix A (Luke 1:47) in our book, *op. cit., One God & One Lord.*

Sometimes Scripture refers to Jesus as being anointed without specifically saying that he was anointed with holy spirit. For example, in their prayer in Acts 4, Peter, John and the other disciples said:

Acts 4:27
Indeed Herod and Pontius Pilate met together with the Gentiles and the people of Israel in this city to conspire against your holy servant Jesus, whom you anointed.

Psalm 2:2 also refers to "...the LORD and...his Anointed One," which we can tell from the context does not refer to just any anointed one, but to Jesus Christ and his still future ministry to Israel. On the Day of Pentecost, the Lord Jesus began the Christian Church by anointing each one who believed with holy spirit. This anointing occurred when Jesus "poured out" the gift of holy spirit, and Peter pointed this out to the crowd.

Acts 2:32 and 33
(32) God has raised this Jesus to life, and we are all witnesses of the fact.
(33) Exalted to the right hand of God, he has received from the Father the promised Holy Spirit [holy spirit] and has **poured out** what you now see and hear.

Since Pentecost, Jesus Christ has "anointed" each one who believes on him at the moment of the person's New Birth. When a person becomes a Christian, he is born again and receives the gift of holy spirit, which is poured out into his entire body. He has a new nature and becomes a new creation. In pouring out holy spirit to Christians, Jesus passes on to us the gift of holy spirit he himself received from his Father. Thus, from the time of his salvation, each Christian is an anointed minister of the Gospel, with the power to walk in the steps of the Lord.

The word "anoint" is used only once in the Church Epistles (Romans through Thessalonians), and this use makes it clear that every Christian is anointed with holy spirit from the moment of his New Birth:

2 Corinthians 1:21 and 22
(21) Now it is God who makes both us and you stand firm in Christ. He **anointed** us,
(22) set his seal of ownership on us, and put his Spirit [spirit] in our hearts as a deposit, guaranteeing what is to come.

Verse 21 above makes it very clear that each Christian has been anointed. Note the past tenses of "anointed," "set his seal," and "put his spirit." These are accomplished realities. Each Christian is equipped for service today and is sealed with the guarantee of everlasting life in the age to come. Furthermore, as we have already seen, and cover in more detail in Appendix A, once a person is saved he cannot lose the holy spirit he has received. This is an important point, because it means that a Christian is "anointed" **once and for all** at the time he is saved. He can never be anointed again, because the holy spirit will never be poured out on him again.

Jesus pours out holy spirit when a person is born again and, because it never leaves, he never pours it on him again. : A "re-anointing" would have been possible in Old Testament times because holy spirit was "conditional" for people and God could take it from them. Thus it would be possible before Pentecost to be anointed multiple times. However, that is not possible for Christians, because we receive holy spirit once, and are sealed with it, and it becomes part of our very nature.

Samson may have lost holy spirit and later, after his prayer to regain strength, have been re-anointed (though it is not specifically stated that way in the Bible), but no Christian would ever have that experience. Nevertheless, there is no record that states, or any reason to believe, that faithful men and women such as Moses, Joshua, Deborah, Samuel, etc., lost holy spirit and then had to be anointed with it again, which tells us that God stands with those whom He has anointed and supports them even when they do not obey Him. After all, David did not lose it when he committed adultery and had Uriah killed (but also, he prayed to God not to take it). However, God did take His holy spirit from Saul, which shows that even God, as merciful and longsuffering as He is, has limits. In the

Old Testament and Gospels, if a person hardened his heart against God, as King Saul did, God might take back His gift of holy spirit.

This anointing—the gift of holy spirit—is the key to us being able to live spiritually balanced lives. As our perfect connection to Jesus Christ, the Head of the Body, holy spirit gives us the ability to hear from our Lord and separate truth from error, as the following verses show:

> **1 John 2:25–27 (AMP, brackets and parentheses are theirs; bold print is our emphasis)**
> (25) And this is what He Himself has promised us—the life, the eternal [life].
> (26) I write this to you with reference to those who would deceive you [seduce and lead you astray].
> (27) But as for you, the **anointing** (the sacred appointment, the unction) which you received from Him abides [permanently] in you; [so] then you have no need that anyone should instruct you. But just as His anointing teaches you concerning everything and is true and is no falsehood, so you must abide in (live in, never depart from) Him [being rooted in Him, knit to Him], just as [His anointing] has taught you [to do].[8]

The Amplified Bible accurately picks up the sense of the verb in verse 27 and translates it "abides [permanently]." How wonderful and how comforting. No Christian has to worry that if he sins he will lose the gift of holy spirit. No, it is part of his nature, born and sealed inside him, and it will stay in him, as the Amplified Bible says, "permanently."

The heart of each Christian should be filled with thanksgiving because of all that is contained in the gift of holy spirit with which we have been forever anointed. God's love, joy, and peace are within us. Through His

---

8. Sometimes you hear people quote verse 27a to defend the obvious error that "the Holy Spirit" will teach you all you need to know, independent of the written Word of God. Why then would there be "teachers" set by Christ in the Church (Eph. 4:11)? In context, the above verses are speaking of counterfeit "believers" teaching doctrinal error about Jesus Christ among true believers. John is saying that Christians should listen to the spirit of God within them rather than to such false teachers. We know that the spirit of God never contradicts the written Word of God, which should remain in our hearts as the ultimate standard for truth (Heb. 4:12).

Son Jesus Christ, our heavenly Father has called us, consecrated us, and empowered us for a life of joyful service to Him. At the moment He gave us life, He gave us all we will ever need to live it. Let us do so for His glory.

There is one more point that we should make in our striving for unity in the Body of Christ. We know there are Christians who use the word "anointed" in reference to temporary spiritual enablements or empowerings that usually occur as they minister, pray, sing, etc. We recognize that there are such genuine spiritual experiences they are trying to describe. God does work with us as we step out in faith to obey Him. He energizes His gift of holy spirit in His people, resulting in manifestations (such as a message of knowledge, a message of wisdom, miracles, and healing) that are not available for us to do by the flesh alone.

Nevertheless, we assert that Christians have the responsibility to study the words in God's Word and to use the vocabulary of Scripture the way God uses it. We will not come to a "...unity in the faith and in the knowledge of the Son of God..." (Eph. 4:13) if we do not use the vocabulary of the Word of God as God does. How are Christians from diverse cultural and denominational backgrounds going to reach a common understanding if each uses his own denominational jargon and ignores how the Word of God uses its own vocabulary?

New Christians and Bible students alike can be confused by hearing about "the anointing" as if it were a temporary empowering but never seeing it used that way in Scripture. In listening to many people talk about "the anointing," we have decided that the biblical equivalent to what they are saying is a "working," or, an **energizing** of the gift of holy spirit that is already within a believer. The word "energize" is used in the Greek text, and gets translated in many versions as "working" or "workings."

> **1 Corinthians 12:6**
> There are different kinds of working [*energemata*, energizings], but the same God works [*energeo*, energizes] all of them in all men.

We feel it is more accurate to call God's temporary spiritual empowerings "energizings" than "anointings," because for Christians, "anointing" specifically refers to the one-time event of the New Birth.[9] Of course, if a person wanted to use, "workings," or something similar, that would be biblical also. The point is that we should attempt to use the vocabulary of the Bible the way the Bible uses it.

The gift of holy spirit is the "equalizing factor" among all members of the Body of Christ. Each one has the power of God to serve in whatever capacity he is called and directed by the Lord. Obviously, these callings of God are extremely varied, depending upon people's unique desires and abilities, and how God is able to work with them according to their faith. Each Christian, however, can rest assured that he has been anointed by the Lord, and that his anointing, and the spiritual power that comes with it, is permanent.

Baptism in Holy Spirit

Another "liquid" word that is used of receiving God's gift of holy spirit is "baptized." In the Administration of Grace, baptism in holy spirit, like the anointing, is a one time occurrence that happens at the time a person is saved and becomes a Christian. Appropriately, it was John the Baptist who first mentioned baptism in holy spirit. The phrase is not used in the Old Testament at all.

> **Mark 1:7 and 8**
> (7) And this was his message: "After me will come one more powerful than I, the thongs of whose sandals I am not worthy to stoop down and untie.
> (8) I baptize you with water, but he will baptize you with the Holy Spirit [No "the." Read "holy spirit"]."

The liquid connotation of baptizing in holy spirit is figurative. God's gift of holy spirit is intangible, and cannot literally be poured out, nor can one literally be immersed in it. But using the word "baptized" (immersed in) makes the point that holy spirit soaks one entirely.

---

9. We realize that strictly speaking, "energizings" is not in most versions of the Bible, but it is in the Greek, and using it would still be clarifying, similar to using the word "Rapture," which, though not in any English text, is the Latin word in 1 Thessalonians 4:17 for "caught up."

Before we consider baptism in holy spirit, we should talk about water baptism. Many people believe that John the Baptist was the first person to baptize in water, but this is clearly not the case. Hebrews 9:10 mentions "various ceremonial washings" in the Law, and the Greek word for "washings" is *baptismos* (immersions, baptisms). There are other Greek words for washing that God could have easily used, such as *pluno*, which is used of inanimate things; *nipto*, used of washing or of washing a part of the body; or *louo*, which means "to bathe" or "to wash the entire body." Instead, He chose "baptisms" to refer to the Old Testament washings.

A careful reading of the Old Testament will reveal various types of washings. Exodus 30:17–21 mentions the bronze basin that was placed between the door of the Tabernacle and the altar so the priests could wash their hands and feet. According to Exodus 40:12, Aaron and his sons were brought to the Tabernacle and washed with water. When Solomon built the Temple in Jerusalem, he had a basin cast of bronze that was so large the Bible calls it "the Sea." Scholars estimate that it held about twelve thousand gallons of water and, according to 2 Chronicles 4:6, the priests washed in it.

The Mosaic Law was full of regulations about washing. Many different things could make a person unclean, and often the Law said he had to wash in water in order to re-enter the congregation (cp. Lev. 14:9, 15:7–27, 16:26 and 28, 17:15 and 16). In that sense, bathing in water, beside being a sanitary regulation, had some typological significance. The same was true of John's baptism—the water was symbolic of the rinsing off of sin and of one showing desire to enter the congregation of the kingdom of heaven. Also, the Levites were sprinkled with water before they started ministering in the Tabernacle (Num. 8:5 and 7). The Law even had a special water of purification that was used in certain cases of uncleanness (e.g., Num. 19).

By the time of John the Baptist, there were ritual washing pools all over Israel. Today many of these pools can still be seen in the archaeological excavations, with good examples at Qumran, Masada, New Testament Jericho, and in Jerusalem itself. There were a large number of ritual baths discovered when the steps on the south end of the Temple were excavated.[10] That makes good sense, because a person going to the Temple might touch

---

10. Benjamin Mazar, *The Mountain of the Lord* (Doubleday and Company, Inc., New York, 1975), p. 146.

something unclean, and then not be able to enter. Having a *mikvah* (the Jewish word for the ritual bathing place) right on the stairway into the Temple would assure the pious worshipper that he was ritually clean.

It is also believed that the Jews of the time of Christ required a new convert to be water baptized. Hastings *Dictionary of the Bible* says:

> A stranger who desired to become a Proselyte of the Covenant, or of Righteousness, i.e., in the fullest sense an Israelite, must be circumcised and baptized, and then offer a sacrifice; circumcision alone was not enough. Three of those who had instructed the stranger in the Law…took him to a pool, in which he stood up to his neck in water, while the great commandments of the Law were recited to him. These he promised to keep. Then a benediction was pronounced and he plunged beneath the water, taking care to be entirely submerged."[11]

The Jews at the time of Christ were very familiar with ceremonial and symbolic washing, which explains why none of them asked John what his baptism meant, and also explains why the people were so willing for him to baptize them. Also, when the priests and Levites came to question John (John 1:19–27), they did not act surprised, as if baptism were a new ritual.

What Christians should understand is that the ritual washings and baptisms of the Old Testament were symbolic in nature and have been done away in Christ. There is no more Temple; no more basins [lavers], or ritual bathing places; no more water of purification; no more required washing of body or clothes before one can enter the presence of God. When the reality of Christ came, these ritual things were done away. John clearly saw that, and stated it. We have already quoted Mark 1:7 and 8, but we quote it here with a different emphasis:

Mark 1:7 and 8
(7) And this was his message: "After me will come one more powerful than I, the thongs of whose sandals I am not worthy to stoop down and untie.

---

11. James Hastings, *A Dictionary of the Bible* (Hendrickson Publishers, Peabody, MA, originally published by T. & T. Clark, Edinburgh, *1898*, reprinted in 1988), "Baptism," Vol. 1, p. 239.

(8) I baptize you with water, but he will baptize you with the Holy Spirit [No "the." Read "holy spirit"]."

John knew the temporal nature of water baptism, which was a ritual symbolizing a greater coming reality, and he correctly pointed out that Christ would baptize with holy spirit. Not with holy spirit **and** water, because when the greater reality came, the ritual that pointed to it, the water, was no longer needed. As we have said, baptism, immersion in water, pointed to the greater reality that believers would one day be totally immersed in holy spirit.[12] When a Christian receives God's gift of holy spirit, it is not just his lower body that receives, or his head, or any other separate part of his body. He is totally immersed in holy spirit. When a person becomes saved, he is completely "soaked" in holy spirit.

Just as John understood that the greater reality of holy spirit baptism would replace the water rituals of the Law, so did Jesus, who taught it to his disciples just before he ascended.

Acts 1:4 and 5
(4) On one occasion, while he was eating with them, he gave them this command: "Do not leave Jerusalem, but wait for the gift my Father promised, which you have heard me speak about.
(5) For John baptized with [in] water, but in a few days you will be baptized with [in] the Holy Spirit [No "the." Read "holy spirit]."

These verses are packed with truth. First, the reason the disciples had to "wait" for the holy spirit was because it had not been available up until

12. We will not take the time in this book to develop the thesis that baptism in holy spirit has replaced water baptism such that baptism in water is no longer necessary for Christians. Also, we do not think it is relevant to get involved in the ongoing debate about whether a person should be baptized by total immersion or by sprinkling or partial immersion. Historically, the Jews at the time of Christ immersed totally, and so did John. More to the point, however, is that we believe that water baptism was a ritual that, like the other water rituals of the Law, passed away with the coming of the baptism in holy spirit, which was the greater baptism the Law pointed to. For a much more thorough treatment of the subject of water baptism, see our booklet, *What is True Baptism?* by John A. Lynn (The Living Truth Fellowship, Indianapolis, IN, 2010).

then in the way God was going to make it available on Pentecost; Jesus had not yet poured it out. Now it has. No longer does anyone have to "wait" or "tarry" for the holy spirit—it is born inside a person when he is saved. He may not manifest the power of the spirit at that time, but that is not because he does not have it.

Second, it is clearly called a "gift," as we have seen before. Third, the word "but" between John's baptism and the baptism in holy spirit clearly indicates that there was a change coming. "**But**" is a contrasting conjunction that sets in contrast that which precedes it with that which follows it. Christ told the disciples that "…John baptized in water, **but** you will be baptized in holy spirit." Baptism in holy spirit is the greater reality that has replaced baptism in water, and is the reason why Ephesians 4:5 says that the Church has only "**one baptism**," which is baptism in spirit.

It is a tremendous truth that no one was baptized with holy spirit until Jesus poured it out on the Day of Pentecost. John did not baptize with holy spirit, but specifically stated that he baptized with water only, and that it would be Jesus who would baptize with holy spirit. Although Jesus oversaw his disciples baptizing people in water (John 4:1 and 2), he never did so, because the baptism he would bring was the greater baptism of holy spirit. But Jesus could not baptize anyone with holy spirit until he himself had received it from God, which happened after his ascension into heaven, as Peter made clear:

> **Acts 2:33**
> Exalted to the right hand of God, he has received from
> the Father the promised Holy Spirit [holy spirit] and has
> poured out what you now see and hear.

The Apostles were "baptized" in holy spirit on the Day of Pentecost, the very first day that Jesus poured out the spirit, and the first day it was available to be born again of God's holy spirit. From that day forward until the Rapture of the Church when Christians are taken off the earth and the Tribulation begins, every person who is saved is "baptized" in holy spirit.

The baptism in holy spirit is a one-time occurrence, and it happens the instant a person gets saved. This is clear from 1 Corinthians, which says that we were baptized in holy spirit into one body, that one body being the Body of Christ.

1 Corinthians 12:13
For we were all baptized by [in] one Spirit [spirit] into one body—whether Jews or Greeks, slave or free—and we were all given the one Spirit [spirit] to drink.[13]

When does a person become a member of the Body of Christ? When he is saved, and Corinthians tells us we are "baptized" into the Body, so therefore our baptism with holy spirit occurs when we are saved. It is of the utmost importance to understand that the Word of God teaches that a person is "baptized" in holy spirit **when he is saved**, and that it is a **one-time occurrence**. In Christian circles today, it is common to hear "the baptism of the Spirit" used to refer to something a person receives at some point after he has been saved, and which he manifests by speaking in tongues. Thus, in most Charismatic circles, a person is not considered "baptized in the Holy Spirit" until he speaks in tongues or otherwise manifests the power of God.

We believe God chose the words that are in the Bible because they best communicate spiritual truth. If we all use our own jargon, there may be two serious consequences. First, we may lose the impact of what God said because the words we choose may not properly communicate the same thing that God is saying. Second, it will be difficult to achieve unity among Christians, especially if the way we use words contradicts the way they are used in Scripture. The Bible uses "baptized in holy spirit" to refer to the reality that occurs when a person is saved, and that is how we Christians should use the phrase. In regard to manifesting the power of God, we should say, for example, that "Bob has been baptized in holy spirit, he has been saved, but he has not yet manifested speaking

---

13. The Greek text is worded in such a way as to make the verse an **Amphibologia** (Bullinger, *op. cit, Figures*, pp. 804–806). It can be read: "…we were all baptized by [in] one spirit [i.e., holy spirit] into one body…" or it can read: "…we were all baptized by one Spirit [Jesus Christ] into one body.…" Either way, at the time a person is baptized/born again/saved he joins the One Body of Christ. No one becomes a member of the Body of Christ without being saved.

in tongues." That sentence is biblically sound, and the vocabulary can be documented from Scripture. If all Christians will hold themselves to the way words are used in the Word, we will find we can discuss theological issues with much more clarity and will have more unity in the Body of Christ as a result.

God is working hard to communicate to us that we are completely filled with holy spirit. Under the Law, when someone was immersed in water, he was totally covered. Similarly, when we are immersed in holy spirit, which happens the instant that we are saved, every cell of our being is totally saturated with holy spirit. This makes perfect sense, because as we have seen, when we receive holy spirit it becomes part of our very nature.

Filled To Overflowing

We have seen that Scripture says when a person is born again he is "anointed" and "baptized" with holy spirit. Scripture also uses the phrase, "filled with holy spirit." When a person becomes a Christian, the holy nature of God is born in him, which is why Scripture says that Christians are "… partakers of the divine nature…" (2 Pet. 1:4-KJV). A person's nature is in every part of him, so when a person is saved, the holy spirit born in him "fills" him. When he is saved, a Christian gets all the divine nature he will ever get. That is not to say that he will not manifest more power outwardly, because he can and he should, but he will never get more holy spirit inwardly. Consider this verse:

> **Ephesians 1:3 (ESV)**[14]
> Blessed be the God and Father of our Lord Jesus Christ,
> who has blessed us in Christ with every spiritual blessing
> in the heavenly places,

If a Christian could receive more holy spirit from God than he gets when he is saved, then God has not given each Christian "every spiritual

---

14. We feel the ESV translation really captures the heart of this verse. First, we Christians are "in Christ," and so that phrase belongs after "us." Furthermore, the phrase "in heavenly places" is where God has the blessing and from whence He gives it. "…in heavenly places" does not go after "us" as if we were the ones in heaven now. Ephesians 2:6 does not mean we are in heaven now, it means we will be in the future.

blessing." Furthermore Colossians 2:10 (KJV) says we are "complete" in Christ. If when we got saved we received only **some** holy spirit, and could be filled with more, we would not be complete. The truth of the matter is that when we get born again we have all the holy spirit we are ever going to get. Now it is up to us to utilize the spiritual power we have.

We have seen that once a person is saved, he is filled with holy spirit, and cannot lose it. However, we must be aware that God often uses the phrase, "filled with holy spirit" to indicate one being **filled to overflowing into evidence**. This overflowing does not occur constantly, it is a temporary overflowing. For example, when a person speaks in tongues, he is filled to overflowing with holy spirit. However, he is not always speaking in tongues, even though he always has holy spirit sealed inside him. When Scripture says a Christian is "filled" with holy spirit, it almost always means he is bringing into manifestation the holy spirit born inside him. Thus the phrase, "filled with holy spirit" is referring to an already full vessel overflowing out into the senses world where it can be observed by others.

A study of the phrase "filled with holy spirit" shows that the context in which it appears determines whether it means filled to capacity or filled to overflowing.[15] By "overflowing," we mean where the person who is "filled" manifests or shows forth the gift of holy spirit within him in an evident way. An example of a verse where "filled with holy spirit" meant "filled to capacity" is Luke 1:15, referring to John the Baptist.

> **Luke 1:15**
> for he will be great in the sight of the Lord. He is never to take wine or other fermented drink, and he will be filled with the Holy Spirit [No "the." Read "holy spirit"] even from birth.

John was filled with holy spirit from his birth, but not everything he did was a result of the spirit inside him overflowing into evidence. Thus "filled" in Luke 1:15 means filled to capacity. However, in the following verses it is clear that when Scripture said a person was "filled" with holy

---

15. This is true of both *pleroo* and *pimplemi* which both mean "filled" (*pletho* is a form of *pimplemi*, but it is not found in the New Testament).

spirit, it was a way of indicating that the action they took was by the spirit of God, not from their flesh.

Luke 1:41b and 42a
(41b) ...Elizabeth was filled with the Holy Spirit [No "the." Read "holy spirit"].
(42a) In a loud voice she **exclaimed**...

Luke 1:67
...Zachariah was filled with the Holy Spirit [No "the." Read "holy spirit"] and **prophesied**:

Acts. 4:8
Then Peter, filled with the Holy Spirit [No "the." Read "holy spirit"], **said** to them [i.e., to the rulers who stood against him]...

Acts 4:31b
...And they were all filled with the Holy Spirit [No "the." Read "holy spirit"] and **spoke** the word of God boldly.

In the examples above, being filled with holy spirit meant the person was filled to overflowing, the inward spirit being manifested outwardly in various actions. The first use of the phrase "filled with holy spirit" in the writings to the Christian Church is Acts 2:4, regarding the initial outpouring of holy spirit on the Day of Pentecost. Here it refers to an outward evidence of the inward reality of holy spirit.

Acts 2:4
All of them were filled with the Holy Spirit [No "the." Read "holy spirit"] and **began to speak in other tongues**...

The Apostles saw tongues like fire "rest" upon each other and they heard the rushing mighty wind. These two signs showed them that they had received within themselves the promise of the Father that Jesus had told them to expect.

John the Baptist had said that the Messiah would baptize with "... holy spirit and with fire" (Matt. 3:11; Luke 3:16). Also, between his resurrection and the Day of Pentecost, and shortly before his ascension, Jesus had appeared to the Apostles, "...breathed on them and said, "Receive the Holy Spirit" [No "the." Read "holy spirit"] (John 20:22). When Jesus breathed on them, the sound would have been very similar to wind, the same sound a person makes when he breathes out. So, hearing the wind and seeing the fire on the Day of Pentecost, the Apostles took the cue and realized that the gift of holy spirit they were waiting for had been given. They had been "filled" inwardly, then, as they began to speak in tongues, they were "filled" to overflowing, and showed the outward evidence of the inward presence of holy spirit.

In Acts 13:9, Paul confronted Elymas the sorcerer and, being "... filled with the Holy Spirit...[No "the." Read "holy spirit"]," received revelation about Elymas' devilish purposes and spoke by the spirit to invoke the power of God to thwart him. Here we see another clear illustration where to be "filled with holy spirit" means to manifest the power of holy spirit.

Other uses of "filled" in the New Testament show that it can refer to being filled to overflowing. Matthew 27:48 and John 19:29 portray a sponge "filled" with vinegar, which would have been indicated by some dripping out of the sponge, supports the idea that "filled" can mean "filled to overflowing." Ephesians 5:18 also supports the idea that "filled" can mean "filled to overflowing."

> **Ephesians 5:18**
> Do not get drunk on wine, which leads to debauchery.
> Instead, be filled with the Spirit [No "the." Read "spirit"]."

The words, "be filled with spirit" (Author's translation) are in the imperative mood in the Greek text, and thus are a command. If Christians are filled with holy spirit at the time they are saved, what is the meaning of the command, "be filled with spirit"? The answer is that, as we have seen, "be filled" can mean to be filled to overflowing, in other words, bring the holy spirit into outward manifestation. The command to be filled with spirit fits with many other verses, such as God wanting us to speak in tongues (1 Cor. 14:5), wanting us to be eager to prophesy (1 Cor. 14:39), etc. God commands us to "be filled," so the filling must refer to an *action* we can take. Thus, our being filled is not God giving us more spirit, it is us walking in the power of the gift of holy spirit He has already given us.

Scripture makes a distinction between the filling God does at one's New Birth, and a particular "filling" into manifestation that is "energized" by God and "activated" by the obedience of the believer. In studying the biblical uses of the phrase, "filled with the spirit," it is important to grasp that it usually refers not to a filling up of holy spirit, but to an overflowing into evidence in the world. The difference is very important. A Christian need not ask for holy spirit. Rather, he is to utilize the holy spirit he already has, bringing it into powerful external evidence.

Chapter 8

Walking in Power
The Manifestations of Holy Spirit

Each Christian has God's gift of holy spirit. Therefore, each Christian has spiritual "power" and should be exercising that power. Remember that Jesus said that when holy spirit came, believers would have power.

Acts 1:8
But you will receive power when the Holy Spirit [holy spirit] comes on you; and you will be my witnesses in Jerusalem, and in all Judea and Samaria, and to the ends of the earth."

What is the power Jesus was speaking of? It is the power to hear from God, to speak in tongues, prophesy, do signs, miracles, and wonders, and much more. In short, we can bring into evidence, into manifestation, the gift of holy spirit inside us. The gift of holy spirit, the divine nature, that is sealed in each Christian, cannot be detected by the five senses. No one can see, hear, smell, taste, or touch it. However, holy spirit inside can be manifested, brought forth into evidence, in the nine ways set forth in 1 Corinthians 12:8–10.

1 Corinthians 12:7
Now to each one the **manifestation** of the Spirit [spirit] is given for the common good.

The word "manifestation" is a good translation of the Greek word *phanerosis*, which means "a manifestation, a making visible or observable."[1] Manifestation comes from two Latin words: *manus* = hand and *festare* = to touch. A manifestation is detectable by the five senses. We experience manifestations all the time. Electric energy in a light bulb is manifested in the form of light and heat. A manifestation of the chicken pox disease

---

1. Spiros Zodhiates, *The Complete Word Study Dictionary New Testament* (AMG Publishers, Chattanooga, TN, 1992), p. 1436.

is a rash with small pimple-like sores. We cannot see the virus that causes the chicken pox, but we can see the manifestation of the disease.

The multipurpose "Swiss Army" knife is a good example of the difference between a gift and a manifestation. The traditional knives have red handles, and many come with two blades (big and little), two screwdrivers (flathead and Phillips), a can opener, an awl, scissors, a file, and a pair of tweezers (Nine manifestations!). If you receive one multipurpose knife as a gift, you can use (bring into manifestation) any or all of its implements, and cut, snip, tweeze, etc. The one gift has many manifestations. Similarly, the one gift God gives each believer is holy spirit, which can be manifested in nine ways.

The examples of the light bulb, chicken pox, and Swiss Army knife are intended to show the difference between a gift and a manifestation, and every example has limitations. The examples are intended to make the point that there can be one gift with many manifestations, and when a person has the gift, he has the capacity to manifest it.

The gift of holy spirit is not observable or detectable by our five senses. Its presence inside the Christian becomes known when it is manifested, made obvious, in the senses world.[2] It may be obvious only to the one with holy spirit, such as when God gives a message of knowledge to someone, and that message is known only by the one receiving it, but it is obvious in the senses world nonetheless.

The Bible says that to "each one" (1 Cor. 12:7) is given the manifestation of the spirit. Each and every Christian can manifest holy spirit because each Christian has holy spirit. We know there are many Christians who have never manifested the gift of holy spirit in a way that they themselves recognize, and this has caused them to doubt that they can. We trust that

---

2. There has been much scholarly discussion about the exact nature of the genitive, "of," in the phrase, "the manifestation of the spirit." The confusion is in large part due to the fact that most theologians think the "Spirit" is God. The spirit in this verse is the gift of God, holy spirit, and the genitive is the genitive of origin. The gift of holy spirit is the source of the manifestations. A parallel phrase occurs in 2 Corinthians 4:2, which has "the manifestation of the truth" (KJV, which has the articles accurately placed) [that's the only other use of "manifestation" in the Bible]. This also is a genitive of origin. One cannot see the "truth" in the Apostles' minds, but it is there, and it is the origin of their behavior, which can be seen by everyone. The gift of holy spirit and "truth" are invisible in a person, but they produce manifestations that can be clearly seen in the senses world.

this book presents convincing evidence that a Christian can manifest holy spirit even if he has never done so.

What are the manifestations of holy spirit? The Bible tells us.

1 Corinthians 12:8–10 (Author's translation)
(8) For to one is given through the spirit **a message of wisdom**; and to another [*allos*] **a message of knowledge** because of the same spirit;[3]
(9) to a different one [*heteros*] **faith** by the same spirit; and to another [*allos*] **gifts of healings** by the one spirit;
(10) and to another [*allos*] working of **miracles**; to another [*allos*] **prophecy**; to another [*allos*] **discerning of spirits**; to a different one [*heteros*] **various** kinds of **tongues**; and to another [*allos*] the **interpretation of tongues**.

We will study each of these manifestations separately, but before we do, we need to address some basics about the manifestations. First, these verses seem to indicate that each Christian gets only one manifestation, something that has confused many people. Even though these verses use the term, "to another," it does not mean that each person will manifest only one of the manifestations. As we have seen somewhat already, and will see in much more detail later, every person can manifest all nine manifestations. However, not everyone will manifest the spirit in the same way at any given time and place. To make sure that things in the Church are done "decently and in order" (1 Cor. 14:40-KJV), at any given time the Lord energizes different manifestations in different believers. Thus at a Christian meeting, one person will speak in tongues and interpret, another will prophesy, another will minister healing, etc.[4] It is important

---

3. It is "because of the same spirit," the gift of holy spirit inside him, that a person can receive revelation. The word *kata* (because of) has a variety of meanings. Bauer's Greek Lexicon lists two major concepts, with more specific meanings under those, and even more specific meanings under those. For this verse, he notes "the mng. [meaning] 'in accordance w. [with]' can also disappear entirely, so that k. [*kata*] means simply *because of, as a result of, on the basis of....*" William Arndt and F. Wilbur Gingrich, *A Greek-English Lexicon of the New Testament and Other Early Christian Literature* (University of Chicago Press, Chicago, 1979), p. 407.

4. The use of "to one...to another..." has caused great confusion in the Church, and so we deal with it in great detail in Chapter 9, "To one...to another."

to point out that believers need to step out on what the Lord is energizing in them. It often happens that he is working in someone to pray, speak in tongues and interpret, prophesy, etc., but the person will be too timid to step forth and manifest. The Lord will do his part, we need to be sure we are doing ours.

Second, the Bible specifically says that the manifestation of holy spirit is for the "common good." Some benefit is missed, or some consequence occurs, when Christians do not walk with the power of the manifestations of holy spirit. Imagine the Bible with no such manifestations—no record of Moses smiting the rock, or Joshua stopping the Jordan River, or Samson pushing down the pagan temple, or God telling Samuel to anoint Saul as king, or Elijah calling down fire from heaven, or God telling Jonah to go to Nineveh.

The Bible would be much less exciting and would bring much less hope and blessing if the power of God were absent from its pages. Had Ananias not walked in the power of the manifestations, he would not have had the blessing of healing Paul (Acts 9:10–18). Had Peter not walked in the power of the manifestations, he would not have had the blessing of being the first to lead Gentiles into the New Birth (Acts 10:9–46). If Paul had not walked in the power of the manifestations, Eutychus would have remained dead (Acts 20:9–12). If a Christian does not speak in tongues, he misses out on the fact that it is a sign from God that he is saved (1 Cor. 14:22). Similarly, if the manifestations are absent or misused, there are consequences. If everyone in the congregation speaks in tongues at the same time, for example, an unbeliever may get the wrong impression (1 Cor. 14: 23).

Third, we must take note that God has placed the manifestations into three groups, or categories. In the above verses most versions read "to another" eight times. However, there are actually two different Greek words, *allos* and *heteros*, translated "to another." In Greek, *allos* was generally used to express a numerical difference and denotes "another of the same sort," while *heteros* means a qualitative difference and denotes "another of a different sort." When a list is put together, and the items are said to be *allos*, they are of the same kind or nature. When they are said to be *heteros*, they are different in nature. Thus, what we see in this section is God separating the manifestations into three groups, separated by the word *heteros*, which we showed in brackets when we quoted the verses.[5] In our translation, we used "another" when the Greek word was *allos*, and "different one" when it was *heteros*.

As we study the groupings of the manifestations, it is clear that two of them are revelation (hearing from God), five are related to the power of God, and two are worship oriented.

Revelation	Power	Worship
• A message of knowledge • A message of wisdom	• Faith • Gifts of healings • Miracles • Prophecy • Discerning of spirits	• Speaking in tongues • Interpretation of tongues

Before we examine these manifestations separately, we need to be aware that they are listed separately in the Bible and discussed separately in this book for the sake of clarity. God never intended them to be separate and distinct in the lives of the believers who experience them. He is our Father and He wants a relationship with us, and He wants us to be effective fellow-workers with Him (1 Cor. 3:9). In order to do that, we must be able to worship God (the worship group), hear from Him (the revelation group), and work for Him (the power group). In the day-to-day life of a believer who is striving to love God, live a holy life, and do God's will, the manifestations will often work seamlessly and result in great blessing for the believer and the people affected. For example, a Christian woman, Susan, may be by herself enjoying worshipping God by singing in tongues to some Christian music she is playing. Then the phone rings and it is her friend who needs prayer because many things seem to be going wrong in her life and today she is sick. Susan immediately feels the leading of the Lord to pray for specifics about her friend's life (the revelation manifestations

---

5. The groups of the manifestations are also explained in more detail in Chapter 9, "To one…to another."

at work) and then commands healing to take place in the name of Jesus Christ (faith and healing). By the time she gets off the phone, her friend is feeling better.

In the above scenario, Susan did not think to herself, "Now I need a message of knowledge. Now I need a message of wisdom, Now I need faith. Now I need the manifestation of gifts of healings." No, she had a relationship with God and love for her friend, and the manifestations worked together to produce the "common good" mentioned in 1 Corinthians 12:7.

The manifestatons work together, but it is still important to understand them individually. For years, scholars have discussed the manifestations of holy spirit and there are many differing opinions. The reason for the discussion and the uncertainty is that the manifestations are not clearly defined in 1 Corinthians. There is a good reason for this. It is common in all writing that authors leave out details and descriptions that everyone knows. Books and magazines are full of words that refer to things that in other cultures or ages may not be understood. Writers today commonly mention cars, planes, the Internet, and thousands of other things that we do not explain in detail because the readers know what they are. There are many examples of this in the Bible also.

A good example occurs in Luke, where, in his day, Luke did a good job of dating the birth of Christ by telling us it was about the time of the first census that took place while Quirinius was governor of Syria (Luke 2:2). No doubt everyone in Luke's day who read that said, "Ah, now I know when the birth of Christ occurred." Today, however, not much information about Quirinius has survived the centuries, and so there is controversy about the date of the birth of Christ.

Another example involves biblical animals. No doubt when Job was written, everyone knew what the "behemoth" was (Job 40:15). Today we do not know enough information for scholars to agree on what the animal is. Another example involves nations. Genesis and other books of the Bible mention the "Hittites" (Gen. 10:15), but that nation was lost in history so completely that until the nineteenth century, when archaeologists uncovered entire Hittite cities, some scholars even doubted their existence.[6]

---

6. Joseph Free, *Archaeology and Bible History* (Zondervan Publishing House, Grand Rapids, MI, 1982), p. 108.

Nevertheless, the Bible never describes them because the biblical readers knew exactly who they were and where they lived.

The people of Corinth and other Christians in the first century were familiar with the manifestations of holy spirit, so there was no need for Paul to explain what they were or how they worked. God's people had been manifesting holy spirit for generations (except for speaking in tongues and interpretation of tongues, with which the Corinthian Church was very familiar). God had put holy spirit upon people in the Old Testament such as Moses, Joshua, Deborah, David, Elijah, and many others, and those people could then hear knowledge or wisdom from God (thus, the message of knowledge and wisdom). They had the faith to do what God asked of them even when it seemed impossible, they did miracles, and when Jesus came on the scene, he taught his disciples to heal and cast out demons. The believers of Corinth were familiar with all these manifestations, and of course Paul, who founded the Church in Corinth on his second missionary journey (Acts 18:1–18), had also instructed them.

Some scholars have tried to look in Greek culture to find the meaning of the manifestations based on the definitions of the Greek words themselves (for example, "wisdom" was very important in the Greek culture). That misses the point, and for the most part has been unhelpful in discovering the nature of the manifestations, and is one reason why there is so much debate about the manifestations by scholars. The manifestations were not Greek experiences or concepts, but the timeless manifestations, outward evidences, of the inward presence of holy spirit. These manifestations were not to be found in Greek culture, vocabulary, or history, but in the experiences of the men and women of God.

English culture today is somewhat similar to the Greek culture in that there has been very little accurate exposure to the power of holy spirit and very little accurate teaching on it. Therefore, we need a clear explanation of the manifestations so we can understand them. As the Greeks of old, we need to get our understanding from the Bible itself and then add to our understanding by utilizing and experiencing the manifestations. We will start our study of the manifestations by giving a basic definition for each of them, and then examining them in more detail.

A message of knowledge is God or the Lord Jesus Christ providing you with information, insight, and understanding about something.[7]

A message of wisdom is God or the Lord Jesus Christ providing you with direction, or how to apply the knowledge you have about something.

The manifestation of faith is you having the confidence or trust that what God or the Lord Jesus Christ has revealed to you by a message of knowledge or a message of wisdom will come to pass at your command.

The manifestation of gifts of healings is you exercising your God-given spiritual ability to heal by the power of God, according to what God or the Lord Jesus Christ has revealed to you by a message of knowledge or a message of wisdom.

The manifestation of working of miracles is you exercising your God-given spiritual ability to do miracles by the power of God, according to what God or the Lord Jesus Christ has revealed to you by a message of knowledge or a message of wisdom.

Discerning of spirits is God or the Lord Jesus Christ revealing to you information about the presence or non-presence of spirits (including both holy spirit or demons), and sometimes including the identity of demons present, whether or not you may cast them out, and providing the power to do it.

Prophecy is speaking, writing, or otherwise communicating a message from God to a person or persons.

Speaking in tongues is speaking a language of men or angels that you do not understand, which is given to you by the Lord Jesus Christ.

Interpretation of tongues is giving the sum and substance, in your own language, of what you have just spoken in tongues.

As we study these manifestations and understand what they are and how they enable each Christian to walk in spiritual power, it will be clear

---

7. In the context of this book, "you" refers to you the Christian. The manifestations of holy spirit can be utilized only by people who have holy spirit.

that every Christian can utilize all of them. The prophets of old utilized all of them but the two that God hid in Himself for the Administration of Grace—speaking in tongues and the interpretation of tongues. If the prophets who had holy spirit upon them by measure utilized seven manifestations to walk powerfully before God, then surely God has not done less for us who have been filled and sealed with the gift of holy spirit.

It is very important to realize that when the Bible says "manifestation of the spirit" it means exactly that—these are evidences of holy spirit, not natural abilities God has given to the person. They are the presence of holy spirit being made visible. We make this point because some people treat these manifestations as if they were talents that some people have, with no specific connection to the gift of holy spirit they received when they were saved. It is true that God does give different people talents. Some people sing well; some people are very athletic; some are very intelligent; some people are great artists, etc. These are all God-given talents, but they are not manifestations of holy spirit.

We will examine the manifestations in the order and groups that they are presented to us in the Word of God.

A Message of Knowledge and a Message of Wisdom

We will cover the two "revelation" manifestations together because they are the first group of manifestations God mentions. They often work seamlessly together, with a single revelation from God consisting of both a message of knowledge and a message of wisdom. We call these the "revelation" manifestations because they deal with God or the Lord Jesus "revealing" something. We translate these manifestations as a "message" because the Greek word *logos* means an intelligible communication. The first definition of *logos* in *Thayer's Greek Lexicon* is "*a word,* yet not in the grammatical sense (equivalent to *vocabulum,* the mere name of an object), but language, *vox,* i.e., a word which, uttered by the living voice, embodies a conception or idea."[8] The NIV uses "message," and other versions, such as the RSV, NRSV, and NJB, use "utterance," which would be fine as long as

---

8. Thayer, *op. cit., Thayer's Greek-English Lexicon,* p. 380.

it is understood that it is the Lord who "utters" the message to the person and not that the person speaks a message of wisdom to someone else.

The translation "message" communicates accurately exactly what the Lord gives by revelation: a message. The message may come as an audible voice, as a picture or vision, as a physical sensation, or even as a firm realization, an inner knowing. The King James Version says "word of wisdom" and "word of knowledge" and so those terms are widely used, and "word" is used for "message" in Christian jargon. Nevertheless, it could be misleading to a new Bible student who might think of revelation as "words," especially because in our experience the majority of the revelation any person receives is not a "word" and not even by "words," but much more often by an impression or picture.

Since the time of Adam and Eve, it has been important for mankind to hear from God. When He speaks to individuals, if what He says is knowledge, i.e., information and insight, the revelation is "a message of knowledge." If what He says is wisdom, i.e., direction or what to do about a given situation, the revelation is "a message of wisdom."[9]

The prophets had holy spirit upon them, which is why they could hear from God and then powerfully act on what He said, and why they were so revered in their culture. It is possible for God to speak to people audibly, and not via the holy spirit upon or in them, but this is rare. When God wanted to communicate to people, He usually did so via holy spirit. That is why, as we saw in Chapter 3, all through the Old Testament and the Gospels, when God wanted a person to prophesy or, like Joseph, to be a wise ruler, He put holy spirit on him. Today, many Christians realize that it is possible to hear from God, and there are a number of books available on the subject by popular preachers.[10] It is a great blessing that today, in

---

9. Knowledge is information about a situation, while wisdom is what to do about the situation. The first definition of "wisdom" in *Webster's 1828 Dictionary* captures its essence: "the right use or exercise of knowledge." Noah Webster, *American Dictionary of the English Language*, (Foundation for American Christian Education, San Francisco, CA, 1828, reprinted 1967), "wisdom."

10. One example is Joyce Meyer, *How to Hear from God* (Warner Faith, USA, 2003). Joyce writes in her introduction: "We talk to our children all the time—why wouldn't our heavenly Father talk to His children?" God does want to talk to us, and He will if we open our spiritual ears and have faith.

the Administration of Grace, each and every Christian can hear from God and the Lord Jesus Christ.

When we speak of revelation from God, a message of knowledge or wisdom, we are speaking of God or the Lord Jesus giving direct revelation to the person via holy spirit. Sometimes people point out that God "speaks" via other people's advice, or nature, etc. He can "speak" to us that way, but that kind of communication from God is not a manifestation of holy spirit. Furthermore, a message of wisdom or knowledge is the Lord giving information to the believer, not the believer giving it to others. The Living Bible, for example, calls "a message of wisdom," "…the ability to give wise advice.…" Many people, saved and unsaved, give wise advice. That is not a manifestation of holy spirit. The manifestation of a message of wisdom occurs when God gives a Christian a message about what to do in a given situation via the gift of holy spirit.

As we saw from its definition above, the manifestation of **a message of knowledge** is when God or the Lord Jesus Christ gives a believer information about something. It may be only a little bit of information, but it is knowledge nevertheless. A good example would be Joseph interpreting Pharaoh's dream (Gen. 41:25–27). God gave Joseph knowledge about the meaning of the dream, which was that there would be seven years of plenty, then seven years of famine. That revelation is **a message of knowledge** because it only gives information, the facts of the case.

When God gives someone a message of knowledge, He may or may not need to give a message of wisdom so the person will know what to do. For example, if a person has lost his car keys, all God has to do is let the person know where they are, He does not have to give a message of wisdom and say, "Go get them." The person will do that without having to have a message of wisdom. Often, however, God will give a message of wisdom when He gives a message of knowledge. What if God had told Joseph about the years of plenty and the years of famine, but then never said what to do about it? The best Joseph could have done in that case would have been to pick a reasonable solution. However, God did give Joseph a **message of wisdom**, and Joseph told Pharaoh to store up twenty percent of the harvest during the plenteous years for the upcoming famine years (Gen. 41:33–36). When God gives a person direction, and tells him what to do, then it is "a message of wisdom."

It is important to realize and keep in mind that a message of knowledge and a message of wisdom are manifestations of holy spirit, and are not part of the natural human mind. They work together with the human mind, but they are separate from it. They are not superior knowledge, insight, awareness, or wisdom, which comes from the ability of the mind. Many unsaved people have great knowledge and wisdom, but these are not manifestations of holy spirit. Neither is it giving knowledge or wise advice to someone else, for many unsaved people give wise counsel to others.

A message of knowledge and a message of wisdom are God "speaking" to us to guide and help us. It is inconceivable that He would not do that for each and every Christian. Surely He would not give guidance to one Christian and not to another. Every Christian can, and needs to, manifest holy spirit in these two ways to live a rich and successful Christian life. No doubt most Christians have heard from God via the manifestations without even realizing it. Although there are times when God gives a message of knowledge or wisdom in such a clear and powerful way that it cannot be missed, usually God speaks in a "gentle whisper" or "a still small voice" (1 Kings 19:12-NIV, KJV).

An example of the Lord giving a very clear and powerful message of knowledge and wisdom was when the Lord wanted Peter to go to the Gentiles and present the Christian message to them. The Lord gave Peter a vision and an audible revelation (Acts 10:11–13). However, in our experience, the whisper of God can be so gentle, so quiet, that often we cannot distinguish it from our own thoughts. This is especially true in these modern times when there is probably music or television in the background, and we are so busy and distracted that we are not really paying attention to Him. That is a major reason why the definition of a message of knowledge and a message of wisdom is "God or the Lord Jesus Christ **providing** to you" information or direction. The Lord "provides" the information or direction, but sometimes we do not recognize it for what it is. Many times it is only after the fact that we recognize that the "thought" we had was actually revelation from the Lord.

Sometimes it is because of the timing of a thought or idea that we come to recognize it as revelation. Many Christians have the experience of doing something that turns out to be at "just the right time." A believer may "get the idea" to call a friend that he has not called in a long time, only to find out when he is on the phone that the timing of the call was so godly that the "idea" had to have come from the Lord. A person may "feel an urge" to stop by someone's house when he is on his way home from work, only to find that the timing of the visit was so perfect that the "urge" had to be revelation. Although sometimes these things happen by coincidence, a Christian endeavoring to walk with God and bless people will recognize them happening too frequently for that to always be the case. Often he will be able to think back to the "idea" or the "urge" and begin to recognize that it was somehow different from a "normal thought," even though he did not recognize that at the time.

In the above examples the Lord gave the revelation at just the right time, and the effect of the believer acting on the revelation he received was that people were helped and blessed. This is a good example of how the manifestations work for the "common good" (1 Cor. 12:7). It is often when there is a tangible blessing in the Body of Christ that people recognize that the Lord is at work in those Christians who walk by the power of holy spirit.

Revelation from God or the Lord Jesus rarely comes like a flash of lightning and a crash of thunder, so very different from our own thoughts that we cannot miss it. Usually the Lord is working to help us do what we are already doing. Thus, revelation sometimes makes us aware of something that we already know, jogging our memory or "connecting the dots" for us. A good example of that is when Paul stood on trial before the Sanhedrin. Paul had been a Pharisee (Phil. 3:5), and was very aware of the tension between the Pharisees and Sadducees, who were both vying for control of the religious system in Israel. As he was brought before them he could have been in serious trouble. They hated him, and the Romans dealt harshly with troublemakers. However, just at the right time, Paul "perceived" (Acts 23:6-KJV) that part of the Sanhedrin was Pharisees and part was Sadducees, and he cried out that he was a Pharisee and on trial over the issue of the resurrection of the dead. The counsel broke into pandemonium, and Paul was taken from there by the Romans who feared he would be hurt.

That Paul received revelation is quite clear from the scope of Scripture. He knew very well that part of the Sanhedrin was Pharisees and part was Sadducees, and he knew the issues over which they were divided. Therefore, it would make no sense to say that he "perceived" or "noticed" (NRSV) it as if he did not already know it. He knew it, but it had not occurred to him to use their division to save himself. The Lord provided the insight for Paul and it probably saved his life.

While it is important that we do not become prideful or "spooky spiritual" and attribute all our thoughts and ideas to God, there are times when we have an "Aha" moment, or a "gut feeling," that is from God and not from our own mind. The holy spirit sealed inside of us is part of our very nature, and therefore God can communicate through it seamlessly and effortlessly to our minds.

We have now discussed the revelation manifestations, a message of knowledge and a message of wisdom, and seen how they work in the lives of Christian believers. What God did for the people who had holy spirit in the Old Testament, He does for Christians because He knows we need His help and guidance to be successful in life and accomplish what He would have us accomplish. Each and every Christian should strive to live a holy life and do the work God has for Him, and then expect to receive messages of knowledge and wisdom to help and bless him.

One of the great benefits of a message of knowledge or of wisdom is that it builds our faith. It is a powerful faith-building experience to hear from heaven, and we need faith in order to accomplish that which the Lord asks us to do. Faith is the third manifestation listed in 1 Corinthians 12.

Faith

The **manifestation of faith** is the first manifestation that God places in the second group of manifestations, which we call the "power" manifestations. We believe that faith is the foundation of the power manifestations. "Faith" is the translation of the Greek word *pistis*, which means "trust," "confidence" or "assurance."[11] We like to use the word "trust." It is important to distinguish the biblical definition of faith from today's definition that has permeated the Christian Church and society. When most people think of "faith," they think of it in terms of the modern definition: "firm belief in something for which there is no proof."[12] When religious people have no proof for what they believe, we often hear them say, "You just have to take it by faith." It is vital to understand that "belief in something for which there is no proof" is far from the biblical definition of "faith."

The biblical definition of faith is "trust," and we trust things only after they have been proven to us. Jesus never asked anyone to believe he was the Messiah without proof. He healed the sick, raised the dead, and did miracles, such as healing the man born blind (something that had never been done in the history of the world), and he asked people to believe the miracles that he did (John 10:38). Similarly, God does not ask us to believe Him without proof. He has left many evidences that He exists and that His Word is true. Thus, when God asks us to have faith, He is not asking us to believe something without proof. God proves Himself to us, and because of that we trust Him, that is, we have faith.

We must distinguish between faith as it is commonly used in the Bible and the "manifestation of faith." All of us have "faith" (trust) in a large number of things. In fact, ordinary life would be impossible without trust. A person would not sit down if he did not trust that the chair would hold him. People plan their entire evening based upon faith (trust) in a recorded announcement by a total stranger as to what time the movie they want to see starts. God asks us to trust that Jesus has been raised from the dead because the Bible, history, and life give plenty of evidence for it.

In contrast to ordinary faith, the **manifestation of faith** is necessary to accomplish the special tasks that God, by revelation, asks us to do. For example, Jesus said that a person with faith could tell a mountain to be cast into the ocean and it would be done (Mark 11:23). Well, many of us have seen mountains, and we know that we do not have the human power

---

11. For more on what biblical faith really is, see our book, Chapter 11, "Keep the Faith," *Don't Blame God!* by Mark Graeser, John A. Lynn, & John Schoenheit (The Living Truth Fellowship, Indianapolis, IN 2011).

12. *Merriam-Webster's Collegiate Dictionary* (Merriam-Webster, Incorporated, Springfield, MA, 2003), p. 450.

to move them, so doing that requires the power of God. We need God to make that kind of miracle available to us by first giving us the revelation to do it. When He does, then the faith we must have in order to get the job done is "the manifestation of faith."

Moses brought water out of a rock by the manifestation of faith (Exod. 17:5 and 6), Gideon defeated the Midianites by the manifestation of faith (Judg. 6:16), Elijah multiplied the oil and bread by the manifestation of faith (1 Kings 17:14–16), and the other great miracles of the Bible were done by the manifestation of faith. When it comes to miracles and gifts of healings, we need the manifestation of faith because we cannot heal the sick or do miracles by our human power. God must give us a message of knowledge and a message of wisdom, letting us know that it is His will for us to heal someone or do a miracle, and then we must have the faith to do it.

Every Christian needs to utilize the manifestation of faith. Christ said that when people received holy spirit they would receive power (Acts 1:8), but no one can operate the power of God without the faith to do so. Since every Christian needs to use the manifestation of faith to bring to pass the revelation that God gives him, every Christian has the ability to manifest faith. Thus, we see that the manifestation of faith, like a message of knowledge and a message of wisdom, is for every Christian, not just certain ones.

Gifts of Healings and Working of Miracles[13]

We cover these two manifestations together because they are similar in many ways. The "gifts [plural] of healings [plural]" is so called because God does multiple healings, and each of them is a gift, done out of His grace or mercy. Gifts of healings and working of miracles are manifestations of holy spirit because it takes a believer to do them by the power of God that he has been given. It is very important to realize that it is people, empowered by holy spirit within, who do healings and miracles. On rare occasions God heals or does a miracle without human agency, but that is

---

13. The word "working" is perhaps more properly, "energizing," and it is plural. However, we felt that saying "energizings of miracles" was unclear. The phrase "working of miracles" is working more than one miracle and thus adequately covers the plural in the Greek.

not "the manifestation" of gifts of healings or miracles because the gift of holy spirit inside a Christian was not employed.

To do a healing or miracle, several manifestations come into action. First, the person needs a message of knowledge and/or a message of wisdom to know what the situation is and what to do about it. Second, he needs the manifestation of faith to bring to pass the healing or miracle. Third, he must represent Christ on earth and, via the power of God, bring to pass the miracle as God supplies the energy for it. Notice how Peter raised Tabitha.

> **Acts 9:40**
> Peter sent them all out of the room; then he got down on his knees and prayed. Turning toward the dead woman, he said, "Tabitha, get up." She opened her eyes, and seeing Peter she sat up.

Peter spoke the miracle into being. First, Peter prayed. Then, when he had revelation from the Lord to go ahead, he raised her from the dead by the power of God. Once Peter received the revelation to raise Tabitha, he performed the miracle. We believe that there would be more miracles and healings in Christendom today if Christians would step out in faith and do what the Lord tells them to do. Too often we are waiting for God to do what He has given us the spiritual power to do.

It is not our intention to demean the power of prayer in any way. Christians are commanded to pray, and should do so as much as possible. However, when God or the Lord Jesus gives us the revelation to do a healing or miracle, that is not the time to pray, it is the time to step out in faith and boldly do the miracle. If the miracle or healing takes time, the one receiving the revelation must stay in faith and prayer to see it accomplished.

The book of Exodus has a great example showing that it is our choice to use the spiritual power inside us. God told Moses to take the Israelites out of Egypt. By the time they reached the sea, Pharaoh's army was close on their heels, and the people were terrified.

Exodus 14:13–16

(13) Moses answered the people, "Do not be afraid. Stand firm and you will see the deliverance the LORD will bring you today. The Egyptians you see today you will never see again.

(14) The LORD will fight for you; you need only to be still."

(15) Then the LORD said to Moses, "Why are you crying out to me? Tell the Israelites to move on.

(16) Raise your staff and stretch out your hand over the sea to divide the water so that the Israelites can go through the sea on dry ground.

Once God gave the revelation of what to do, it was Moses' turn to act, using the power God had given him. Moses utilized the manifestation of faith, and performed the miracle of splitting the sea. Had Moses not had faith to raise his staff and do the miracle, Israel would not have escaped from the Egyptians. Likewise, we Christians must recognize the power we have, and then step out and use that power.

Jesus' Apostles and disciples had holy spirit upon them (John 14:17), which is why he could send them out to heal the sick, raise the dead, and cast out demons (Matt. 10:8; Luke 10:9). Furthermore, Jesus said that when people have holy spirit, they have power (Acts 1:8). It is clear that since every Christian has the gift of holy spirit, then every Christian has the power to do healings and miracles (Mark 16:17 and 18; John 14:12), just as the disciples of Christ and the prophets of old did. We need to increase our faith and step forth boldly to do what the Lord directs us to do.[14]

The manifestations of gifts of healings and working of miracles are often interwoven. There are certainly miracles that are not healings, such as when Moses parted the sea so the Israelites could escape Egypt. Also, there are healings that are not miracles, when, although the natural power of the body to heal itself is augmented by the healing power of God, the

---

14. We realize that although the presence of holy spirit gives each Christian the spiritual power to do healings and miracles, not everyone is called to walk in that kind of ministry. There is a difference between inherent spiritual ability and how that ability will actually be evidenced in the life of an individual Christian. Nevertheless, we assert that many more Christians would be doing healings and miracles if they knew they had the ability, and were confident to act on the spiritual power they have.

healing is not instantaneous. However, there are many miracles of healing in the Bible, such as the instantaneous healing of Bartimaeus, who was blind (Mark 10:46–52). Also, casting out a demon can be a miracle (Mark 9:39).

Prophecy

The manifestation of prophecy is speaking, writing, or otherwise communicating a message from God to another person or persons. God or the Lord Jesus gives the Christian a message of knowledge or a message of wisdom via the holy spirit born inside him, and when he gives that message to someone else, it is prophecy. The revelation that is spoken as prophecy can come in the moment, coming almost word-by-word as the speaker says them, something we call "inspirational prophecy." It can also come as a complete revelation given to the speaker before it is spoken as prophecy, and it can come as a combination, with some revelation coming beforehand and some coming as the prophecy is spoken. In the Old Testament, when a person had holy spirit, he or she almost always prophesied. That is why Joel said that when holy spirit would be poured out on all Millennial Kingdom believers, they would prophesy (Joel 2:28), and why Peter, in his teaching on the Day of Pentecost, referenced Joel.

> **Acts 2:17b and 18**
> (17b) …I [God] will pour out my Spirit [spirit] on all people. Your sons and daughters will prophesy, your young men will see visions, your old men will dream dreams.
> (18) Even on my servants, both men and women, I will pour out my Spirit [spirit] in those days, and they will prophesy.

God says His servants will prophesy, so there should be little argument about it. The manifestation of prophecy is to strengthen, encourage, and comfort people (1 Cor. 14:3). It can reveal the secrets of people's hearts so that they can be closer to God (1 Cor. 14:24 and 25). A study of prophecy in Scripture shows that prophecy is part of the power of God, which is why God places prophecy in the "power" group of the manifestations. Some Bible teachers have placed prophecy in the "worship" group of manifestations, but prophecy is not worship, it is speaking a message from

God to people. It is used in a worship service, yes, but that does not make it worship. At any given Christian service all the manifestations may come into play, depending on the needs of the people.

Many Christians do not prophesy, but it is not because they do not have the spiritual ability. The presence of holy spirit inside a Christian gives him that ability. If a Christian does not prophesy, either he has not been sufficiently instructed, or he does not have the faith to step out on what he has been given, or he does not want to prophesy. 1 Corinthians 14:24 states that the whole church can prophesy, and 1 Corinthians 14:39 (KJV) says "covet to prophesy."

There is a reason why each Christian should covet to prophesy. Bringing God's messages to His people is not only a tremendous privilege, it is essential for the wellbeing of the Church. A study of the Bible, especially the Old Testament, reveals how valuable prophets were in the spiritual wholeness of the people of Israel. Prophecy is not only speaking about the future. Not only can every Christian prophesy, as the Scripture says, but we should want to. That every believer can prophesy gives us more conclusive evidence that each believer can manifest all nine manifestations.

Discerning of Spirits[15]

The manifestation of **discerning of spirits** is necessary if men and women of God are going to deal effectively with the spiritual realities of this fallen world. There are many "spirits" in this world, including angels and the gift of holy spirit.[16] Nevertheless, because of the spiritual battle that rages around all of us, the most important aspect of discerning of spirits is dealing with the demonic forces of this world.

---

15. The Greek word translated "discerning" is plural. Nevertheless, we used "discerning" because it has the overtones of plurality. If a person is "discerning," it is because he has exhibited discernment in a multitude of situations.

16. The word "spirits" in the phrase "discerning of spirits" does not refer to "attitudes." Although that is one of the meanings of *pneuma*, it is not the meaning in this context. There are many very gifted people that are very sensitive and can "read" people and situations very well, but many of them are unsaved. That discernment is a natural ability, just as is native intelligence and other natural abilities.

Ephesians 6:12 (KJV)[17]
For we wrestle not against flesh and blood, but against principalities, against powers, against the rulers of the darkness of this world, against spiritual wickedness in high places.

Our Adversary, the Devil, walks about as a roaring lion, seeking people to devour (1 Pet. 5:8). God has not left us helpless, but has empowered us to deal with him. The manifestation of discerning of spirits is more than just recognizing them, it also involves entering into battle against them and casting them out. Recognizing demons, protecting the believers, and casting them out is all part of "discerning of spirits."

The Greek word translated "discerning" (*diakrisis*) has several meanings. It can mean a "distinguishing" or "differentiation." Also, it can mean to quarrel.[18] One of the definitions in *Liddell and Scott's Greek Lexicon* is "decision by battle, quarrel, dispute."[19] Thus *diakrisis* can be much more than just "discerning," it has the overtones of quarreling or fighting. Since "discerning of spirits" is a total package of recognizing "spirits" and dealing with them, God places it in the "power" group of manifestations.

The manifestation of discerning of spirits is interwoven with the other manifestations. For example, a believer manifesting discerning of spirits may be simultaneously aware of the presence of the demon, know what to do about the situation, and begin to command it to come out of the person. Receiving the information about the demon and knowing what to do is similar to and interwoven with a message of knowledge and a message of wisdom, while the casting out of the demon can be in the category of a miracle (Mark 9:38 and 39), even as a healing can be a miracle (Acts 4:16).

Every Christian will encounter demons, whether he recognizes them or not. What a great blessing and comfort to know that God has equipped

---

17. We like the KJV because it uses the word "wrestle," which is literally what the Greek text says. As in any wrestling match, there is an opponent that must be fought and overcome.

18. Arndt and Gingrich, *op. cit., A Greek-English Lexicon*, p. 185.

19. Henry Liddell and Robert Scott, *A Greek-English Lexicon* (Oxford University Press, NY, 1992), p. 399.

each of us to deal with any demon that comes against us. Ephesians 6:12, which says we wrestle with demonic powers, is written to every Christian. Therefore, every Christian can manifest discerning of spirits.

Speaking in Tongues

Speaking in tongues is a Christian speaking a language of men or angels that he does not understand, which is given to him by the Lord Jesus Christ. It is one of the great blessings that God has given to the Christian Church, and He desires that every Christian speak in tongues.

> **1 Corinthians 14:5a**
> I would like every one of you to speak in tongues...

The fact that God says He wants each Christian to speak in tongues should end the discussion about each person getting only one "gift" of holy spirit. If each of us can speak in tongues, then that would be the one manifestation we all would get, and there would be no need to list the other eight. This verse makes it clear that each of us can manifest holy spirit in more than one way.

The manifestations of speaking in tongues and interpretation of tongues did not exist before the Day of Pentecost. We believe that speaking in tongues is so valuable to Christians that we have dedicated Chapter 10 to it.

Interpretation of Tongues

The interpretation of tongues is interpreting, or giving the sum and substance, in one's own language, that which he has just spoken in tongues. The interpretation of tongues, like speaking in tongues itself, is given by the Lord. No one understands what he is saying in a tongue, so no one could give an interpretation of what he is saying. The interpretation comes from the Lord Jesus Christ, just as the tongue does. The manifestation of interpretation of tongues works just like speaking in tongues and prophecy do—the words come from the Lord Jesus Christ to the individual via the gift of holy spirit inside him. When a person speaks in tongues in a believer's meeting, he should interpret so that the people in the meeting may be edified.

1 Corinthians 14:5
I would like every one of you to speak in tongues, but I would rather have you prophesy. He who prophesies is greater than one who speaks in tongues, **unless he interprets**, so that the church may be edified.

The interpretation of tongues is to be done by the one who spoke in tongues, just as 1 Corinthians 14:5 says. Furthermore, because speaking in tongues is praise and prayer to God, the interpretation will also be to God. That is the big difference between prophecy and the interpretation of tongues. Prophecy is a message to the people (1 Cor. 14:3), while interpretation of tongues is to God (or the Lord Jesus Christ), but is heard by the congregation, who are then edified by it.

This section of the book has shown that each Christian has the spiritual ability to manifest all nine manifestations of holy spirit. Every Christian can talk with the Lord and receive revelation, every Christian can and should have faith and do some of the works of Jesus, every Christian should enter into the spiritual battle and deal with demons, every Christian should prophesy, speak in tongues, and interpret. It is by manifesting holy spirit that Christians can walk in the power that Jesus Christ gave to the Church. We must trust God in order to boldly manifest holy spirit in our daily lives.

Gifts or Manifestations?

In the previous section, we spoke over and over about the "manifestations" of holy spirit. At this point we want to once again make the point that we Christians should use biblical words when we talk about the things of God. Most Christians commonly use the word "gifts" to describe what the Bible calls "manifestations" of the spirit, and this causes problems in Christianity. Why? Because words have definitive meanings, and it is through those meanings that clear communication is made possible. "Manifestation" does not mean "gift." What's the difference? A gift is individually given, and no one has a gift unless it was given to him. A manifestation is an evidence, a showing forth, of something that a person already has. There are spiritual gifts, which include holy spirit,

God-given ministries such as that of an apostle or a prophet, and the gift of everlasting life (Rom. 6:23). But, the nine manifestations are not gifts and calling them "gifts" can have a negative effect on the quality of believers' lives.

The theology of many Christians, however, reduces the difference between "gifts" and "manifestations" to a non-issue, which is one reason most commentaries make so little of it. If a person believes that he will be given at most only one of the manifestations (which is the most common teaching about the "gifts of the spirit"), then to him there is no difference between a gift and a manifestation. If the Swiss Army knife has only a knife blade, then there is not much difference between the gift of the knife and the manifestation of the blade. But, if the Swiss Army knife has many blades and tools, there is a huge difference between the knife as a whole and just one blade. The difference between gift and manifestation becomes very clear and very important when one realizes that the one gift of holy spirit has many "manifestations," or evidences.

The major problem that occurs when the manifestations of holy spirit are thought to be "gifts" is that it causes many Christians to be spiritually passive. Instead of realizing that they can utilize the nine manifestations and walking in faith to speak in tongues, some believers wait on God, hoping that one day He will give them the "gift" of tongues. Other believers who would love to heal people wait for the power to heal. Such people are waiting for something they already have! They may even plead with and beg God, and end up disappointed with Him for not answering their prayers. Christians need to know that they *have received* the power of holy spirit, and that God is waiting for them to act. They must move their mouths and speak in tongues, or use their voice to prophesy, or stretch forth their hands to heal, all with faith in the power God provided.

The theology of Bible translators is in large part responsible for people thinking that the manifestations of the spirit are gifts. Notice how often the word "gift," "gifts," or "gifted" appears in most translations of 1 Corinthians 12–14. Yet not one of these uses of "gift" is in the Greek text.

1 Corinthians 12:1a
Now about spiritual **gifts**, brothers…."[20]

1 Corinthians 13:2a
If I have the **gift** of prophecy…."

1 Corinthians 14:1
Follow the way of love and eagerly desire spiritual **gifts**, especially the **gift** of prophecy.

1 Corinthians 14:12
So it is with you. Since you are eager to have spiritual **gifts**, try to excel in **gifts** that build up the church.

1 Corinthians 14:37a
If anybody thinks he is a prophet or spiritually **gifted**…."

---

20. The improper addition of "gifts" to the Greek text is one reason why Christians should purchase and learn to use Bible study helps such as interlinears and lexicons. An "interlinear" is a Bible in the original Greek or Hebrew, with the English in an interlinear (between the lines) form. Looking at an interlinear version of the Greek text shows conclusively that "gifts" was added by translators to the English version. This same thing could be done for all the verses listed where "gifts" was added. Note that, although Greek and English word order are not the same, the sense of the verse can be well followed in the interlinear. Well-stocked Christian bookstores have Interlinear Bibles or visit www. Christianbook.com or www.Half.com.

1 Corinthians 12:1. 1) Greek text, 2) Transliterated Greek text 3) English literal translation, 4) English rendition

1) Περὶ δὲ τῶν πνευματικῶν, ἀδελφοί, οὐ θέλω ὑμᾶς ἀγνοεῖν.

2) *Peri de ton pneumatikon adelphoi ou thelo humas agnoein.*

3) concerning but the spirituals brothers not I want you (plural) ignorant.

4) Now concerning the spiritual things, brothers, I do not want you ignorant.

It is easy to see why the average Christian thinks of prophecy and the other manifestations as "spiritual gifts." It is difficult to read the Bible and come away with an accurate understanding of it when the translators have allowed their theology to distort the clear reading of the text. What is the Christian to do when he reads a version with "gifts" improperly inserted in the text? He can cross out "gifts" and make an accurate reading in the margin.[21]

One good thing about the King James Version, American Standard Version, and New American Standard Version is that the translators *italicized* many words that are not in the Hebrew or Greek text, but which they added in an attempt to clarify what a verse says. In today's English writing, words are sometimes *italicized* for emphasis. A Christian reading those versions needs to remember that the *italicized* words are not being emphasized, they were **added** to the original text.

> **1 Corinthians 12:1 (KJV)**
> Now concerning spiritual *gifts*, brethren, I would not have you ignorant.

> **1 Corinthians 14:1 (KJV)**
> Follow after charity, and desire spiritual *gifts*, but rather that ye may prophesy.

> **1 Corinthians 14:12 (KJV)**
> Even so ye, forasmuch as ye are zealous of spiritual *gifts*, seek that ye may excel to the edifying of the church.

In each of the above verses, the *italics* show that the word "*gifts*" has been added. A better translation than "spiritual *gifts*" is "spiritual *matters*" or "spiritual *things*," which fits the subject of 1 Corinthians 12–14, which are about spiritual matters, including "gifts" (1 Cor. 12:4), "service" (1 Cor. 12:5), "working" (energizings) (1 Cor. 12:6), and "manifestations" (1 Cor. 12:7–10).

---

21. Helpful hint: Over time ball point pen ink runs through the thin India paper most Bibles are printed on and becomes visible on both the front and back of the page. Writing in a Bible with pencil lasts for years and can even be changed if necessary. Colored pencils are good for different emphases.

The Greek word translated "spiritual" in 1 Corinthians 12:1 and 14:1 is *pneumatikos*, which is an adjective, and thus needs a noun to complete the sense of the sentence. That is why the translators have supplied the noun "*gifts.*" It is common for translators to try to get the sense of the context and supply a noun to complete the sense of *pneumatikos*. For example, Romans 15:27 says the Gentiles share in the *pneumatikos* of the Jews. The NIV and ESV supply "blessings," while the KJV and ASV say "things." 1 Corinthians 2:15 uses *pneumatikos*, and the NIV supplies "man," reading "spiritual man," while the ESV supplies "person" and reads "spiritual person," and the KJV reads "he that is spiritual." In 1 Corinthians 9:11, *pneumatikos* is used in the context of spiritual things that are sown into a person's life, so the NIV supplies "seed," reading "spiritual seed," while the KJV supplies "things" reading "spiritual things," and the NRSV says, spiritual "good."

The wide variety of spiritual matters being discussed in 1 Corinthians 12–14 dictates that "matters" or "things" be supplied to complete the sense of "spiritual" in 1 Corinthians 12:1, 14:1, etc. Those chapters in 1 Corinthians are speaking about spiritual matters of many kinds, not just spiritual "*gifts.*" Adding the word "*gifts*" obscures what God had so clearly stated in the original text and causes people to be confused about the manifestations of holy spirit.

In conclusion, it is important to use the word "manifestations" rather than "gifts" when referring to speaking in tongues, interpretation, prophecy, message of knowledge, etc., for a number of reasons. That is the wording that God uses, and we are always on solid ground when we use the language of the Bible. Furthermore, the word "manifestations" points to the fact that we are dealing with outward evidences of something, which in this case is the gift of holy spirit. So if speaking in tongues, etc., are manifestations of the gift, then everyone with the gift has the ability to manifest it. Are you a Christian? If so, you have holy spirit, and with it comes the power of its nine manifestations just as Christ said in Acts 1:8.

Chapter 9

"To one...to another"
An Explanation of 1 Corinthians 12:8–10

We studied the nine manifestations of holy spirit in the last chapter, and showed that each Christian can manifest all of them. Nevertheless, 1 Corinthians 12:8–10 seems to say that each Christian is given only one of the manifestations, and this has confused and weakened the Church. It is important that we properly translate and understand these verses.

> **1 Corinthians 12:7–11 (Author's translation)**[1]
>
> (7) Now to each one is given the manifestation of the spirit for the common good.
>
> (8) For to one is given through the spirit **a message of wisdom**; and to another **a message of knowledge** because of the same spirit;[2]
>
> (9) to a different one **faith** by the same spirit; and to another **gifts of healings** by the one spirit;
>
> (10) and to another working of **miracles**; to another **prophecy**; to another **discerning of spirits**; to a different one *various* kinds of **tongues**; and to another the **interpretation of tongues**.
>
> (11) Now all these the one and the same Spirit energizes, distributing to each one individually just as he purposes.

We have seen in Chapter 8 of this book that each Christian can manifest, or bring into evidence, the gift of holy spirit in the nine different ways

---

1. We use our own translation here primarily because of the lower case and upper case "s" on spirit and because of the names of the manifestations themselves.

2. It is "because of the same spirit," i.e., because of the gift of holy spirit, that a person can receive revelation. The word *kata* (because of) has a variety of meanings. *Bauer's Greek Lexicon* lists two major concepts, with more specific meanings under those, and even more specific meanings under those. For this verse, he notes "the mng. [meaning] 'in accordance w. [with]' can also disappear entirely, so that k. [*kata*] means simply *because of, as a result of, on the basis of....*" (Arndt and Gingrich, *op. cit., A Greek-English Lexicon*) p. 407.

that are listed in the verses above. Each Christian can hear from God (a message of wisdom or knowledge), speak in tongues, interpret tongues, prophesy, have faith, and do miracles, healings, and cast out demons. In spite of that, there has been great confusion in the Church about how many of the manifestations an individual is able to operate. At first glance, 1 Corinthians 12:8–10 does appear to say that any one person will be given only one of the manifestations. This contradicts the evidence we gain from other Scriptures, so what do these verses mean? The explanation of why the Bible says, "to one…to another," becomes clear as we study the context of 1 Corinthians 12:8–10.

The Church in Corinth was deeply divided. This is apparent from the very first chapter of Corinthians, when Jesus, via Paul, appeals to them so that there would be "no divisions" among the people (1 Cor. 1:10). There was jealousy and quarreling among the believers (1 Cor. 3:3). They were even suing one another in the Roman courts (1 Cor. 6:1–7). They would not share their food with each other, and when they came together to eat, one got drunk while another stayed hungry (1 Cor. 11:21). They were even trying to use the divisions between them to determine who had the approval of God (1 Cor. 11:18 and 19).

The division and quarreling in the Church at Corinth is the background of 1 Corinthians 12, and is a major factor in why the "spiritual things" of 1 Corinthians 12–14 are presented to show that God and Jesus work in harmony to produce different spiritual gifts, energizings, and manifestations that bless and build up the entire Body of Christ. The great lesson of 1 Corinthians 12 that was essential for the Corinthians (and us) to understand is that spiritual things may be different, but it is the same God, same Lord, and same gift of holy spirit that produces them. No man is spiritually gifted in and of himself. The gifts, the power, and the manifestations all come from God and the Lord. Based on that, we can all be thankful for who we are, what we have, and that we can work together.

1 Corinthians Chapter 12 opens by saying we should not be ignorant of spiritual *things*. This should be obvious, but in their pride the Corinthians believed they knew more than they actually did. This is why they needed so much teaching, reproof, and correction about spiritual *things*. Then verses 4–6 emphasize that nothing comes from the believers themselves,

but all things come to them from God and the Lord via the one gift of holy spirit.[3]

1 Corinthians 12:4–6 (R. C. H. Lenski)[4]
(4) Now there are distributions of charismata [gifts] yet the same Spirit [spirit];[5]
(5) and there are distributions of ministrations, and the same Lord;[6]
(6) and there are distributions of energies, yet the same God who energizes all things in all ways.

Note the three repetitions of "distributions." The focus here is not on what a person has, but rather that there has been a "distribution" to the person by the Lord Jesus. Had the Corinthians understood that, it would

---

3. When it comes to spiritual *things*, God is the primary or "first" cause, and Jesus is the "immediate" cause. For example, God gave the gift of holy spirit to Jesus, who gave it to us (Acts 2:33). God gave the information contained in the book of Revelation to Jesus, who then made sure it was given to mankind (Rev. 1:1). God puts people in the Church as it pleases Him (1 Cor. 12:18), but Jesus is said to actually give the ministries (Eph. 4:7–11). These examples could be multiplied many times, and the Christian should not be confused just because sometimes God is said to do something while other times Jesus is said to do it. Both are sources of the blessings, and at different times both are said to do the same things. Unlike the divided Church at Corinth, God and Jesus always work in harmony.

4. We use Lenski here because of the literal nature of his work and his accurate rendition of "distributions," which is important to see in order to properly understand verse 11, which uses the verb form of the word *diairesis*. "The term *diairesis* appears only here in the New Testament and means, not "diversities" as our versions translate (for the fact that the gifts are diverse is too obvious to require statement), but 'distributions.' The gifts are parceled out…." (R. C. H. Lenski, *The Interpretation of I and II Corinthians* (Augsburg Publishing House, Minneapolis, MN, 1963), p. 495 (We changed the Greek letters in Lenski's book into English letters). Furthermore, he uses "energizes" in verse 6, which is also used in verse 11, tying the two verses together. Vincent also points out the connection between the distributions in verse 6 and verse 11, and notes that although *diairesis* can be translated "diversities" or "distributions," the connection with v. 11 favors "distributions" (Marvin Vincent, *Vincent's Word Studies in the New Testament* (Hendrickson Publishers, Peabody, MA), Vol. 3, p. 255).

5. In this verse, "spirit" refers to the gift of holy spirit that each believer has received. This section echoes Ephesians 4:3–6, which also encourages believers to be unified and mentions seven important things around which to build their unity, among them one spirit, one Lord, and one God. This is not a reference to the Trinity, which is the three being "one," it is making the point that all three are involved with spiritual manifestations.

6. The word "ministrations" is a plural noun and means ministries or services.

have gone a long way toward unifying them. Instead of being proud of their differences, they would have been proud that the Lord cared for the entire Body and equipped people differently so that everyone in the Church would have all their needs met. Verse 4 speaks of the *charismata* gifts that are distributed, and gifts are individually given. Each person receives his own gifts, which include salvation (Rom. 6:23), a gift ministry (i.e., the personal ministry one has been given by the Lord, Eph. 4:7–13), healing (1 Cor. 12:9, 28, 30), and even an individual's particular sexual drive (1 Cor. 7:7). Verse 5 speaks of services, and verse 6 speaks of energies and energizings, and they point out that even though those can be different, it is the same God who energizes them.

Verse 7 changes the subject, and switches from gifts, ministries, and energizings, to the "manifestation," or bringing into evidence, of the holy spirit. This change is indicated by the change of the subject, and by the word *de* in the Greek text, which indicates a break in the subject or a mind contrast, and is usually translated "now" or "but."

> **1 Corinthians 12:7**
> Now to each one the manifestation of the Spirit [spirit] is
> given for the common good.

It is vital that we properly understand this verse if we are going to properly understand this section of Scripture. The verse starts out with "Now," which some versions have as "But." The point is that there is a change between verses 4–6 and verse 7. In verses 4–6 the subject was "distributions," but now Paul is speaking of something that "each one" has, which is the "manifestation" of holy spirit. Each Christian has the "manifestation" of the spirit, which is singular because if a person has holy spirit, then he naturally has all of the ways it can be shown in the senses world. If a person has a light bulb, he naturally has the manifestation of it—light, heat, and a higher electric bill. If a person has a Swiss Army knife, he naturally has the manifestation of that particular knife; usually a blade, screwdrivers, scissors, etc. The individual evidences are "manifestations," plural, but the singular noun "manifestation" is used in the Bible to inclusively refer to all the ways holy spirit is brought into evidence in the life of a believer, and it is clear from the context of these verses and the scope of Scripture that every believer can operate all of the manifestations.

A good way to think about the fact that the holy spirit is singular but has nine manifestations is to think of a beautiful diamond set in a diamond ring. The diamond is a singular stone, but it has many facets. It is impossible to have the diamond without having all the facets, as they are part of the diamond itself. That is quite a good metaphor for holy spirit. It is impossible to have holy spirit without having the capacity to manifest it, because the manifestations are an inherent part of it. In fact, God placed holy spirit on believers in the Old Testament so they would manifest it, walk in its power, and thus do the work He wanted them to do. Of course, a person can have holy spirit and not walk in the power it gives. He can quench the spirit by not speaking in tongues, not walking in faith, etc. This is in part what makes a "carnal" Christian (1 Cor. 3:3-KJV), one who lives by what his flesh dictates, and not by the Word of God or the spirit of God.

> **It is impossible to have holy spirit without having the capacity to manifest it, because the manifestations are an inherent part of it.**

It is important that 1 Corinthians 12:7 is set apart from verses 4–6 to help us understand that even though we have individual "gifts" from God, we can operate all of the manifestations. Thus, each one is challenged to push himself in the faith so that he can help other people. There is only so much we can do of our own ability. Sooner or later, to really help someone, we have to use spiritual power. We will need to pray in tongues (1 Cor. 14:14), interpret or prophesy for the edification of the Church (1 Cor. 14:4 and 5), hear from God to know what to do and how to do it (Acts 9:10–16), heal someone (Acts 3:1–8), or cast out a demon (Luke 10:17). These things require spiritual power, and the believer has such power (Acts 1:8), "Christ" in him (Col. 1:27). Remember, every Christian is filled with holy spirit.

The operation of spiritual power has its origin in God, who works through believers who trust and obey Him. Thus, the operation of the power of holy spirit is directed by the Lord, either directly or by the written Word and love. For example, a believer can speak in tongues at will, but is directed by the Lord how to do it decently and in order (cp. 1 Cor. 14:23). When it comes to a message of knowledge or wisdom, or doing a healing, miracle, or casting out a demon, one cannot do these things without the Lord's direct provision. He gives the revelation and he supplies the power for the healing or miracle. Believers must recognize this and give credit to the Lord. 1 Corinthians 12:7 and 8 remind us that the Lord is the one who deserves the credit. They repeat that Christians are "given" the manifestation of the spirit, and because it was "given" to them, they should not boast about it—and the Corinthians were boasting about the things they had been given, taking the credit for them as if they were spiritually powerful on their own.

1 Corinthians 4:7
For who makes you different from anyone else? What do you have that you did not receive? And if you did receive it, why do you boast as though you did not?

There is no place in the Christian life for boasting in oneself and taking the credit for what God and the Lord Jesus have done. Another way the Lord reminded the Corinthians that the manifestations were operated only with his provision was to repeat that it was only because of the gift of holy spirit that they had any manifestation at all. We all need to remember that, "to one is given **through the spirit**…and to another… **because of the same spirit**; to another…**by the same spirit**; and to another…**by the one spirit**." The fourfold repetition of "spirit" places great emphasis on the source of the manifestation.

In the Greek text there is an even further emphasis on the fact that the manifestations come from the one gift of holy spirit.

1 Corinthians 12:8 and 9 (Author's translation)
(8) For to one is given through [*dia*] the spirit a message of wisdom; and to another a message of knowledge because of [*kata*] the same spirit;
(9) to a different one faith by [*en*] the same spirit; and to another gifts of healings by [*en*] the one [*heis*] spirit;

In verse 8 we are told that a message of wisdom comes "through" the spirit. Then we are told that the message of knowledge comes "because of" the same spirit. Then we are told in verse 9 that faith comes "by" the same spirit, and healings "by" the "one" spirit. Seeing the words, "is given," "through," "because of," and "by," there should be no question that it is the Lord who is working, and working through holy spirit. If there is any division and quarreling among the people, it is only because they are so proud and carnal that they cannot see that it is the Lord himself who energizes people differently so that the needs of the entire Body of Christ can be met.

The different "energizings" that the Lord distributes at any given time to the people of the Church reflect the needs of the Church. That is why in verses 8–10 the manifestations are said to be "to one…to another…to another…." The Corinthians never doubted that they each had the spiritual ability to utilize all of the manifestations of the spirit that are listed in verses 8–10. However, the Lord does not energize all the manifestations in every person at the same time. In fact, Paul directs the Corinthians to manifest the spirit in a way that is a blessing to the Church. He says, "… When you come together, everyone has a hymn, or a word of instruction, a revelation, a tongue or an interpretation. All of these must be done for the strengthening of the church" (1 Cor. 14:26b). He also reminds them that if they all speak in tongues when an unbeliever is in the room it could give him the wrong idea (1 Cor. 14:23).

It is not the case, as some teach, that each individual can utilize only one manifestation (usually miscalled "*gifts*"). We have heard some people say, for example, "God has not given me the gift of tongues." The book of Corinthians and other writings to the Church (such as Acts) are very clear that every Christian has the spiritual ability to speak in tongues, even if he never has. What this section of Scripture is saying is that at any given gathering of believers the Lord will energize different manifestations in different people. He will give one person a message of knowledge, "another" will prophecy, "another" will speak in tongues and then interpret, "another" may minister healing to a sick person, and so forth. Every Christian has the power of holy spirit, but the way that power will be used at any given time depends on the purposes of God, and upon our faith and willingness to step out and use what we have been given. No matter who does what, it is always the same Lord who distributes the power and always the same gift of holy spirit that is energized.

That each person can manifest all nine manifestations is clearly implied in the Greek text of verses 7 and 8. The words "to one" at the beginning of verse 8 are the masculine singular relative pronoun, "who." Any pronoun can be replaced by its antecedent and the sentence will still make sense. For example, in the sentence, "Bill married Sally, who is a journalist," the pronoun "who" can be replaced by its antecedent, Sally, and the sentence be perfectly clear: "Bill married Sally; Sally is a journalist." If we replace the relative pronoun in verse 8 with its antecedent, "each," in verse 7, then it would read, "Now to each one the manifestation of the spirit is given… to each one is given the message of wisdom…."[7] However, even though each Christian can receive a message of wisdom from the Lord Jesus, he will speak to different people at different times.

After speaking of the nine manifestations, Scripture returns to the theme of distributions, reminding believers that the Lord distributes to each as he purposes.

1 Corinthians 12:11 (Author's translation)[8]
Now all these the one and the same Spirit energizes, distributing to each one individually just as he purposes.

Verse 11 is a summary of what we have just seen in verses 4–10. It is the Lord Jesus who energizes, as he purposes, "all" the manifestations and spiritual *things* talked about in this chapter, and the words "distributing" (also in vv. 4, 5, and 6) and "energizes" (also in v. 6) help tie the whole section together. This brings up a point that should loom large in the life of every believer: if it is the Lord who energizes in individuals according to his purposes, how do we get to the point that he energizes us more?

---

7. In the Greek text of verse 7, *hekastos* is the natural antecedent of the *ho* that begins verse 8. *Hekastos* is the subject in the sentence and matches *ho* in case, number, and gender.

8. We use our own translation here for several reasons, but primarily to show the connection between the "distributions" of verses 4, 5, and 6 and the distribution in this verse and to show clearly that "energizes" is a verb (many versions translate it as a noun).

The answer to that question is that if we want to be energized by him, we need to obey the Word of God and live a holy and faith-filled life.

Occasionally there is some discussion about whether the "he" near the end of verse 11 refers to the Lord or to the believer. It has to refer to the Lord. He is the one doing the distributing, and he does so according to his own purposes, which is why "one" believer "is given" one manifestation and "another" believer "is given" another. If the "he" in the verse referred to the believer, then the Lord would not be able to coordinate the worship service and distribute things "...in a fitting and orderly way" (1 Cor. 14:40). The believers at the fellowship, even if kindhearted and selfless, would not know what their particular purpose should be at the meeting. In contrast, the Lord knows the hearts and abilities of all men, and his own purposes as well, and distributes spiritual *things* so that the people are most blessed.

So far in 1 Corinthians 12 we have seen how it is the "same" Lord Jesus and the "same" God who distribute to, and energize, each believer. No Christian has anything that he has not been "given." Starting in verse 12 and going to the end of the chapter, the Lord gives another example of what he distributes. He distributes members in the Body of Christ. Verse 12 starts with, "For even as" or, "For just as."[9] Thus the way the Lord works with spiritual *things* is "just as" the way he works with the Body, that is, he distributes as it pleases him.

It is now clear why the spiritual *things* of 1 Corinthians 12:1–11 are in the same chapter as the members of the Body of Christ (verses 12–31). All of them are distributions of the Lord, given as he sees fit. Do Christians differ? Yes, but that is no reason to boast or to elevate one person above another, because all that we are and have are the Lord's work. It is due to his great love for the Body and his desire that each person be taken care of that he distributes different things to different people. If we all walk powerfully in what he gives us, the Body of Christ will function as well as a perfectly tuned engine.

The chapter closes with the way things actually work in any given body of believers.

---

9. Verse 12 opens in the Greek with *kathaper gar*, which means "For just as," or, "For even as," or, "For as," and almost every version recognizes that fact (the NIV does not).

1 Corinthians 12:28–31[10]

(28) And in the church God has appointed first of all apostles, second prophets, third teachers, then workers of miracles, also those having gifts of healing, those able to help others, those with gifts of administration, and those speaking in different kinds of tongues.

(29) Are all apostles? Are all prophets? Are all teachers? Do all work miracles?

(30) Do all have gifts of healing? Do all speak in tongues? Do all interpret?

(31) But eagerly desire the greater gifts. And now I will show you the most excellent way.

This section of Scripture blends the manifestations and the ministries, pointing out that not everyone will be energized in the same way at the same time. This is exactly what we have seen earlier in this chapter. It confuses some readers that the manifestations (e.g., tongues, interpretation, miracles, etc.) are blended with ministries (e.g., apostles, prophets, teachers, etc.), and some thus conclude that not everyone can speak in tongues or interpret. However, we must remember that these verses are a summary statement, we dare not lose sight of the point of 1 Corinthians 12 when reading them. The Lord distributes to every person, and at any given time he will energize spiritual gifts and manifestations differently in different people, even though each person can manifest all nine manifestations. Verses 28–30 are a fitting conclusion to the chapter, reflecting the reality that at any given time, in any given meeting, not every person will do everything. It is the Lord who distributes and energizes as it pleases him.

Another lesson 1 Corinthians 12:7–10 teaches is how God groups the manifestations of holy spirit. In order to understand it clearly, let us quote those verses again.

---

10. These verses contain some manifestations and some ministries. The manifestations of holy spirit are miracles, healing, tongues, and interpretation. The gift ministries are apostles, prophets, teachers, those able to help others (Rom. 12:7), and there are those with gifts of administration (Rom. 12:8).

1 Corinthians 12:7–10 (Author's translation)
(7) Now to each one is given the manifestation of the spirit for the common good.
(8) For to one is given through the spirit a message of wisdom; and to another (***allos***) a message of knowledge because of the same spirit;
(9) to a different one (***heteros***) faith by the same spirit; and to another (***allos***) gifts of healings by the one spirit;
(10) and to another (***allos***) working of miracles; to another (***allos***) prophecy; to another (***allos***) discerning of spirits; to a different one (***heteros***) *various* kinds of tongues; and to another (***allos***) the interpretation of tongues.

Notice in the above verses that there are two different Greek words, *allos* and *heteros*, translated "to another" and "to a different one" (in most versions, both words are translated "to another"). *Vine's Lexicon* clearly states the difference between the two words:

Allos and *heteros* have a difference in meaning which, despite a tendency to get lost, is to be observed in numerous passages. *Allos* expresses a numerical difference and denotes "another of the same sort"; *heteros* expresses a qualitative difference and denotes "another of a different sort."[11]

When a list is put together, and the items are said to be *allos*, they are of the same kind or nature. When they are said to be *heteros*, they are different in nature. Thus, what we see in this section is God grouping the manifestations into three groups, which are:

1) A message of wisdom and a message of knowledge, which are of the same sort (*allos*).

2) Faith, healings, miracles, prophecy, and discerning of spirits, which are of the same sort (*allos*) but different (*heteros*) from Group 1.

3) Tongues and the interpretation of tongues, which are different (*heteros*) from Group 2, but of the same kind (*allos*) as each other.[12]

---

11. Vine, *op. cit., Vine's Complete Expository Dictionary*, "another," p. 29.
12. It is not the people who are *allos* and *heteros*, but the people as they are functioning, utilizing the manifestations.

Many scholars have seen and acknowledged the grouping of the manifestations (which most of them refer to as gifts).

Paul himself indicates three groups: 1) *ho men...allo*; 2) *hetero* followed by four *allo*; 3) again, *hetero...allo*. The first two gifts are a pair, so also the last two.[13]

The interchange of the two words in the Greek text (*alloh* = another of the same kind and *hetero* = another of a different kind) shows that Paul divided the gifts into three categories.[14]

Aware that Paul frequently organizes his thought in patterns of three, such classic commentators on 1 Corinthians as Johannes Weiss and Ernest-Bernard Allo thought that Paul's list was a triad of triads. Paul's own use of language, however, indicates a different pattern of organization, 2 + 5 + 2, in an A-B-A arrangement. Paul begins with two gifts of the word (v. 8). "To someone else" (*hetero*) introduces a new series of five charisms (vv. 9–10c). Another "to someone else" introduces the final pair.[15]

...if we take each *hetero* as marking a new category, we get an intelligible result. Of the three classes thus made, the first is connected with the intellect, the second with faith, and the third with Tongues.[16]

[After pointing out that *allos* is varied with *heteros*] Accordingly, the third (faith) and eighth (tongues) in the chain of gifts indicate points of transition, in the writer's thought, from one sort of endowment to another; and the nine thus fall into three divisions, of two, five, and two members respectively....[17]

---

13. Lenski, *op. cit., The Interpretation of I and II Corinthians*, p. 499 (We changed the Greek letters in Lenski's book into English letters).

14. Troy Welch, *Bible Doctrine 102: A Syllabus* (Channel Island Bible College and Seminary, Oxnard, CA), p. 37.

15. Raymond Collins, *Sacra Pagina: First Corinthians* (The Liturgical Press, Collegeville, MN, 1999), p. 451.

16. Alfred Plummer and Archibald Robertson, *The International Critical Commentary: 1 Corinthians*, (T&T Clark, Edinburg), p. 265. We changed the Greek letters to English letters. We assert that God does not vary His vocabulary simply to avoid monotony. He has a divine purpose for what He writes.

17. G. G. Findlay, *The Expositor's Greek Testament*, (Wm. B. Eerdman's Publishing Company, Grand Rapids, MI, reprinted 1990), Vol. 2, p. 888. Findlay also makes the

The reason for the three groups of manifestations, as they are given, becomes clear from the study of the Word of God and from living them out. There are many things in the Bible that are fully understood only when acted upon and lived out. God did not design His Word to be understood by academicians, but by disciples. Jesus made this clear.

John 7:17
If anyone chooses to do God's will, he will find out whether my teaching comes from God or whether I speak on my own.

No one will truly understand prayer until he is faithful to pray, and no one will understand the manifestations of holy spirit until he walks in the power of them and speaks in tongues, interprets, prophesies, etc. The first manifestation group, the message of knowledge and the message of wisdom, is information by revelation. All information that we receive from the Lord will be either knowledge or wisdom. The last group of two manifestations relates to the worship of God. Speaking in tongues is a language

Both speaking in tongues and interpreting tongues are to God, and worship Him.

spoken to God, not to men (1 Cor. 14:2). It is prayer, praise, and giving thanks. The interpretation of tongues is speaking in the language of the group of people present, the gist, i.e., the sum and substance, of what has been spoken to God in a tongue. Thus, both speaking in tongues and interpreting tongues are to God and worship Him. The second group, which consists of five manifestations, relates to the power of God. Faith, gifts of healings, workings of miracles, discerning of spirits, and prophecy are "power" manifestations in that they work to help, strengthen, and protect the Church.[18]

---

following observation: the first two are through the mind, the second in distinction from the mind, and the third in suppression of the mind.

18. God does not name the three groups of manifestations, so different scholars have seen different emphasis in the groups, and "named" them accordingly. We would call the groups, "Revelation; Power; and Worship," or something similar. Plummer sees the groups connected with "Intellect; Faith, and Tongues" (Plummer and Robertson, *op. cit., The International Critical Commentary*, p. 265), while Lenski says, "intellect; faith; the tongue" (Lenski, *op. cit., The Interpretation of I and II Corinthians*, p. 499). Welch

In conclusion, we see the Lord was very serious when he said he did not want us to be ignorant about spiritual *things* (1 Cor. 12:1), and thus he has laid out in great detail in 1 Corinthians 12–14 many of the spiritual things he does for the Church. It is the same God and same Lord who give spiritual gifts, ministries, and energizings. Each Christian has been given the gift of holy spirit, which has nine manifestations that, although manifested by the individual Christian, are energized by the Lord Jesus. They are meant to be operated decently and in order, such that at any given time at any given place, the ministries and manifestations will work together in harmony for the blessing and building up of the Body of Christ.

---

groups them as based on the Word, "miracle gifts" and "sign gifts" (Welch, *op. cit.*, *Bible Doctrine 102*, p. 37).

Chapter 10

Speaking in Tongues

Speaking in tongues is one of the great blessings that God has given Christians. Nevertheless, there is confusion about it in the Church with some people saying it is for every Christian, some people saying it is for some Christians, and even some people saying it does not exist any more but was only for the first century Church. In this chapter, we will set forth some of the fundamentals about speaking in tongues and why God says in 1 Corinthians 14:5 that He would like every Christian to do it. Speaking in tongues is a manifestation of holy spirit that contributes greatly to the quality of our lives as followers of the Lord Jesus Christ. Speaking in tongues is a Christian speaking a language that he does not understand, a language that has been given to him by the Lord Jesus Christ via the gift of holy spirit.

Why should every Christian speak in tongues? A primary reason is that speaking in tongues is the only absolute proof a Christian has that he is born again and guaranteed everlasting life in Paradise. Second, speaking in tongues illustrates to the believer the most basic principle of the Christian walk, which is *trusting the Word of our heavenly Father*. Third, speaking in tongues allows each Christian to be a "witness" to the resurrection of Jesus Christ. Furthermore, when we speak in tongues in a fellowswhip of believers, we are able to obey God's exhortation in 1 Corinthians 14:12 (KJV), "...seek that ye may excel to the edifying of the church," by then giving the interpretation of what we have just spoken. We will now expand upon these primary reasons why God wants every Christian to speak in tongues, as well as give even more benefits for using this God-given supernatural ability. However, before we elaborate on what speaking in tongues is, it is helpful to understand what it is not.

What Speaking in Tongues is Not

It is not a gift. No properly translated verse of Scripture calls speaking in tongues a gift. It is a manifestation of holy spirit.[1]

It is not gibberish, babble, or a made-up language. Even though the tongues that some people speak may seem very strange to our ears, speaking in tongues is a genuine language of men or angels.

It is not speaking a language you already know. When a person speaks in tongues, he does not know the language he is speaking. The Bible makes this very clear.

> **1 Corinthians 14:14**
> For if I pray in a tongue, my spirit prays, but my mind
> is unfruitful.

The mind is "unfruitful" because the individual speaking in tongues does not understand what he is saying. Another verse teaches that same truth:

> **1 Corinthians 14:2 (NASB)**
> For one who speaks in a tongue does not speak to men,
> but to God; for no one understands, but in his spirit he
> speaks mysteries.

The NASB has "spirit" with a lower case "s," which is accurate because it refers to the gift of holy spirit inside the person. Also, it has the phrase, "for no one understands," which is an accurate translation of the Greek text. The point the verse is making is that when someone speaks in tongues, he does not understand what he is saying. That is why the verse says, "no one understands." Many versions add the word "him" at the end of the phrase, saying, "for no one understands **him**." Adding the word "him," when it is not in the Greek text, changes God's intended meaning and causes the verse to be in error.

There are times, such as in Acts 2 and as has been reported in Christian history, when someone in the audience will understand what another

---

1. This is covered in greater detail in Chapter 8, "Walking in Power: The Manifestations of Holy Spirit."

person says in tongues. Thus, if 1 Corinthians 14:2 is made to say that no one listening to someone speaking in tongues will ever understand what the speaker is saying, it creates a contradiction in Scripture and confuses people who want to be able to read and understand the Bible. 1 Corinthians 14:2 is very clear: when it comes to an individual speaking in tongues, "no one understands," that is, no one understands what he himself is saying.

It is not designed for missionary work. The language one speaks when he speaks in tongues is given by the Lord via the holy spirit, not chosen by the speaker. There are many reasons given in the Word of God for a Christian to speak in tongues, and missionary work is not among them. There is no record in Scripture where anyone used speaking in tongues to do missionary work. This idea came about as a result of what happened in the early Pentecostal movement when God, apparently to show people that speaking in tongues was not gibberish, gave known languages to people as they spoke in tongues, just as on the Day of Pentecost when the audience understood the tongues the Apostles were speaking. For example, when Agnes Ozman manifested speaking in tongues, she spoke in Chinese.[2] Upon hearing these foreign languages, people assumed they were for mission work.

> There is no record in Scripture where anyone used speaking in tongues to do missionary work.

It is not "dead," "gone," or "passed away." Some Christians believe that speaking in tongues was only for the early Church and is now gone, but that cannot be the case. Tongues is prayer in the spirit, is giving thanks well to God, is proof of one's salvation, and more. Surely these things are as necessary in the Church today as they were in the first century, and it is as important to be confident of our salvation today as it was 2,000 years ago. 1 Corinthians 13:8–12 (KJV) says that speaking in tongues will pass away when "…that which is perfect is come…," and when we know even as we are known. "That which is perfect" is the Lord Jesus Christ, as verse 12 makes clear when it says we will be "face to face" with him, and we will know as we are known only when the Lord comes. Until then we

---

2. Roberts Liardon, *God's Generals* (Whitaker House, New Kensington, PA, 1996), p. 119.

will continue to know "in part" (1 Cor. 13:12) and only "...see through a glass, darkly..." (1 Cor. 13:12-KJV). Until that time, speaking in tongues will continue to be a blessing to the Church, which is why God tells us not to forbid it (1 Cor. 14:39). Speaking in tongues is unique to the Church Administration, and when the Lord "raptures" us to meet him in the air, speaking in tongues will cease because it will no longer be necessary.

What Speaking in Tongues Is

It is something that God wants us to do. He says in the following verse:

> **1 Corinthians 14:5**
> **I would like every one of you to speak in tongues,** but I would rather have you prophesy. He who prophesies is greater than one who speaks in tongues, unless he interprets, so that the church may be edified.

Many people have mistakenly allowed the second part of this verse to obscure the first part, but the first clause is very clear. The truth is that God wants us to speak in tongues, interpret, and prophesy, but you cannot do all three unless you do each one, and each is very important for the growth of the Church. Some versions, such as the NASB, have "wish," as if God "wishes" that we spoke in tongues, but that is not a good translation in this context. God gave the gift of holy spirit; Jesus said that those who received it would have power, and the manifestations of the spirit are for "each" believer (1 Cor. 12:7). God wants (ESV, RSV) or "would like" (NIV), or "desires" (DHB), for us to speak in tongues. J. E. Styles, a Charismatic teacher who led many people into speaking in tongues during his ministry, wrote: "From our own experiences, and from the testimony of many others, both ministers and laymen, we are convinced that every Spirit-filled child of God should speak with tongues every day in his own private prayer life."[3] We are also convinced of this, and we will see why.

---

3. J. E. Styles, *The Gift of the Holy Spirit* (Fleming H. Revell Company, Old Tappan, NJ, 1971), pp. 37 and 38 (author's emphasis removed).

It is the absolute proof to a Christian that he is saved, born again, and guaranteed everlasting life in Paradise. Speaking in tongues is a manifestation of holy spirit (1 Cor. 12:7–10), so the only people who can speak in tongues are those who have holy spirit, and every Christian was sealed with holy spirit when he believed (Eph. 1:13). 1 John 3:24b says: "…this is how we know that he lives in us: We know it by the Spirit [spirit] he gave us." The primary way that we "know" from the spirit that Christ is in us is speaking in tongues. For various reasons, none of the other manifestations are absolute proof. This is such an important point that we will expand it in the next section.

It vividly illustrates the most basic principle of the Christian walk, which is trusting and obeying the Word of our heavenly Father. Every Christian should learn to trust and obey the written Word of God. When it comes to speaking in tongues, God says to do it, and gives information about how to do it. Nevertheless, to speak in tongues a Christian must have faith that what God says is true, and then he must walk out on that faith and obey what God says. As we will see, this is why the Bible says speaking in tongues is the only way to really make Jesus "Lord." We will expand this point in the next section.

It is a witness of the resurrection of Christ to the believer, and also a sign to unbelievers (1 Cor. 14:22). Throughout history, the Jews asked for signs. Moses turned his stick into a snake as a sign, Joshua set up rocks as a sign, Gideon wanted a sign from the angel that spoke to him, and the Jews were constantly asking Jesus for signs. Now, God has given us a sign of His work, the presence of His holy spirit within us, and it is an open and bold witness of the resurrection of Jesus Christ. We will expand this point in the next section.

It is speaking a language of men or of angels (1 Cor. 13:1) that is not understood by the person speaking in tongues. Speaking in tongues can be a language of angels, which explains why there are so many tongues that are not known human languages. The person speaking in tongues does not understand what he is saying, as we have seen above.

It is speaking to God, not to men (1 Cor. 14:2).

It is speaking sacred secrets. When a person speaks in tongues, he speaks sacred secrets to God, his heavenly Father (1 Cor. 14:2). Although most versions of the Bible read that Christians speak "mysteries" to God, the Greek word *musterion* means "sacred secret," not "mystery," and it is translated "sacred secret" in Rotherham's Emphasized Bible (RHM). It is a blessing and a privilege for Christians to be able to speak sacred secrets to God by speaking in tongues.

It is speaking the wonders of God (Acts 2:11). On the Day of Pentecost, the audience could understand what the Apostles were speaking in tongues, something that generally does not occur (1 Cor. 14:2). Even the skeptics in the audience, however, had to admit that the Apostles were speaking the wonders of God.

It is praise to God (Acts 10:46; 1 Cor. 14:16 and 17).

It is edifying to the one speaking (1 Cor. 14:4; Jude 20).

It is giving thanks well to our heavenly Father (1 Cor. 14:17).

It is prayer in the spirit (1 Cor. 14:14 and 15). It is very important to realize that prayer in the spirit is speaking in tongues. Sometimes Christians call fervent or emotional prayer "prayer in the spirit," but in the Bible that phrase refers **only** to speaking in tongues.

It is under the speaker's control. Speaking in tongues is under the speakers control, so it can be misused and operated incorrectly, which is why the Word dedicates many verses in 1 Corinthians 14 to how to do it properly. A Christian speaking in tongues can start and stop when he wants to. He can speak loudly or softly, he can sing or shout in tongues. It is precisely because speaking in tongues is under the speaker's control that God gives us directions about its proper use. For example, there is no profit in someone standing up in front of a group and only speaking in tongues, because those listening will not understand the tongue and the speaker will be speaking "into the air" (1 Cor. 14:6–9). Similarly, if the whole church has gathered and everyone is speaking in tongues at the same time, if an unbeliever or someone who does not understand comes in, he will probably say you are all out of your mind (1 Cor. 14:23).[4]

---

4. The translation "out of your mind" (some versions read "mad") is the translators' attempt to represent the Greek text in this context of public worship, which, unfortunately, cannot be easily translated into English. In the Greek pagan worship, it occasionally happened that the devotees were taken over by demons and acted in a frenzied, frantic, raving manner. The New Testament scholar, C. K. Barrett, writes: "*You are mad…does not mean, You are suffering from mental disease, but, You are possessed…*" (C. K. Barrett,

God never wants His people to look foolish or have others turn away because of a Christian's behavior, so He instructs us in the proper use of tongues. On rare occasions God will work so powerfully in someone that they start speaking as a result of what He does. However, otherwise their speaking in tongues is totally under their control. If the person does not "speak," i.e., move his mouth, his tongue, and make the sounds, he will not speak in tongues. Something else we need to be aware of is that, on rare occasions, a person who is demonized ("possessed") is taken over by the demon, which then makes them speak in a language they do not understand. This is not speaking in tongues because it is never under the control of the speaker.

When sung instead of spoken, it is "singing in the spirit" (1 Cor. 14:15). A person can sing in tongues. In Scripture, "singing in the spirit" is singing in tongues.

Speaking in tongues is speaking a language that does not come from your mind, but by way of God's spirit within you. Speaking in tongues is primarily designed for one's personal edification and use, but it is also to be utilized in a gathering of Christians by following it with its companion manifestation, the interpretation of tongues, so that the Church is edified by one's praise to God. Speaking in tongues followed by the interpretation of tongues enables each believer to obey God's exhortation to "...strive to excel in building up the church" (1 Cor. 14:12b-ESV). What an awesome privilege to be able to build up the Royal Family of God, but one cannot build up the Church by the manifestation of interpretation of tongues unless he first speaks in tongues.

Speaking in tongues is proof of salvation. Speaking in tongues is the only absolute proof a Christian has that he is born again and guaranteed everlasting life in Paradise. Speaking in tongues is supernatural, i.e., it is beyond man's natural ability. It is a God-given ability made possible by the presence of holy spirit that is born inside each Christian. No non-Christian can speak in tongues. When a person gets saved, born again, he is sealed

---

Black's New Testament Commentary: The First Epistle to the Corinthians, (Hendrickson Publishers, Peabody, MA, 1968), p. 326). God wants to prevent confusion in Christian fellowships. He never wants people who attend church to think that the congregation has been taken over by demons and gone into a religious frenzy. He makes it clear that what is done in the service "...must be done for the strengthening of the church" (1 Cor. 14:26b).

with the gift of holy spirit (Eph. 1:13). Speaking in tongues is God's witness to us that we are indeed born again of incorruptible seed (1 Pet. 1:23).

Salvation is the world's biggest deal to any person, because a saved person will live **forever**. And you may say: "GREAT! Umm, how do I know I'm saved?"

Some would reply: "Well, because God says so, if you obey Romans 10:9."[5]

"Yes, but I didn't feel anything happen when I got saved, and the next day I smoked, drank whiskey, cursed, and cheated at miniature golf. So how do I know for sure that the holy spirit of God is permanently within me? Is there any evidence in the senses realm, the realm where I've lived from birth and to which I am almost completely attuned? Something I can see and hear?"

Yes, there is, because speaking in tongues is one of the nine "manifestations" of the gift of holy spirit. The English word "manifestation" comes from two Latin words, *manus*, meaning "hand," and *festare*, meaning "to touch." It refers to something concrete and tangible.[6] The gift of holy spirit is not tangible, because it is spirit, which is not in the realm of the five senses. That is why Scripture does not promise that one will feel anything when he gets born again. God may accompany someone's New Birth with a miracle in the senses realm so that he knows it without a doubt, but that is rare and certainly not promised. It is a great blessing, and certainly part of the grace in the "Administration of Grace," that God has provided believers with indisputable proof that we are saved, and there are "no ifs, ands, or buts about it!"

Remember that speaking in tongues and its companion manifestation, interpretation of tongues, were conspicuously absent prior to the Day of Pentecost. The question is: What is so unique about speaking in tongues that God reserved it just for us who are born again of His spirit?

It is not what is unique about speaking in tongues; it is what is unique about salvation in the Church Administration that necessitated speaking

---

5. Romans 10:9 says: "That if you confess with your mouth, 'Jesus is Lord,' and believe in your heart that God raised him from the dead, you will be saved."

6. The Greek word translated "manifestation" is covered in Chapter 8, "Walking in Power: The Manifestations of Holy Spirit."

in tongues as the indisputable proof of that unconditional salvation. In no other administration was salvation equated with seed, birth, and therefore permanent sonship. In neither the Old Testament nor the period of the Gospels was salvation permanent, and no one ever dreamed it would be. Talk about "the world's biggest deal." This is it! God came up with proof that to the ignorant may seem absurd, but which is actually very ingenious and practical.

In no other administration was salvation equated with seed, birth, and therefore permanent sonship.

In 2 Corinthians 1:22, it says God "set his seal of ownership on us, and put his Spirit [spirit] in our hearts as a deposit, guaranteeing what is to come." The Greek word translated into English as the phrase "deposit, guaranteeing what is to come" is *arrabon*, and it means a token, a down payment, a guarantee.[7] In the KJV it is translated "earnest," as in "earnest money" that is put down on the purchase of a house.

The **manifestation** of the holy spirit known as speaking in tongues, which only Christians can do, gives the believer positive proof that he is saved. Speaking in tongues is the most powerful and convincing way in which our holy spirit testifies that we are children of God.[8]

"Tongues" is a language that God gives you, just as He first did on Pentecost when the Church was born. And the record in Acts 2:1–4, where the Apostles spoke in tongues immediately after they were born again and received holy spirit, is the pattern God intended for every Christian, which is that each one speak in tongues right after he is born again.

Why? For many reasons, among them so that each Christian immediately knows once and for all that (a) he has everlasting life, (b) the Word of God is true, (c) Jesus Christ is alive, (d) he is filled with the

---

7. This is a good example of when the meaning of a Greek word cannot be effectively brought into English in just one word. The NIV does a good job of catching the essential meaning of *arrabon*.

8. Both Jesus Christ and our holy spirit testify that we are God's children. The most convincing proof we have from our holy spirit is speaking in tongues, but the other manifestations also testify to our sonship. Furthermore, Jesus Christ testifies to that fact in many ways as we walk and talk with him in our daily lives. Romans 8:16 says, "The Spirit [Jesus Christ] himself testifies together with our spirit, that we are God's children" (Rom. 8:16, R. C. H. Lenski, *The Interpretation of St. Paul's Epistle to the Romans* (Augsburg Publishing House, Minneapolis, MN, reprinted 1961), p. 524).

power of God and can utilize all the other manifestations, and also (e) that he can immediately begin to praise and pray to God in the spirit. That is why God clearly says in 1 Corinthians 14:5 that He would like each Christian to speak in tongues. We think that for our Father, hearing a newborn Christian speak in tongues parallels how a mother feels when she hears her newborn baby make its first cry—it's alive! The difference is that when God hears a child of His speak in tongues, He knows the person will be alive *forever*.

We believe it is tragic that countless Christians never take advantage of this wonderful blessing of God and speak in tongues. In the past 35 years, we have had the awesome privilege of helping to lead thousands of dear saints into speaking in tongues, some of whom were 60–80 years old and had desired to for decades. With a few minutes of instruction, they easily did it, and many cried tears of joy.

Speaking in tongues is a way of trusting God and making Jesus Lord. Speaking in tongues is very practical. How so? The second vital truth about speaking in tongues, and also why God wants every Christian to start doing it immediately, is because it perfectly illustrates the "bottom line" principle of the Christian walk, which is trusting God and His Word. Trusting God is how we find out whether or not He keeps His Word.

How so? Think about it. God goes first, if you will, and gives His Son for us. Jesus takes his turn and goes to the Cross. God raises him and promises us salvation. Now, it's our turn. When we believe Romans 10:9, it's God's turn and the Lord Jesus fills us with holy spirit. Furthermore, God says, "Say, I'd really like it if you'd speak in tongues."

Our turn again: "Huh? You want me to fluently speak a language I've never learned?" God's turn: "That's right."

"Seriously?"

"Yes."

"How?"

"Good question. Remember Pentecost? What happened? They spoke in tongues as I gave them the words. So all you have to do is speak, but don't speak a language you know."

"Let me get this straight. You want me to open my mouth and employ the mechanics of speech, and you're telling me I'll be speaking a real language?"

"Absolutely."

Does that require any faith, any trust in God and His Word? It sure does, and that is what being a Christian is all about. It always comes down to whether or not we really believe what God says.

Do you want to see a biblical record that vividly illustrates exactly the same principle involved in speaking in tongues? Look at Matthew 14:25–33. The disciples are in a boat trying to cross the Sea of Galilee in the middle of a storm. Jesus strolls by—on the water. They freak out.

Jesus says, "Relax, it's I."

Peter pipes up: "Yeah, well, if it's really you, let me walk on the water too."

Jesus: "Come on, brother."

Now put yourself in Peter's potentially soggy shoes. Does he have a promise? Yes. What is it? That he can walk on the water. Jesus would not ask him (or you) to do anything he (or you) could not do. And with the promise comes a provision, "If you step out, I'll help you." Now it's Peter's turn. How will he find out if the promise is true? There's only one way—step out of the boat! And he did! But, it was not until the split second his foot touched the water that God "took His turn" and made it firm under his feet. Had Peter put his foot one inch from the water and said, "Oh, this won't work," he never would have experienced the power of God.

See the principle? We have to **act** on the promise if we want to see the power of God. It is **exactly** the same in regard to speaking in tongues. If you are born again, you can speak in tongues. How do you know? Because God would not ask you to do something you cannot do. He clearly says, "I would like every one of you to speak in tongues..." (1 Cor. 14:5a). Furthermore, as we have set forth, He gives you plenty of incentive and motivation by setting forth its benefits.

So whose turn is it now? Right—yours. What do you have to lose to give it a try? You just open your mouth and utilize the mechanics of speech, but do **not** speak English or any other language you know. What you will be speaking is whatever language God chooses to give you. If it is a language of men, someone somewhere on the earth (among the approximately 6000 or so dialects) could understand it. If it is a language of angels, no one on earth would understand it.

When it comes to speaking in tongues, there is only one way to fail—and that is *not to speak*. Please get this: if you open your mouth and speak (not a language you know), *you cannot fail*—you will speak in tongues. If you **do** move your lips, your throat, your tongue and formulate different words, you will speak in tongues. Why? Because it is impossible for God to lie, and He was the one who asked you to speak in tongues.

Through the years, we have shared these same truths with many people. Some have come back to us and said, "I tried it and it didn't work."

We always ask: "Did you open your mouth and project sounds? Did you **speak**?"

And they say, "Well, no."

And we say, "Then you did not actually try."

Just as the water did not become firm until Peter's foot actually touched it, so God does not give you the words until you speak. Do you see how this perfectly illustrates what the Christian life is all about? God makes many promises to us, but the only way they come to pass is when we act on them. Our heavenly Father makes wonderful promises to us because He adores us, and oh, how He longs to fulfill them to us for our benefit.

Speaking in tongues is walking out in faith that what God has told us in His Word is true, and demonstrating our obedience to Him, even if we are uncomfortable with the idea, having confidence that we will actually speak in tongues. That is why speaking in tongues is the perfect indicator that we have made Jesus "Lord," because we are willing to do what he asks and obey him. Consider the following verse:

> **1 Corinthians 12:3**
> Therefore I tell you that no one who is speaking by the Spirit [spirit] of God says, "Jesus be cursed," and no one can say, "Jesus is Lord," except by the Holy Spirit [No "the." Read "holy spirit"].

1 Corinthians 14 makes it clear that speaking or praying or singing "by the spirit" means doing so in tongues. Think about that in light of the

above verse. Even non-Christians can **say** the words "Jesus is Lord," right? So, there must be a deeper meaning here—and there is. To speak in tongues requires absolute faith in the resurrection and lordship of Jesus Christ, and doing so in response to God's exhortation in 1 Corinthians 14:5 ("I would like every one of you to speak in tongues…") is **really** saying Jesus is Lord. It is "putting your money where your mouth is."

If we refuse to do so, we are, in essence, making ourselves lord in that area of our lives. As Jesus said, "Why do you call me, 'Lord, Lord,' and do not do what I say?" (Luke 6:46). No wonder 1 Corinthians 12:3b says, "… no one can say, 'Jesus is Lord,' except by the Holy Spirit [holy spirit]." The word "can" is *dunamai* in the Greek text, which is "to be powerful, to be able." Thus, The New Living Translation says that no one "is able to say" that Jesus is Lord except by holy spirit. The Amplified Bible reads: "no one can **really** say" that Jesus is Lord except by holy spirit, and we think that captures the essence of what God is saying here. If we are not willing to do what God has told us He wants us to do, then we are not able to **really** say that Jesus is Lord of our lives.

Speaking in tongues is a witness to the resurrection of Christ. Speaking in tongues allows each Christian to be, a "witness" to the resurrection of Jesus Christ. A person cannot speak in tongues without the presence of holy spirit inside him, and so speaking in tongues is a "sign" to each Christian that he has the spirit of God. It is also a sign to unbelievers (1 Cor. 14:22). In a court of law, "hearsay" is not admissible as evidence. Only a firsthand seeing or hearing will stand up under cross-examination. But, we today do not have the luxury of being with Jesus Christ as his disciples did, nor were we there when they crucified our Lord, nor when he arose from the dead, nor when he appeared to his disciples. How then can we be expected to be enthusiastic "witnesses" for him? Is there any comparable sensory connection we can have with our Lord?

We believe that the answer lies in several sections of Scripture, each of which shows the connection between the gift of holy spirit and the **"witness"** that spirit can be to us to the end that we walk in the power of the spirit and **"witness"** God's heart to the world.

Acts 1:8 (NASB)
but you shall receive power when the Holy Spirit [holy spirit] has come upon you; and you shall be My **witnesses** both in Jerusalem, and in all Judea and Samaria, and even to the remotest part of the earth."

Keep that in mind as you read the following verses:

Romans 8:15 and 16 (KJV)
(15) For ye have not received the spirit of bondage again to fear; but ye have received the Spirit [spirit] of adoption, whereby we cry, Abba, Father.
(16) The Spirit itself beareth **witness** with our spirit, that we are the children of God.

Jesus Christ, "The Spirit," bears witness with our spirit, and the more confident we are that we are children of God, the more boldly we live as witnesses of the truth. Exactly **how** does the holy spirit in us **"witness"** to us? We assert that it is via speaking in tongues, because that is the external proof in the senses realm of the internal reality of the gift of holy spirit. Speaking in tongues is the indisputable proof to you that Jesus rose from the dead and is now living in your heart via the gift of holy spirit that he poured into you.

After Acts 4:31 says that the believers were "filled," that is, boldly manifesting the holy spirit outwardly (they were already Christians and thus filled inwardly), we read:

Acts 4:33 (NASB)
And with great power the apostles were giving witness to the resurrection of the Lord Jesus, and abundant grace was upon them all.

It is safe to say that the power with which the Apostles witnessed to the Resurrection included their speaking in tongues and helping others to do likewise.

In the next chapter of Acts, after the Apostles had been miraculously freed from prison and gone right back to the Temple courts to preach the

Word, they were taken before the Sanhedrin. The high priest chastised them for speaking the Word after the council had forbidden them to do so. Watch what Peter says, and note verse 32 especially.

> **Acts 5:29–32 (NASB)**
> (29) But Peter and the apostles answered and said, "We must obey God rather than men.
> (30) "The God of our fathers raised up Jesus, whom you had put to death by hanging Him on a cross.
> (31) "He is the one whom God exalted to His right hand as a Prince and a Savior, to grant repentance to Israel, and forgiveness of sins.
> (32) "And we are **witnesses** of these things; and *so is* the Holy Spirit [holy spirit], whom [which] God has given to those who obey Him."

When the Apostles said that the holy spirit God had given to those who obey Him was a witness that Jesus was raised from the dead, it is obvious that the clearest witness, which God calls a sign for unbelievers, is speaking in tongues. The more real the witness of the holy spirit within us, the more real is our witness to others.

The next section we will consider has three uses of the word "spirit" and nine uses of the word **"witness"** in five verses.

> **1 John 5:6–13 (NASB)**
> (6) This is the one who came by water and blood, Jesus Christ; not with the water only, but with the water and with the blood.
> (7) And it is the Spirit [spirit] who [that] bears **witness**, because the Spirit [spirit] is the truth.
> (8) For there are three that bear **witness**, the Spirit [spirit] and the water and the blood; and the three are in agreement.
> (9) If we receive the **witness** of men, the **witness** of God is greater; for the **witness** of God is this, that He has borne **witness** concerning His Son.
> (10) The one who believes in the Son of God has the **witness** in himself; the one who does not believe God has made

Him a liar, because he has not believed in the **witness** that God has borne concerning His Son.

(11) And the **witness** is this, that God has given us eternal life, and this life is in His Son.

(12) He who has the Son has the life; he who does not have the Son of God does not have the life.

(13) These things I have written to you who believe in the name of the Son of God, **in order that you may know that you have eternal life**.

Verse 6 is saying that Jesus Christ was born into the world as a true human being, coming by way of "water and blood" like every other human. Verse 7 says that the spirit of God witnesses to the reality of Jesus' life, and verse 8 is saying the same thing that Romans 8:16 says—the spirit of God bears witness in each Christian. Verse 9 says that the witness of God is that Jesus is who God says he is. Then verse 10 says that whoever believes in Jesus has the "witness" within himself, and verse 11 says that this inner witness is the testimony that we are saved. Verse 13 reiterates that the previous verses were written **so that we who believe in Jesus Christ could know for sure that we have everlasting life.**

Just as "doubting Thomas" touched the nail print in Jesus' hands, and just as the other disciples saw Jesus, heard him, and touched him, so we today have an experiential, "firsthand" sensory knowledge of his resurrection. We have that every time we manifest his holy spirit by speaking in tongues. It is our indisputable proof that **HE IS RISEN!**

Have Faith, Not Fear

Some people do not speak in tongues due to a fear about it. It is important that Christians do not allow fear to keep them from doing the will of God. All of us have some fear, but obedient Christians meet their fear head on and break through into victory.

One of the common fears people have is that they will not really speak in tongues, but instead will have some kind of counterfeit. God never cautions us about that or warns us to beware of such a thing happening. There is no verse of Scripture that says, "Beware of counterfeit tongues."

Thus, believers need not be concerned that when they speak in tongues, it is not genuine. When a Christian is speaking words he does not understand, and is in control of his mouth, he is speaking in tongues. Jesus said,

> **Luke 11:13**
> If you then, though you are evil, know how to give good gifts to your children, how much more will your Father in heaven give the Holy Spirit [No "the." Read "holy spirit] to those who ask him!"

When a person asks God for holy spirit power, he gets the genuine article, not a counterfeit.

Another concern that people have, especially when they first speak in tongues and realize that they are the ones speaking, is that somehow they are making up the language, and thus are "in the flesh" and not "in the spirit." Speaking in tongues allows a Christian to really experience being a "fellow-worker" with God (1 Cor. 3:9). Speaking in tongues is part supernatural and part natural; part spirit and part flesh. Acts 2:4 makes it clear that it is as the Christian speaks that the Spirit gives the utterance, the words. If the Lord did not give the words, one could not speak in tongues. However, if one does not *speak*, neither will he speak in tongues.

1 Corinthians 14:2 says, "...anyone who speaks in a tongue...." There is never a reference to "the Lord" speaking. Neither is there any verse of Scripture that says "the Holy Spirit" will speak through a person. It is the person who is doing the actual speaking. Some Christians do not speak in tongues even when they know it is God's will and want to do so because they expect God to speak through them, i.e., take over their mouths and make them speak. He will not do it. The Bible says the Christian does the speaking. Thus, a believer should never wait for God to move his mouth and speak through him. Instead, he should move his mouth and use the mechanics of speech in faith that the Lord will give him the words to say as he is speaking.

Some people who have heard speaking in tongues may be afraid of "sounding stupid." Tongues can be a language of men or angels, and there are some languages that sound strange to us. However, nothing that comes from the Lord is ever "stupid." It is a great blessing to speak in tongues, and we should be very thankful for whatever language the Lord gives us, and proud that we have the opportunity to speak in tongues and pray and praise God in that way.

Some people are afraid to try to speak in tongues because they are afraid they are somehow not good enough to do so. Remember, speaking in tongues is a manifestation of holy spirit, and if you are saved you already have holy spirit and can therefore speak in tongues. The Bible is to be our rule for faith and practice, and there is not one single verse that even hints that someone has to be "good" to speak in tongues. Besides, God has made us holy and righteous in Christ, and that is about as "good" as you can get! Remember also that speaking in tongues is prayer and praise in the spirit. No one thinks to himself, "I am not good enough to pray." Even the worst criminal may pray for God to help him. Similarly, God would never keep someone from praying in the spirit because he was "not good enough."

> **It is important that Christians do not allow fear to keep them from doing the will of God.**

Scripture is clear that God wants us to speak in tongues. There is nothing to fear and every reason to want to obey God and receive the blessings and benefits of speaking in tongues.

How much should we speak in tongues?

God's Word never directly tells us how much we should speak in tongues, but there are good reasons to believe that each person should speak in tongues much in his private prayer life. First, speaking in tongues is prayer in the spirit, and the Bible tells us to "pray continually" (1 Thess. 5:17), "Be…faithful in prayer" (Rom. 12:12), and "Devote yourselves to prayer" (Col. 4:2a). Furthermore, speaking in tongues is praise to God and giving thanks to Him, and it is hard to see how one could do that too much. The Apostle Paul wrote to the Church at Corinth:

> **1 Corinthians 14:18**
> I thank God that I speak in tongues more than all of you.

Paul was highly disciplined in his prayer life and spoke in tongues more than all the Corinthians. Only a few chapters earlier, Paul exhorted the Corinthians to "Follow my example" (1 Cor. 11:1a). We also should follow the example of Paul and speak in tongues much in our daily lives.

How to Speak in Tongues

1. Relax and have faith that what God has promised, He will perform. God has said He wants you to speak in tongues (1 Cor. 14:5), and Jesus said that God would give holy spirit to those who ask (Luke 11:13). If you are a Christian, you have it.
2. Remember that you will not understand what you are saying.
3. **You** must do the speaking. Scripture says of the Apostles on the Day of Pentecost that *they* spoke in tongues.
4. You must **speak**. Right now, say out loud: "I know that God wants me to speak in tongues," and pay attention to what you are doing as you speak. **You** move your mouth, you move your tongue, and you make the sounds. Speaking in tongues is **speaking**. If you will not move your mouth and make the sounds, then you will not speak in tongues, or any other language for that matter.
5. The language forms syllable by syllable **as you speak**. Because no one understands what he or she is saying in tongues, you cannot wait until you know what you are going to say and then speak. The Lord will not give you a sentence in tongues ahead of time that you then speak forth. Rather, he will "put on your tongue" a syllable, which will come out **as you speak**. It is a walk by faith. You open your mouth to speak, and as you speak the Lord provides the syllables.

   The New American Standard Bible translates the last phrase in Acts 2:4 very accurately: "And they were all filled with the Holy Spirit [holy spirit] and began to speak with other tongues, as the Spirit **was giving them** utterance." Notice that Scripture tells us that they were speaking **as** the Spirit **was giving them** utterance. The Lord does not tell us ahead of time; we step out in faith word by word. Notice also that the Lord gave the "utterance," i.e., what to say. A great Bible teacher once said, "**What** you speak is God's business, but **that** you speak is your business."

6. Speaking in tongues will probably seem very strange at first, but just keep on doing it. Remember, when you speak in tongues, the words

come from the gift of holy spirit inside you and not from your brain, and this will be new to you. You are not used to speaking words without understanding them, but that is what you have to do to speak in tongues. Practice makes it easier.

7. You may tend to repeat the same syllables or words over and over. Although that is speaking in tongues, it is not the developed language that you should desire. Remember that **you** are doing the speaking, so relax and let the Lord help you expand your vocabulary with different sounds. If you get stuck and find yourself saying the same word over and over, force yourself to try different vowel and consonant sounds so that you will get unstuck.

8. The Devil may try to tell you that you are just making up words. If so, make up these words for him: "Get lost." The best defense is a good offense, and the best offense is knowing and acting upon God's Word. Scripture tells us that the Lord wants us to speak in tongues and makes it clear that we can. It tells us that we will not understand what we are saying. Furthermore, it is clear in Scripture that we are the ones who do the actual speaking. Speaking in tongues is under your control, and you are doing the speaking, so it may seem like you are making up the language, but you are not. Remind yourself of all that and "… Resist the devil and he will flee from you" (James 4:7). Then, "Humble yourselves…under God's mighty hand…," "…standing firm in the faith…" (1 Pet. 5:6 and 9), and boldly speak in tongues.

So relax, take a deep breath, let it out slowly, and focus your mind on the God and the Lord who love you immeasurably. Thank them for having filled you with the holy spirit, take another breath, and go for it—speak forth words of praise, thanksgiving, and worship. That is exactly what you will be speaking. Be **BOLD**—the words you are hearing are the proof that Jesus is alive and well—and you are too—forever! It cost him his life for you to be able to praise and worship God in this wonderful way, so get into it!

One more thing. Not only will you **hear** the words you are speaking, like when you speak in your native tongue, but because you are not using your mind to speak in tongues, you can also **listen to** what you are saying. That is why it may sound really strange at first, but so would any language you have never heard before. The Lord is with you. Go for it! And know that as you are speaking in tongues, you are praising your wonderful heavenly Father and touching His heart with your love for Him.

Chapter 11

Revelation and the Gift of Holy Spirit

It is important for us to know how God and the Lord Jesus communicate with us via the gift of holy spirit that has been born inside us. Although there are many facets to revelation, and although God can communicate to people in many ways, the primary way God and the Lord communicate with Christians is through holy spirit.

What is Revelation?

The word "revelation" comes from the word "reveal," which means "to make known." Biblically, the word "revelation" refers to something made known by a spiritual source, which may be God, the Lord Jesus Christ, the Devil, or demons. In this book, we deal primarily with revelation that comes via the gift of holy spirit.

In its secular usage, "revelation" can refer to something that has a profound impact on a person or when someone learns something that helps him understand some aspect of life. For example, someone might say, "It was a revelation to me to learn that my headaches could be cured by getting more sleep." However, that is not the way "revelation" is used in its biblical context.

Revelation Is Not

1. What someone learns from reading the Bible. When the Bible was originally given, it was revelation to that individual who then communicated it to others. When a person reads it, he learns, but that type of learning is not revelation, it is using our faculties of logic, memory, etc.
2. What someone feels very strongly about. When a person feels very strongly about something, there is a danger that some of those strong opinions will "leak over" into what he says comes from God. This is as true in regard to doctrine as it is for personal feelings and opinions.

3. What someone knows from his five senses (seeing, hearing, smelling, tasting, and touching). What a person observes through his senses may be accurate, but it is not "revelation" unless it comes from a spiritual source.

Revelation Is

Information that is revealed to someone by a spiritual source.

God's "Categories" of Revelation

The Bible places revelation into two categories, knowledge and wisdom. The manifestations of holy spirit that are revelation are "a message of knowledge" and "a message of wisdom" (1 Cor. 12:8).[1] It is fitting that God categorizes all revelation as either knowledge or wisdom because all information is either knowledge or wisdom. Knowledge is the "facts concerning the case," and is information. "Wisdom" has many aspects and in today's language can have several definitions. However, the first definition of wisdom in the first edition of Webster's Dictionary (published in 1828) captures its meaning in the phrase, "a message of wisdom": "the right use or exercise of knowledge."[2]

When God gives revelation to an individual, it may involve either or both a message of knowledge and a message of wisdom. For example, when God gives a message of knowledge (i.e., gives a person information), He will often give with it a message of wisdom so the person knows what to do with the information he has received. If He does not give a message of wisdom, it usually means that what to do is clear from either the Word of God or from natural wisdom based on the five senses world. God gave a message of knowledge and wisdom to Samuel when the people wanted him to anoint a king over them. Samuel did not want to, but God gave him a message of knowledge and a message of wisdom, saying, "And the LORD told him: 'Listen to all that the people are saying to you; it is not you they

---

1. Information can be a part of the manifestation of discerning of spirits, but God places that manifestation in the "power" category of the manifestations. See Chapter 9, "To one…to another: An explanation of 1 Corinthians 12:8–10."
2. Webster, op. cit., American Dictionary of the English Language, "wisdom."

have rejected, but they have rejected me as their king'" (1 Sam. 8:7). This one revelation contained knowledge that reminded Samuel (i.e., they have not rejected you, but me) and also wisdom, what to do ("Listen" to the people).

The Sources of Revelation

The actual source of revelation is either God, Jesus Christ, the Devil, or a demon. All revelation comes from one of these four spiritual sources. God and Jesus Christ both originate communication to people, and so do the Devil and his demons. Angels are not a "source" of revelation, although they bring revelation messages. Both the Hebrew transliteration *mal'ak* and the Greek transliteration *aggelos* mean "messenger," and angels deliver messages for God, however they are not the source of the message.[3]

Ways a Revelation Message Can Be Communicated

When looking at the ways God, Jesus, the Devil, or demons can give a revelation message, the first major distinction we must recognize is that it will come either internally (from inside the person) or externally (from outside the person). All revelation will either come to a person externally and thus usually be perceivable by others, or it will be internal, given directly to the person's mind.

Revelation from God or the Lord Jesus that comes to us externally can come in a multiplicity of ways. Examples of how God has communicated a message of knowledge or wisdom externally include His speaking audibly. When God spoke the Ten Commandments to the Israelites, everyone heard it and became so fearful they asked God not speak to them directly anymore.[4] Other "external" ways God has given a revelation

---

3. In Greek, a double "g" is pronounced "ng," so *aggelos* is pronounced "angelos," of which our English word "angel" is a translation. The meaning of *aggelos* is "messenger." Translators usually deal with *aggelos* according to its context, so if the messenger is human they translate it "messenger" or a similar word, and if it is a spirit being they translate it "angel." Cp. Matthew 1:20, "angel," with Matthew 11:10 where John the Baptist is God's "messenger."

4. It is believed by most Christians that God first gave the Ten Commandments by writing them on tablets of stone, but that is not the case. He first gave them in an audible voice,

message include: sending an angel (Judg. 13:3–5; Luke 1:26–37), sending a prophet with a message (2 Sam. 12:1–12), having Balaam's donkey give the message (Num. 22:28–30), putting dew on a fleece (Judg. 6:36–40), and writing on a wall (Dan. 5:5).

Demons also come into concretion and give revelation to people. The Devil did so to Eve in the Garden of Eden, and a demon manifested himself and spoke to Job's friend Eliphaz.[5] No one else heard what the demon said to Eliphaz, but had there been someone with Eliphaz he could have heard, because the demon spoke externally, in the senses world. This is often what happens with mediums, who contact the spirit world, and necromancers, who contact the dead, although sometimes they hear the voices or see the visions in their heads. Demons are also expert at manipulating physical objects to communicate a message, and thus all forms of divination are an abomination to God (Deut. 18:10–13). Crystal ball divination, tea leaf reading, and similar practices are all ways that demons communicate messages in the senses world.

Both God and the Devil give revelation "internally" also. In certain circumstances, demons can enter into people and communicate directly to their minds (this is often known as being "possessed," but a better translation is "demonized"). If a demon enters a person's body and

which frightened the Israelites, and they asked God not speak with them any more, but instead speak to Moses (Exod. 20:1, 18–20; Deut. 4:9–11, 36, 5:4, 23–27; Heb. 12:18–21). Edersheim writes "…God Himself 'spake all these words' of the commandments. …The "ten words" were afterwards written on two tables of stone, which were to be kept within the ark of the covenant,…" Alfred Edersheim, *Bible History: Old Testament* (William B. Eerdmans Publishing Company, Grand Rapids, MI, reprinted 1975), pp. 108 and 111.

5. A demon manifested himself to Eliphaz and spoke to him. This occasionally happens and has been reported by witches, mediums, and others who deal with spirits, as well as others to whom demons appear. That Eliphaz saw a "demon" is not specifically stated in the Bible. He called it a "spirit" (Job 4:15), but it is easily discernible as a demon. The demon came at night (4:13) and scared Eliphaz to the point that he shook (4:14 and 15). The demon's form was mostly hidden in the dark (4:16) and it said things that are not true. The spirit claimed that God does not trust his servants and charges His angels with folly (4:18), something a demon would naturally think but that is not true. It also said that men die without anyone regarding it (4:20), when the truth is that God not only regards our lives but counts every hair on our heads. Sadly, Eliphaz was not very knowledgeable or discerning and believed the demon, even repeating some of its "theology" to Job (cp. Job 15:15). That still happens today, and many pagan beliefs, superstitions, and theological errors originated as demonic revelation.

communicates with his mind, the individual will see visions, hear voices, or "just know" things. Psychics usually think they have a "gift," but in actuality there is no such gift. Psychics are demonized but are tricked into thinking they have a gift because their intentions are good, i.e., they are attempting to do good things. Contact with demons is never "good," because they blend truth with error just as the Devil did with Eve in the Garden, and they do "good" only to gain the opportunity to do evil. They use good to "hook" people, because after all, if all their information were erroneous, and all they did was evil, they would never fool anyone, and eventually would have no followers at all. People who go to psychics, mediums, etc., are led away from the true God, and in the end, if they gain the world because of good financial advice or whatever, it is of no lasting profit (Mark 8:36).

How God and Jesus Christ Give Revelation Via Holy Spirit

When an unsaved person becomes saved, the Lord Jesus gives him the gift of holy spirit (Acts 2:33 and 38; Eph. 1:13), which then becomes an integrated part of him, filling him completely. It is through holy spirit that God or the Lord Jesus Christ can speak to him, and that is why in the Old Testament God gave holy spirit to those He wanted to communicate with, and why each and every Christian can manifest a message of knowledge and a message of wisdom.

The way that revelation via the gift of holy spirit works is that a message of knowledge or wisdom originates with God or the Lord Jesus, who communicates to the holy spirit in the Christian, which then communicates with that Christian's mind or body. The gift of holy spirit born inside the Christian is part of him (2 Pet. 1:4-KJV), and so holy spirit can communicate easily with the mind, just as the body can communicate with the mind. Revelation can come to one's mind or to one's body. Revelation that comes to one's mind comes as a thought, emotion, or senses experience (i.e., a sight, sound, etc.). When revelation comes via holy spirit to one's body, it comes as a feeling or sensation (pain, pressure, heat, cold, etc.). It is not always easy to tell whether a thought or feeling is from God or from one's own mind or body. That is why the Bible tells us it takes "constant use" (Heb. 5:14) to be able to accurately discern whether a thought is coming into our mind from God or whether it is one of our own thoughts.

Hebrews 5:14
But solid food is for the mature, who by constant use have trained themselves to distinguish good from evil.

The "solid food" the believer is to feed on includes revelation from God. The mature believer has made it his goal to please God (2 Cor. 5:9), so he lives a holy, obedient, sacrificial life, and will receive more revelation than someone who is not serious about his Christian life (John 14:21). As one matures in the Lord, he learns to more reliably discern the revelation of God from his own thoughts, ideas, emotions, and feelings.

The principle of how revelation works can be charted as follows:

Revelation as a thought	Revelation as a feeling
God (or Jesus Christ) ⇩ holy spirit in you ⇩ your mind ⇩ a thought or emotion	God (or Jesus Christ) ⇩ holy spirit in you ⇩ your body ⇩ a feeling or sensation

Once we understand that revelation usually comes as a thought or feeling, we can understand why "constant use," or "practice," is essential if we are going to reliably discern revelation from our own thoughts and feelings. Actually, a number of Bible versions actually have the word "practice" in Hebrews 5:14, including the ESV, NASB, RSV, and NRSV. We must properly understand the word "practice." It is good in that it implies continual repetition, which is what we should be doing, especially with speaking in tongues, interpretation of tongues, and prophecy, which are more directly under our control. The weakness of the word "practice" is that every time you operate the manifestations, you are not just "practicing," but "in the game," in touch with God and the Lord, and operating the power of God.

The Seven Distinct Ways Revelation Comes to an Individual

Revelation via holy spirit, a message of knowledge and a message of wisdom, comes in seven distinctive ways. You get information from the Lord the same way you gather information from the world around you. The Lord will give you revelation that you (1) see, (2) hear, (3) smell, (4) taste, or (5) touch, or sometimes you (6) "just know." Also, the Lord may give you (7) an emotion.

When the Lord gives a person a vision, sound, smell, etc., via holy spirit, it may seem as real as if it were actually happening in the physical world, but it is happening only in the person's mind. Other people around him are not experiencing what he is. For example, when Stephen saw heaven open and the Lord Jesus standing at God's right hand (Acts 7:55 and 56), he "saw" it as clearly as if it had physically occurred. It was as real to him as his natural sight. Nevertheless, it was a revelation vision via the gift of holy spirit and the others who were with Stephen did not see it. Similarly, when the Lord gives revelation smell, the one receiving the revelation will smell something, but others will not.

Once we understand that a message of knowledge and a message of wisdom come to us by (1) seeing, (2) hearing, (3) smelling, (4) tasting, (5) touching, (6) "just knowing" and (7) emotion, we can expand the chart (see next page) explaining how revelation works.

Receiving revelation works the same basic way for all seven ways God gives it. It comes via the brain like the information of other thoughts and experiences, so Christians must become sensitive to it in order to recognize it consistently, which is why, as we have already pointed out, the individual needs "practice" to do it. Revelation given via holy spirit is usually a very quick experience. It does not usually "hang around" so we can confirm it, study it, etc. God wants us to love Him with all our heart, soul, mind, and strength, and if we do, we are focused on Him and what He tells us.

Revelation is usually a "still, small voice" (1 Kings 19:12-KJV, or as the NIV states, a "gentle whisper"), coming soft and fast, so we must become practiced in recognizing it. A person usually has to be quiet, peaceful, and focused to hear the voice of the Lord.

For revelation vision	For revelation sound
God (or Jesus Christ) ⇩ holy spirit in you ⇩ your mind (the visual center) ⇩ you see a vision as if it were real.	God (or Jesus Christ) ⇩ holy spirit in you ⇩ your mind (the auditory center) ⇩ you hear a sound or voice as if it were real.[6]

Scripture tells us to "Be still, and know that I am God…" (Ps. 46:10), and it is our responsibility to obey that verse and have quiet minds, ready to listen to Him. God tells us to seek Him first in our lives, and He means what He says. In our experience, neither God nor Jesus are usually willing to speak over the music or television that is blaring in the background of our lives. They will usually not "turn up the volume" of their revelation just to accommodate us if we are not willing to obey their commands.

The Bible has many examples of revelation.

---

6. Revelation from demons works in a similar way. When a demon inhabits a person's mind and stimulates the visual center, the person will see a vision. If the demon feeds information to the auditory center of the brain, he will hear voices. Society acts as if people who hear voices are of an unsound mind. They are, but usually not for the reason psychiatrists think (although it is possible to see visions, hear voices, etc., because of mental illness or narcotics). Their minds are unsound because they are inhabited by demons, who are feeding visions and sounds to them. Because many people are ignorant about the true nature of demon spirits and how they operate, and because demons are invisible, a psychic who is demonized may believe he has a "gift" because he "sees," "hears," or " just knows" information about other people. In reality, the demon spirit is feeding information to his mind.

1. **Seeing:** 2 Kings 6:17, "And Elisha prayed, 'O LORD, open his eyes so he may see.' Then the LORD opened the servant's eyes, and he looked and saw the hills full of horses and chariots of fire all around Elisha." When God gave this revelation, which was a message of knowledge by way of a vision, the servant could see the angelic army just as if it were physically there, but no one else could see it. This vision was only a message of knowledge. There was no message of wisdom because there was nothing to do. God simply wanted to comfort Elisha and his servant.

2. **Hearing:** 1 Samuel 9:15 and 16a (KJV), "Now the LORD had told Samuel in his ear a day before Saul came, saying, 'To morrow about this time I will send thee a man out of the land of Benjamin....'" God gave this message of knowledge by speaking it into Samuel's ear, and Samuel heard the voice as clearly as if someone had been there talking with him. It is evident from this record that most translators do not understand how revelation works because, in their versions, they leave out the part about Samuel's ear, despite it being an important part of the biblical record and clearly stated in the Hebrew text.

3. **Smell:** Mark 9:25 (KJV), "When Jesus saw that the people came running together, he rebuked the foul [or "unclean"] spirit, saying unto him, *Thou* dumb and deaf spirit, I charge thee, come out of him, and enter no more into him." Sometimes the Lord will reveal the presence of a demon by way of a terrible stench. The smell is not in the senses world but is a message of knowledge coming from God via holy spirit to the person's olfactory center of the brain where it is interpreted as a terrible smell.[7] Only the one receiving the revelation will smell it. In this record Jesus smelled a bad odor and knew that God was showing him a demon. In this particular record, there was also the manifestation of discerning of spirits because Jesus moved against the demon and cast it out.

4. **Taste:** 2 Kings 4:40, "The stew was poured out for the men, but as they began to eat it, they cried out, 'O man of God, there is death in the pot!' And they could not eat it." That the men (who were prophets) spoke by revelation, and not from their five senses, is clear from reading the verse and its context. The word "death" is a major key. One of the ingredients of the stew was an unknown gourd (v. 39),

---

7. When dealing with demons, information about them from the Lord may also be part of the manifestation of discerning of spirits.

but when the prophet tasted the stew, he knew it was "death." Even if it tasted terrible, one would not confidently say it was deadly. We all have eaten food that tasted positively horrid that may have been good for us. Furthermore, there is nothing in the verse that indicates the food even tasted bad. People sometimes accidentally eat poisonous mushrooms simply because things that are deadly do not always taste bad. The prophets put some stew in their mouths and knew it was "death." That is a good example of how revelation by taste works. In this case, God gave him a message of knowledge by taste. The prophets did not need a message of wisdom because once God showed them the stew was "death," their human wisdom could guide them.

5. **Touch:** Jeremiah 1:9, The LORD touched Jeremiah's mouth. In Mark 5:30, Jesus apparently felt the power leave when his garment was touched. Some ministers report they have felt the sensation of being spiritually drained after ministering the power of God to others, and many ministers say they occasionally receive a physical sensation by revelation. Many times when someone is ministering healing, for example, he "feels" the pain of the one he is ministering to.

6. **Knowing:** Matthew 9:4, "Knowing their thoughts, Jesus said, 'Why do you entertain evil thoughts in your hearts?'" Jesus "knew" their thoughts by revelation. There are times when the message of knowledge or wisdom we receive comes in the form of "just knowing" what is going on. The knowledge is not specifically discernible by seeing, hearing, smelling, tasting, or touching, the person receiving the revelation "just knows" because God (or Jesus) puts the thoughts in his mind.

7. **Emotion:** 1 Samuel 11:6, "When Saul heard their words, the Spirit of God came upon him in power, and he burned with anger." In this example, when God gave this revelation to King Saul, it came via the holy spirit upon Saul to the emotional center in his brain and was registered as an emotion, with the result being that he became very angry. Ezekiel 3:14 is another example of a prophet feeling strong emotion due to the spirit of God. Just as sometimes revelation is "just knowing," sometimes it comes as an emotion that we "just feel." In Saul's case, the holy spirit upon him allowed God to give him the emotion of anger. Emotion is very important in the life of a godly Christian, and God can give us a revelation emotion, or augment an emotion we already have.

Examples of a Message of Knowledge and a Message of Wisdom

As we said in Chapter 8, "Walking in Power: The Manifestations of Holy Spirit," the reason that the revelation manifestations of a message of knowledge and a message of wisdom were not described in Corinthians is that they were well known to the believers. God has communicated knowledge and wisdom to people since He first talked with Adam and Eve in the Garden of Eden, and the entire Bible is full of records of Him communicating with mankind.[8]

A good example of God giving a message of knowledge and wisdom is in Genesis when He talked with Noah.

> **Genesis 6:13–16**
> (13) So God said to Noah, "I am going to put an end to all people, for the earth is filled with violence because of them. I am surely going to destroy both them and the earth.
> (14) So make yourself an ark of cypress wood; make rooms in it and coat it with pitch inside and out.
> (15) This is how you are to build it: The ark is to be 450 feet long, 75 feet wide and 45 feet high.
> (16) Make a roof for it and finish the ark to within 18 inches of the top. Put a door in the side of the ark and make lower, middle and upper decks.

Verse 13 is a message of knowledge. God gave Noah information about what He was going to do. Verses 14–16 are a message of wisdom, i.e., God directing Noah as to what to do. The complete revelation was a blend of knowledge and wisdom, and this is common. Sometimes God gives only knowledge, sometimes only wisdom, but often there is a blend because we usually need to know both the facts of the case and what to do. Another example from Genesis comes from the life of Abram [Abraham].

---

8. Some of the examples given may not be "manifestations of holy spirit," because God may have spoken them audibly and not given them via holy spirit, but all revelation is either a message of knowledge or a message of wisdom, so the principles apply.

Genesis 12:1–3

(1) The LORD had said to Abram, "Leave your country, your people and your father's household and go to the land I will show you.

(2) "I will make you into a great nation and I will bless you; I will make your name great, and you will be a blessing.

(3) I will bless those who bless you, and whoever curses you I will curse; and all peoples on earth will be blessed through you."

In this example, God gave Abraham the message of wisdom first, directing him. Then, He gave him a message of knowledge (vv. 2 and 3), informing Abraham as to what He would do. An example of God giving only a message of wisdom is in Joshua.

Joshua 4:15 and 16

(15) Then the LORD said to Joshua,

(16) "Command the priests carrying the ark of the Testimony to come up out of the Jordan."

In this case, all Joshua needed was a message of wisdom telling him to have the priests come up out of the dry bed of the Jordan River. God did not have to give Joshua a message of knowledge as to why they needed to come out. It was obvious to everyone that the Jordan River was going to start flowing again and if the priests stayed in the riverbed they would drown. In contrast to giving only a message of wisdom, sometimes God gave only a message of knowledge. That happened with Samuel.

1 Samuel 3:11–14

(11) And the LORD said to Samuel: "See, I am about to do something in Israel that will make the ears of everyone who hears of it tingle.

(12) At that time I will carry out against Eli everything I spoke against his family—from beginning to end.

(13) For I told him that I would judge his family forever because of the sin he knew about; his sons made themselves contemptible, and he failed to restrain them.

(14) Therefore, I swore to the house of Eli, 'The guilt of Eli's house will never be atoned for by sacrifice or offering.'"

In the above verses there is no message of wisdom because there was nothing for Samuel to do about the situation. The whole revelation is a message of knowledge to Samuel so he would be informed about what was going to happen and why. God wants to keep His people informed, so, there are times that a message of knowledge is all that is needed.

An example from the book of Ezekiel contains the most common way that revelation comes as a blend of knowledge and wisdom. The whole point of revelation is communication with God and with His Son, Jesus. It is important for us to understand that God has categorized revelation into a message of knowledge and a message of wisdom but one need not know that to communicate with Him. Our communication with God should be as natural, complete, and intertwined as our communication with each other, and that is what we see in the following example.

Ezekiel 2:3–8

(3) He [God] said: "Son of man, I am sending you to the Israelites, to a rebellious nation that has rebelled against me; they and their fathers have been in revolt against me to this very day.

(4) The people to whom I am sending you are obstinate and stubborn. Say to them, 'This is what the Sovereign LORD says.'

(5) And whether they listen or fail to listen—for they are a rebellious house—they will know that a prophet has been among them.

(6) And you, son of man, do not be afraid of them or their words. Do not be afraid, though briers and thorns are all around you and you live among scorpions. Do not be afraid of what they say or terrified by them, though they are a rebellious house.

(7) You must speak my words to them, whether they listen or fail to listen, for they are rebellious.

(8) But you, son of man, listen to what I say to you. Do not rebel like that rebellious house; open your mouth and eat what I give you."

The revelation above contains knowledge, such as "...their fathers have been in revolt against me to this very day," and wisdom, what to do, such as "do not be afraid of them or their words." The knowledge and wisdom are intertwined into a single message, which is what we expect in good communication. Once we become aware of the manifestations of a message of knowledge and a message of wisdom and how the Lord gives them to our conscious minds, usually in a gentle whisper, we are in a much better position to stay attuned to his voice.

Proper Conduct for Those Who Receive Revelation

There is nothing more exciting and more fulfilling than to know we are in touch with God, the Creator of the universe, and the Lord Jesus Christ, and that they are working in us. It takes great maturity to handle it well. All of us need to keep in mind the scriptural admonition that to whom much is given, much shall be required (Luke 12:48-KJV). When a person is given revelation, it is "much" in the eyes of God, and we should all be prepared to do much. Obviously, we are all examples for others, so living a holy and obedient life is fundamental. We should also be prepared to obey whatever God tells us. Revelation is not a game of "if we like it, we'll do it." We are God's children, soldiers, athletes, and ambassadors, and we must be prepared to do whatever He tells us.

> Once we become aware of the manifestations of a message of knowledge and a message of wisdom, and how the Lord gives them to our conscious minds and that he usually speaks in a gentle whisper, we are in a much better position to stay attuned to his voice.

Mature Christians do not think "all," or even most, of our thoughts, feelings, or emotions are from the Lord. As humans, we are "fearfully and wonderfully made" (Ps. 139:14), and God has equipped us to deal with life without His minute-by-minute guidance, especially on small matters (though He can and does help us with small matters). The Bible says we need to practice so we can know which thoughts and emotions are revelation and which are not, and there would be no such directive if all our thoughts and emotions were revelation.

Furthermore, when a Christian does receive revelation, he should be wise in speaking about it. Some people seem to need the approval of others, or think it will elevate them in the Christian community if they constantly say, "The Lord showed me…" or "The Lord told me…." It is rarely the right thing to do, or wise, for a Christian to parade the revelation he has received in front of others. If the Lord really did give him revelation, it will show up in the form of his living a joyful and victorious life, and people will be aware that he is walking by revelation without him constantly telling them.

It is very helpful to know how the Lord communicates to us via the gift of holy spirit inside us. It magnifies the importance of holy spirit in our eyes, and it makes the whole process of revelation much less mysterious. The more clearly we understand how easy and natural it is for the Lord to communicate to us through holy spirit, our divine nature, the easier it is for us to have confidence that he will speak with us.

Chapter 12

Co-workers with God

We have seen that each Christian can walk in the power of God via the nine manifestations of holy spirit. God wants each of us to step forward and be a blessing to ourselves, our families, other Christians, and the world in general. God gave the manifestations so that His people could live the abundant life that Jesus spoke of in John 10:10 (KJV)—in intimate relationship with God and able to help themselves and others. Also, these spiritual abilities we have enable us to engage in the spiritual battle and stand against the Devil and his kingdom.

In spite of the many blessings that come to a believer as he manifests holy spirit, many Christians do not do so. Before one will walk in the power of God, he must first be convinced that it is the will of God for him to manifest holy spirit, and then he must understand that doing so requires his cooperative effort with God and the Lord Jesus Christ. Sometimes the Lord "leads," and we follow his leading. Sometimes, however, we act first, and the Lord backs up our faith by supplying the spiritual power to get the job done.

There are Christians who feel that if they were to take the initiative to manifest the power of God in tongues, interpretation, or prophecy, or lay their hands on someone and ask the Lord for a message of knowledge about that person, etc., it would be overstepping the will of God. They have been schooled to think that unless they have specific guidance from the Lord, they are wrong to take action. They mistakenly think that they have little or no control over how they manifest holy spirit, usually believing that "the Holy Spirit" manifests "Himself" through them. The notion that they have already been enabled and now must simply act in faith makes such believers feel uncomfortable, and perhaps even carnal or blasphemous.

We know from Scripture that God wants us to do certain things (pray, read the Word, share our faith, give, fellowship with others, etc.), so we do them. Most Christians do such things without feeling uncomfortable or without sensing "the leading of the Lord" because they know that what

God says to do in the Bible is "leading" enough. We do not need direct revelation in order to obey God. When it comes to the manifestations, the same thing is true. Scripture tells us to manifest holy spirit. His purpose in giving us His power is for us to use it. God wants us to speak in tongues, praising Him and edifying ourselves, so He says, "I would like every one of you to speak in tongues…" (1 Cor. 14:5a). That should be "leading" enough for any Christian. He wants us to prophesy, which is why He says, "be eager to prophesy" (1 Cor. 14:39). He would not tell us to "be eager" if what He really meant was, "Wait until I tell you, then go ahead."

Similarly, God wants us to ask Him for information by way of a message of knowledge and a message of wisdom. He may not answer our every request, but Scripture often instructs us to ask God for whatever we need, e.g., wisdom (James 1:5). If He then gives it to us via our holy spirit, that is the manifestation of a message of wisdom. We can manifest holy spirit without first hearing from God, and step out on faith in the written Word to speak in tongues, interpret, prophesy, and ask for the revelation to help God's people.

As we said, the Christian's walk with God and the Lord Jesus Christ is a reciprocal and cooperative effort, as the following verse makes clear:

1 Corinthians 3:9a
For we are God's fellow workers…

This verse does not say we are spectators, watching God as He does great things. No, it says we are fellow workers, and if we are going to be effective for God, we must understand what it means to be a fellow worker. Walking in the power of holy spirit involves a reciprocal relationship between God and each believer. He cannot work His work in us if we will not step out in faith and act. We must work together with God, allowing Him to energize His spirit within us, but realizing that we must act in faith in order to accomplish what God is working in us.

Sometimes the Lord "goes first," that is, he tells us what to do. At other times, however, we act first and the Lord backs up our faith by supplying the spiritual power to get the job done. We understand this concept when it comes to prayer. The Bible says to pray, so the obedient Christian prays for all kinds of things, expecting the Lord to "follow" and answer the prayer. However, sometimes we may feel the specific "leading" of the Lord to pray for a specific thing, and then we "follow" by prayer. For example, the Lord Jesus may wake up a Christian in the night and direct him to pray for a friend or relative. In that case, the Lord led and the individual followed. However, the next day he may pray for a friend solely because he knows of something his friend needs. We know that we do not always need the leading of the Lord to pray for others in need. The Word says to do it, and that is enough. When we do, the Lord "follows" our lead by supplying the spiritual power that answers our prayer.

In the same vein, let us consider speaking in tongues, which is prayer and praise to God. He tells us to speak in tongues, so we should. As with praying with our understanding, we may at times feel a specific leading of the Lord, a powerful urge, to speak in tongues, and so we obey. However, most of the time we speak in tongues simply because it is obeying the written Word of God. When we do, the Lord always "follows" by supplying the words.

The same is true with prophecy. Many times the Lord will "lead" by giving us the revelation to deliver a prophecy even if we are not expecting him to work in us that way. This happens a lot, and there are many examples in the Old Testament, like God giving Nathan a prophetic message for King David after he had sinned with Bathsheba (2 Sam. 12:1–12). However, there are times when we recognize a prophecy would be a blessing to someone, so rather than waiting for the Lord to say, "Give that person a prophecy," we ask the Lord for guidance about whether or not to give one. In that case, we initiate the process. We know from the Word of God that prophecy is a blessing, so we assess the situation and then go to the Lord for the "green light" to speak.

Keep in mind that we Christians are "fellow workers." We are not simply sitting around on our thumbs waiting for direction from the Lord. No, we are to help him with the work. What we have seen with prayer, tongues, and prophecy is also true of the revelation manifestations. Sometimes the Lord leads us and we get revelation without asking, and sometimes we should take the lead and ask for the revelation. A good example of the Lord giving revelation without the believer asking for it is when he appeared to Ananias and told him to go and minister to Paul, who had recently had a life-changing experience with Jesus. Ananias was surprised by the revelation and did not want to obey it at first. He questioned the Lord as to whether ministering to Paul was the right thing to do (Acts 9:10–17).

On the other hand, there are times when we do not need to ask the Lord for a specific "go ahead" to do his work. When Jesus sent out the twelve apostles, he told them: "Heal the sick, raise the dead, cleanse those who have leprosy, drive out demons. Freely you have received, freely give" (Matt. 10:8). You can bet those disciples did not go to the outskirts of a town and then sit on the road until they received revelation to go and minister. They had all the direction they needed from Jesus. So do we. There is no sick person we cannot pray for, and as we are praying, we should ask the Lord for more revelation about the situation.

Christians must be ready and willing to act if the power of God is to be manifested. The gift of holy spirit is not a person or force that controls us, and neither is it a "mechanism" that we "operate" solely by our own will. Rather, it is the very divine nature of God in us, and it is via holy spirit that God and the Lord Jesus Christ usually communicate with us. We cannot do the work God has called us to do without His help, and God cannot accomplish His work on earth without our help. A verse in Colossians clearly shows the Christian's reciprocal relationship with the Lord:

Colossians 1:29
To this end I labor, struggling with all his energy, which
so powerfully works in me.

Notice the fellow-laborer relationship between Paul and the Lord. We certainly see Paul laboring in Acts as he traveled from city to city doing what he could to spread the Gospel. As Paul labored, the Lord powerfully worked inside him. The paradigm is this: we labor for the Lord, being energized by the strength he supplies. In the above verse, "powerfully" is the Greek word *dunamis*, from which we get the English word "dynamite." Dynamite is a powerful explosive, but it must be activated by a blasting cap in order to produce kinetic power, that is, power that does work.

Similarly, the "dynamite power" that the Lord will supply to each believer needs to be "set off" by our acting in faith.

From Genesis to Revelation, we see the concept that God supplies the energy (or power) as we act. Moses could throw his stick on the ground, but it would not have become a serpent without God's power. Neither would it have become a serpent if Moses had not obeyed and thrown it down (Exod. 4:1–3). For the sun to stop, Joshua had to tell it to do so, and God had to provide the power (Josh. 10:12–14). Samuel did not have the power to make it rain in Israel during the wheat harvest, but it would not have rained without Samuel calling on God in faith (1 Sam. 12:17).

Too often, little gets done in Christendom because Christians are waiting for God to move rather than acting on what He has already done. If God has already asked us to do something, it will not get done unless we obey. God told Israel to conquer the Promised Land, and He would have supplied the power

> **There are times when we do not need to ask the Lord for a specific "go ahead" to do his work.**

for their victory, but they were not committed enough to act on what He said, so the land remained partially unconquered (Judg. 1:19–36). God wants every person to be saved (1 Tim. 2:4), and He will save them if they obey Romans 10:9. However, if people do not do their part and believe in the Lord Jesus, they will remain unsaved. This same principle works for speaking in tongues. God tells Christians, "I would like every one of you to speak in tongues…" (1 Cor. 14:5a). His will is clear. He will supply the words if we speak, but if we do not speak, it will not come to pass.

In this reciprocal relationship between God and man, the issue of who is in control is central to an accurate and balanced view of the partnership between God and the believer. Neither the believer nor God is completely in control. Viewing God as being in total control can lead a believer into both false humility and utter passivity, i.e., he does nothing without "the Spirit taking over" and acting upon him. This erroneous perspective can cause him to not accept his own responsibility in his relationship with God.

Some Christians may testify that it has been their experience that "the Spirit" did take them over, but, as we stated earlier, no spiritual experience from the true God will contradict the Word of God.[1] "**I can do** everything through him [Christ] who gives **me strength**" (Phil. 4:13) is the genuine. "Christ or the Holy Spirit can do all things through me" is the counterfeit. We are fellow workers, not channels.

We believe this is a great example of how experience alone can be a poor teacher, and why the Word of God must be our only rule of faith and practice. There certainly can be times when the Lord moves so powerfully in a Christian's life that he feels compelled to act, but this is not guaranteed in Scripture. We are to act in obedience to God whether or not we "feel led." Many Christians testify of times when they have "felt compelled" to pray, but also of times when they prayed just because the Bible said to do so, even though they did not feel like it. The same is true for studying, witnessing, speaking in tongues, fellowshipping with other Christians, etc.

In contrast to thinking that the "Spirit" is in control is the view that holy spirit is only a mechanism, an inert battery, or a lifeless source of "potential energy" that must be activated by faith, which puts the believer in total control. He very well may view with distrust any experience of God acting powerfully within him by the spirit, which he thinks should be completely under his control. This closes a Christian off to many profound and personal experiences that might result from his allowing God or the Lord Jesus Christ to deeply "move" him. Such erroneous thinking also puts God in a box. God is God, and He can speak powerfully through holy spirit in the believer.

Many times in our Christian walks we have experienced our moment-by-moment reciprocal relationship with the Lord as a dance—a tango in which the partners must function in split-second cooperation and harmony with one another. Generally, the man leads and the woman follows. In a tango, the woman does not just wait to be thrown around the dance floor. Her "following" involves great independence, knowledge, and self-control. She is not coerced, but rather chooses to execute her role with learned skill.

In the big picture, God "leads," in that He gave us His Word, His Son, and the gift of holy spirit. We follow, with our actions being in response

---

1. For a study of the experience "slain in the Spirit," see Appendix E, "Slain in the Spirit."

to His initiative as expressed in His written Word or in His personal revelation to us. One can easily see the necessity for "dance partners" to become intimately familiar with one another's moves and abilities. The gift of holy spirit makes possible this heart-to-heart relationship between God (and Christ) and each of His children. Not only can the Lord Jesus "coach" us moment-by-moment, but he can also energize our obedient responses.

Let us pursue the dance metaphor in relation to the manifestations of holy spirit. For example, God "leads" by saying in His Word, "I would like every one of you to speak in tongues...." We choose to "follow" by operating the mechanics of speech even though we do not have any words in mind. He then leads again by giving the words to us as we speak, and we follow by continuing to speak.

> **Not only can the Lord Jesus "coach" us moment-by-moment, but he can also energize our obedient responses.**

There are many things about the dance analogy that make it appropriate. Both partners must be willing to dance or there is no dance. Similarly, if the believer refuses to obey, or does not have the faith (trust) to obey, the will of God is not accomplished. The dancers must be very attuned to and focused on each other. Similarly, if the believer is not listening attentively to the voice of the Lord, he will not know what to do. Also, both dancers must be practiced. This is something that does not get much focus in Christendom, but it is vitally important. We will cover the need to practice the manifestations later in the chapter.

We do have to be careful not to take the dance analogy too far. In ballroom dancing, the man leads, and many times God or the Lord Jesus Christ leads us. However, as we saw earlier, it is also true that many times it is the believer who sees a need and goes to the Lord for guidance. There is a tension, or "dance," between the active and passive aspects in the believer's relationship to the gift of holy spirit within him. We can see this by comparing two particular verses of Scripture. The first shows the active aspect, in which the believer's "operation" of holy spirit is emphasized:

1 Corinthians 14:32 (KJV)
And the spirits of the prophets are subject to the prophets.[2]

This verse is set in the context of an exhortation that prophets conduct themselves properly in the Church. They are encouraged to recognize that holy spirit within them does not compel them to act, that they are ultimately in control, and that they can wait for the appropriate time to speak. They do not have to blurt out a message the instant they receive it. The message they speak for God will be best brought forth in love and consideration for all who are ministering and being ministered to. The spirit of God within will not compel obedience to the extent that one cannot resist it. God is not that desperate. If one prophet refuses to speak for Him, He will raise up another who is willing. Our Father is powerful, resourceful, and patient, and He works with His people to engender heartfelt obedience and a true willingness to act upon His leading.

The second verse of Scripture shows the passive aspect of the believer's relationship to holy spirit:

2 Peter 1:21 (KJV)
For the prophecy came not in old time by the will of man: but holy men of God spake *as they were* moved by the Holy Ghost [No article "the." Read "holy spirit"].

In this context, "the prophecy" is synonymous to "the Scripture," or those writings that were inspired by God. These came not by the will of man, but as "holy men of God" freely subjected their wills to the will of God. These were men who had the spirit of God, and it was that holy spirit that "moved" them

---

2. The word "spirits" is the Greek word *pneuma*. Some people believe that it refers to the gift of holy spirit that is born in each believer. Others say that it is the use of "spirit" that means "will," or "attitude." In either case, because the gift of holy spirit can be utilized either properly or improperly, God here reminds the prophets that they are to govern themselves in obedience to His Word. The challenge to the prophet is to speak just what God wants spoken (not necessarily everything God shows him), and not allow anything to keep him from speaking when it is God's will that he speak. This is a great example of why simply **having** the spirit of God is not enough to live a full and vital Christian life. The believer must also learn to recognize the voice of the Lord in order to perfect his or her walk with him.

to speak and write.[3] In 2 Peter 1:21 (KJV), the word "moved" is the Greek word *phero*, which basically means "to bring or to carry." Here it occurs in the passive voice and means "being carried along." This shows that holy men willing to cooperate with God were acted upon by His power. We see this as comparable to a person deciding to swim with the current or walk in the same direction as a "moving sidewalk" in an airport.

Two verses in Acts where *phero* occurs in the passive voice give us insight into the powerful nature of the experience of being "moved" by holy spirit.

> **Acts 27:15**
> The ship was caught by the storm and could not head into the wind; so we gave way to it and **were driven along**.

> **Acts 27:17**
> When the men had hoisted it aboard, they passed ropes under the ship itself to hold it together. Fearing that they would run aground on the sandbars of Syrtis, they lowered the sea anchor and let the ship **be driven along**.

The context of these verses is a powerful storm. This storm "caught" the ship, which could not be turned into the wind. They had no choice as to their direction, but they did drop the sea anchor so as to slow down the ship as it was being carried along by the wind.

We see the wind as analogous to the moving of God via the spirit upon (or in) the men who wrote Scripture. Holy men of God were carried along by God, who inspired them to write via the spirit that was in them. God inspired His Word to be written by communicating to the men via the holy spirit in them. The holy men were not "channels," and they were not out of control of what they were doing. This is an important point, especially because many Christians think and speak of themselves as "channels" for the unstoppable power of God. The men were not "channels," they were co-workers with God. These "holy men" had freely given their wills

---

3. "Men" is historically correct. Men wrote down the Bible we have today. This has nothing to do with spiritual ability, intelligence, seriousness of purpose, or any other such thing, because throughout the Bible there were women with holy spirit who walked powerfully before God. It is primarily due to the roles of women in the cultures of the time.

to the service of God. At the time they were inspired to write Scripture, their wills were in submission to God's will. A study of their lives shows that, in most cases, it took them years of training and discipline to learn to submit to His will.

There are times when men and women of God are in a powerful experience, being moved by God via holy spirit. Believers who experience this view it, not as an abrogation of their freedom of will, but as a profound privilege to work in partnership with God.

The following verse contains the same word *phero* and also illustrates the principle of the believer's reciprocal relationship with the Lord. The context is the resurrected Christ telling Peter about the potential of his service to others once Peter had received the gift of holy spirit.

> **John 21:18**
> I tell you the truth, when you were younger you dressed yourself and went where you wanted; but when you are old you will stretch out your hands, and someone else will dress you and lead [*phero*] you where you do not want to go."

We can see in this verse that it was Peter's choice whether or not to "stretch" out in faith. When he did, it would be the spirit of God working in him that would "lead" him, or carry him along, to places that he would not choose to go if he were concerned only about himself.

Many people have been taught that God will "never overstep our free will," and this is true to a great extent, but not absolutely. All choices are not created equal in their ramifications and consequences. For instance, a man is free to join or not join his nation's army. He has a choice at the point of entry. By entering the army, however, he knowingly limits his choices. As long as he remains in that system, he is required to wear a uniform, report for duty, etc. If he chooses to stop doing what army people are obligated to do, there are severe consequences. The man may object to the discipline and refuse to obey, saying that his free will has been taken away. His military superiors are unsympathetic, reminding him that his free will was exercised at the point he chose to enter the army, and that he knew what discipline would be involved in that choice. They thus expect him to keep his word and his commitment.

Similarly, when a man decides to make Jesus Christ his "Lord," it should mean that he will from then on **obey** his new Master. If he understands this, he learns to discipline himself to do those things that he knows God wants him to do. At times, God moves him to act for Him in a way that the man does not like or agree with, but he does it anyway, not because he is forced to do so, but because his sense of commitment, duty, and responsibility "compels" him. Is his freedom to choose really compromised? No, because he is acting consistently with his prior choice to obey God and submit his will to God's.

God has graciously given each of His children the ability to do whatever He asks us to do. Although doing the will of God may require great effort on our parts, it is effort that God energizes. When we strive in our own strength, apart from His working within us, we burn out. We are so strongly emphasizing the reciprocal relationship between God and the believer because finding and maintaining this balance is essential to radiant Christian living.

Practice Makes Better

It is common knowledge that if a person practices something, he becomes more proficient at it and thus becomes more confident. That is also true when it comes to the manifestations of holy spirit. Nevertheless, it is our experience that most Christians do not consider practicing the manifestations necessary or even possible. That is because most people believe that the "gifts" are the result of the "Person," "the Holy Spirit," acting within them and producing the result, be it tongues, interpretation, prophecy, etc. They believe that because the Holy Spirit is God, who is both perfect and all-powerful, they play very little part in the manifestations, which come out just as God wants.

As we have seen in this book, holy spirit is *the gift of God* that He gives to Christians, which is then part of their nature. Christians are spiritually powerful by nature, and one's holy spirit enables him to speak in tongues, prophesy, heal, do miracles, etc. It is the person who is operating the power of holy spirit, not holy spirit that is using the person. Take, for example, speaking in tongues. Every Christian has the gift of holy spirit, which gives him the power to speak in tongues. To do so, one must trust God and start speaking. If he does not speak, he will not speak in tongues.

God will not "take control" and force a developed language out of a believer who will not walk in faith and work on developing his tongue by speaking a full range of consonants and vowels.[4] Someone might say, "But I thought that the Bible says the Spirit gave the utterance, the words," referring to Acts 2:4 (KJV). True, but God gives the words as the person speaks, so there will be no words if the person does not speak. The Bible says it was the Apostles who "began to speak." What if they had not? There would have been no tongues on that day of Pentecost. For many people it takes time to overcome nervousness and become confident and fluid in the tongue that the Lord energizes via holy spirit. We have led thousands of people around the world into speaking in tongues, and we have consistently seen that when most people begin to speak in tongues they have a few words or a few dozen, but not much more. However, as they "loosen up," overcome their nervousness, and begin to stretch themselves to speak other sounds, the Lord energizes their tongue to be a full language that would stand up to any linguistic analysis. The Bible tells us that practice is important.

Hebrews 5:14
But solid food is for the mature, who by constant use have trained themselves to distinguish good from evil.

We like the translation of the RSV, which uses the word "practice" to describe how to be trained to distinguish good from evil.[5]

---

4. There are rare occasions, as when God was first bringing the manifestations back into the Church in the early 1900's, when people testified that they were compelled to speak in tongues. However, there were extenuating circumstances, not the least of which was God trying to get power back into the Church after it had been almost completely missing for 1800 years. Also, the people involved were seeking the power of God.

5. The ESV, NASB, and NRSV also use "practice." The Greek word is *hexis*, which *Thayer's Greek Lexicon* defines as "…a habit, whether of body or of mind (Xenophon, Plato, Aristotle, others); a power acquired by custom, practice, use." Thayer, *op. cit.*, *Lexicon*, p. 224.

Hebrews 5:14 (RSV)
But solid food is for the mature, for those who have their
faculties trained by practice to distinguish good from evil.

In the context of the above verse, "good" and "evil" have a wide
application, including the truth of God's Word, whether it is from the
Bible or the voice of God. As it applies to the manifestations of holy spirit,
"good" is what comes from God, and "evil" is what does not. For example,
when a person gives a prophecy, it is always
possible for him to add to what God said
from his own mind. Remember, prophecy is
not God taking over the person, but rather
God or the Lord Jesus Christ speaking to the
person via holy spirit within, and then the
person speaking the prophecy. Furthermore,

> **Our trust in our
> own spiritual ability
> grows as we manifest
> power with success.**

we know the voice of God is usually a "gentle whisper" (1 Kings 19:12). It
can be easy to miss or alter what God said by adding to it or subtracting
from it.

In the manifestations of speaking in tongues, interpretation of tongues,
prophecy, a message of knowledge, a message of wisdom, and discerning of
spirits, God or the Lord Jesus communicates to the mind of a believer via
holy spirit. Sometimes it can be difficult indeed for a Christian to separate
his own thoughts from the thoughts that are coming into his mind via holy
spirit. Remember, God seldom shouts. The prophet Samuel recognized the
need for people to grow in the operation of the manifestations, and so he
established what has become known as the "school of the prophets." The
Bible has evidence of companies of prophets joining together for support
and training, such as: 1 Samuel 10:5, 19:20; 2 Kings 2:3 and 5, 4:38 and 6:1.

Another area of the manifestations where practice helps is in the area
of faith (trust) in the spiritual power one has been given. For example, as
a person successfully manifests holy spirit and speaks in tongues over and
over, his faith in his ability to speak in tongues grows. Faith, which as we
have seen is "trust," can grow. Our trust in a person grows or diminishes as
we get to know him. Our trust in God grows as we get to know Him, and
wrong doctrine can destroy people's trust in God if they attribute to Him

things that make Him seem capricious, vengeful, or illogical. Our trust in our own spiritual ability grows as we manifest power with success. The first time a person commands a demon to come out of a person, he may be acting only by trusting that the Bible says he can do it, without the confidence of personal experience. However, after a person has laid on hands to heal, or commanded demons to leave people several dozen times, his faith is built up, and he will manifest power more confidently and fluidly.

God and the Lord Jesus Christ need people who will confidently manifest the power of holy spirit. Jesus trained his disciples to deliver people by using the power of God. This did not take years of seminary study, it took them watching Jesus and trusting that they had the power of holy spirit and could use it just as he did. Jesus even told them, "I tell you the truth, anyone who has faith in me will do what I have been doing..." (John 14:12a). Jesus was neither lying nor exaggerating when he said that. We need to strive to help people by doing the works that he did, and that will take stepping forth and doing them.

When Peter and John healed a man who was lame from his mother's womb (Acts 3:2–8), the religious leaders knew that "...they were unschooled, ordinary men...." Nevertheless, "...they took note that these men had been with Jesus" (Acts 4:13). Peter and John watched Jesus and saw what he did and how he did it. We get to watch Jesus, and others, through the eyes of Scripture, reading the God-breathed accounts and gaining confidence and insight from them. As we act in faith on God's directives to us, we experience our Lord Jesus mentoring us "on the job." Then we too have "been with Jesus," and can in turn bless God's people by manifesting holy spirit.

God has given Christians the wonderful gift of holy spirit so we can do the works that Jesus did: bring light to those in darkness, heal the broken-hearted, and set the captives free. If this great work is going to be done, it is important to understand the gift of holy spirit, because that is the great key to our spiritual power and ability. Then, understanding what we have, let us march forth as people fully equipped to do God's work in this world, with the faith to accomplish all God has for us to do.

The Administration of the Sacred Secret

Different Administrations Have Different Rules

We Christians need to understand the wonderful gift of holy spirit that God has given to us and appreciate His grace. We also need to understand why God called the very time in which we live "…the administration of the grace of God…" (Eph. 3:2-DHB). Why is this age, the age of the Christian Church, singled out by God to be called the administration of "grace"? To understand this, we must understand the uniqueness of the Church and see the difference between what we have today and what God gave to people at other times and other ages.

Throughout history, God has changed the "rules" by which He wants men to live. Every student of the Bible realizes this to one degree or another. For example, before the Church started in Acts 2, God required animal sacrifice, but now He no longer does. Even a cursory study of Scripture shows that God has "administered" the people of earth differently at different times, and so many theologians call the time period covered by a given set of rules an "administration" or "dispensation."[1] The systematic theology that recognizes these different administrations or dispensations is referred to as "Dispensationalism."[2]

---

1. The term "dispensation" refers to God "dispensing" His rules and justice to mankind. Similarly, "administration" refers to Him "administering" His rules and justice.

2. Many theologians think that the systematic theology of Dispensationalism is an invention of man. It is common to hear theologians of other persuasions discount Dispensationalism, saying it was not even believed in the Church until late in the Reformation. That is not actually the case, and in fact "…dispensational-like statements can be found from the writings of the Church Fathers on,…." (Elwell, p. 322). Furthermore, Covenant Theology, the systematic theology that competes with Dispensationalism, was itself a theological latecomer. Covenant Theology "was one of the theological contributions that came to the Church through the Reformation of the sixteenth century. Undeveloped earlier, it made its appearance in the writings of Zwingli and Bullinger…From them it passed to Calvin and other Reformers…." (Elwell, p. 279). Many things Protestants believe today were "rediscovered" during the Reformation, and the real question is not *when* a

Examples of God changing the rules from administration to administration abound. In the Garden of Eden, God told Adam and Eve to eat plants only (Gen. 1:29), but after the Flood, God changed the rules and allowed man to eat meat also (Gen. 9:3), and He still allows us to eat meat today. Another clear example concerns the Sabbath. Before the Mosaic Law, there was no specific law concerning the Sabbath. When God gave the Law to Moses, He changed the rules and commanded that anyone who worked on the Sabbath should be put to death (Exod. 31:14). Today, in the Administration of Grace, God has changed the rules again and it is not a sin to work on the Sabbath (Rom. 14:5; Col. 2:16 and 17). Of course, it is still a good idea to take a day of rest.

Another clear example of God changing the rules from administration to administration involves the rules concerning marriage. Before the Mosaic Law, God allowed men to marry a sister or other close relative. Abraham, for example, married Sarah, his half sister (Gen. 20:12). A man could also have more than one wife in those days. God changed the rules when He gave the Law to Moses, and forbade marrying a half-sister (Lev. 18:9) or other close relative (Lev. 18 and 20), but He still allowed a man to have more than one wife. In the Administration of Grace in which we live today, God has changed the marriage regulations again. Today, He forbids polygamy, saying that each man is to have his "own" wife and each woman her "own" husband (1 Cor. 7:2).

When Christians do not recognize or understand the administrations in the Bible, they cannot resolve its apparent contradictions and become confused as to which commands to obey and which not to obey. It is of the utmost importance that the Christian who wants to obey God's instructions understands the administrations in the Bible. If he does not, he may well end up obeying a command in the Bible that was not written **to him**. For example, what if a Christian took more than one wife, saying

---

certain doctrine was clarified theologically, but whether or not it is stated in Scripture. All Bible scholars acknowledge that God has at certain times changed some of the rules man is to live by. Covenant theologians, for example, recognize "various dispensations of history" (Elwell, p. 280) within their overarching Covenant of Grace, and that the gift of holy spirit has "brought rich gifts unknown in an earlier age" (Elwell, p. 280). [The quotations in this footnote are from Walter Elwell, *Evangelical Dictionary of Theology* (Baker Book House, Grand Rapids, MI, 1984)].

that the Bible said it was okay to do and quoted Exodus 21:10? Can a Christian marry more than one wife just because a verse somewhere in the Bible says it is allowable? No, because we must consider **where** the Bible says that, and **to whom** was God addressing that regulation. If a person has psoriasis (sores and flakes on the skin), does he have to wear torn clothes, not brush his hair, cover his mouth with cloth, live outside of town, and cry "Unclean" when he walks down the street? Yet that is what the Bible says (Lev. 13:45 and 46). Thankfully, those commandments were part of the rules God gave to the Jews, and He has given the Christian Church different rules to live by. Neither do we have to wear tassels on the outside of our garments (Num. 15:38), nor do Christian men have to go to Jerusalem three times a year (Deut. 16:16). Jews under God's Law were commanded to do these things, but now God has changed the rules for Christians. So, if we want to obey God, we must obey the rules written **to us**.[3]

The Administrations in the Bible

There are eight administrations in the Bible and knowing exactly when they begin and end, and the rules distinctly associated with each, is indispensable in explaining many of the apparent contradictions in Scripture. The eight administrations are: 1) Original Paradise (Creation to the Fall), 2) Conscience (Fall to the Flood), 3) Civil Government (Flood to the Mosaic Law), 4) The Mosaic Law (the giving of the Law until Pentecost), 5) the Administration of the Grace of God, also called the Administration of the Sacred Secret (from Pentecost until the Rapture), 6) Tribulation (from the Rapture to the end of Armageddon), 7) Christ's Millennial Kingdom (lasts 1,000 years), 8) Final Paradise (will last forever).[4] Martin Anstey wrote: "In this matter the golden rule is, 'Distinguish the dispensations and the difficulties will disappear.'"[5]

---

3. Many times a rule will be the same from one generation to another. For example, murder has always been a sin. We must study the entire Bible to understand what applies to us and what does not.

4. For more on Administrations go to: www.TheLivingTruthFellowship.org under Bible Teachings/articles/Administrations.

5. Martin Anstey, *How to Master the Bible* (Pickering & Inglis, London), p. 23.

The administration in which we live today began on the Jewish holiday of Pentecost (Acts 2), when the gift of holy spirit was given to everyone who believed. This new administration is called by a couple different names. It is called "...the administration of God's grace..." (Eph. 3:2. We usually call it "the Administration of Grace") and "...the administration of the sacred secret..." (Eph.3:9-RHM). God had specific reasons for using the names that He did. He calls it the Administration of "Grace" because Christians enjoy the grace of God in a manner and to an extent that was not given to people of previous administrations. God has always given grace to mankind, but He has so abounded in His grace to the Church that He calls the very time we live in the "...administration of the grace of God..." (DHB). God kept to Himself the knowledge of the blessings and grace that we have today, and so He also calls this administration the "...administration of the sacred secret..." (RHM).

"Mystery" or "Sacred Secret"?

Rotherham's Emphasized Bible (RHM) calls the administration that we live in "...the administration of the sacred secret...," while the NIV says "...the administration of this mystery...."

> **Ephesians 3:9 (RHM)**
> And to bring to light—What is **the administration of the sacred secret** which had been hidden away from the ages in God, who did all things create.

> **Ephesians 3:9 (NIV)**
> and to make plain to everyone **the administration of this mystery**, which for ages past was kept hidden in God, who created all things.

Why the difference? Throughout the history of the Christian Church, scholars and theologians have propounded doctrines they considered "mysteries" and, therefore, the concept of the "mysterious" things of God has become part of Christian doctrine. Thus many versions of the Bible translate the Greek word *musterion* as "mystery." This is unfortunate because *musterion* does not mean "mystery." "Mystery" is a transliteration of the word *musterion*, not a translation of it. A "transliteration" is when the letters of a word in one language are brought across into another language. The prefix "*trans*" means "across," and the Latin *littera* means "letter." Thus, "transliteration" is literally "bringing across the letters." In contrast, "translation" is bringing the *meaning* of a word in one language across into another language. If we are going to bring the meaning of the Greek into English, we must translate, not transliterate.

The English word "mystery" means something that is incomprehensible, beyond understanding, unknowable. Thus, it is common in religious circles to speak of things such as the "Trinity" or Transubstantiation[6] as "mysteries" because they cannot be understood. In contrast, a "secret" is something that is known by someone but unknown by others.[7] A surprise birthday party is a "secret" to the person having the birthday, but known by those who will attend it. The Greek word *musterion* means "sacred secret," that is, a secret in the sacred or spiritual realm that must be made known by God.

> **If we are going to bring the meaning of the Greek into English, we must translate, not transliterate.**

It is well documented by scholars that *musterion* refers to a secret and not to our standard meaning of "mystery."

> *Musterion:* In the New Testament it denotes not the mysterious (as with the English Word), but that which, being outside the range of unassisted natural apprehension, can be made known only by divine revelation, and is made known in a manner and at a time appointed by God.[8]

---

6. Transubstantiation is the doctrine that the Communion bread becomes the flesh of Christ when blessed by the priest.

7. We are using the word "mystery" and "secret" with great exactness and precision in this book. Unfortunately, they are not used with much precision in our everyday English, and so many people do not see the difference between them. If we are to have any hope of understanding the Bible, it is vital that we use biblical vocabulary precisely.

8. James Strong, *The New Strong's Expanded Dictionary of Bible Words* (Thomas Nelson Publisher, Nashville, TN, 2001), p. 1247.

But whereas "mystery" may mean, and in contemporary usage often does mean, a secret for which no answer can be found, this is not the connotation of the term *mysterion* in classical and biblical Greek. In the New Testament, *mysterion* signifies a secret which is being, or even has been, revealed, which is also divine in scope, and needs to be made known by God to men through his Spirit.[9]

The mystery of the New Testament has been described as an 'open secret'; matters previously kept secret in God's eternal purposes have now been or are being revealed (Eph. 3:3–5; 1 Cor. 2:7–8).[10]

Scholars' assertion that the word *mysterion* does not mean "mystery," but instead refers to a secret that can be known, is confirmed by many verses of Scripture. The verses quoted below make two points that the Bible student must know if he wants to understand the Administration of the Sacred Secret. The first is that the Sacred Secret was hidden from earlier generations and in earlier ages. The second is that God has now made it known. God began to reveal it after the resurrection of Christ and completed revealing it when, via the Lord Jesus, He made it known to the Apostle Paul. Since Christians can know the Sacred Secret, it cannot be a "mystery" in the sense that most people think of today, i.e., something that cannot be known.

Romans 16:25b and 26a
(25b) …the mystery [*mysterion*] **hidden** for long ages past, (26a) **but now revealed and made known** through the prophetic writings by the command of the eternal God….

Ephesians 3:4 and 5
(4) In reading this, then, you will be able to understand my insight into the mystery [*mysterion*] of Christ,

---

9. Howard Marshall, editor, *New Bible Dictionary* (Intervarsity Press, Downers Grove, IL, 1997), p. 795. Some sources use the English "Y" to translate the Greek letter *upsilon*. Thus some sources have *musterion*, while others have *mysterion*.

10. Trent Butler, editor, *Holman Bible Dictionary* (Holman Bible Publishers, Nashville, TN, 1991), p. 998. (Other sources documenting that *musterion* means "secret" and not "mystery" include: William Smith, *Smith's Dictionary of the Bible*, (Baker Book House, Grand Rapids, MI, reprinted 1981), Vol. 3, p. 2047, and Merrill Tenney, editor, *The Zondervan Pictorial Encyclopedia of the Bible* (Regency Reference Library, Grand Rapids, MI, 1976), Vol. 4, p. 330).

(5) which was **not made known** to men in other generations as it has **now been revealed** by the Spirit to God's holy apostles and prophets.

Colossians 1:26

the mystery [*musterion*] that **has been kept hidden** for ages and generations, **but is now disclosed to the saints.**

1 Corinthians 2:7–10a

(7) No, we speak of God's secret [*musterion*] wisdom, a wisdom that **has been hidden** and that God destined for our glory before time began.

(8) None of the rulers of this age understood it, for if they had, they would not have crucified the Lord of glory.

(9) However, as it is written: "No eye has seen, no ear has heard, no mind has conceived what God has prepared for those who love him"—

(10a) but **God has revealed it** to us by his Spirit…

The Sacred Secret was hidden so completely that verse 9 says that before God revealed it, no mind had even conceived what God prepared for us. That is why it is called a "sacred secret," why it needed to be revealed by God (Eph. 3:3), and why it was "unsearchable" (Eph. 3:8) in Scripture. Sadly, these verses in Corinthians often get quoted out of context. It is not uncommon to hear a preacher read them and then teach that God has things in store for us in the future that no eye has seen or ear heard, but that is not what the verses are saying. Quoting the Old Testament, they say that what was not known or even thought about back then has now been revealed to the Christian Church. The evidence is clear: the *musterion* of the Church is a sacred secret that was hidden but is now known by those who care to take the time to learn it.[11]

---

11. All the examples of *musterion* quoted here refer to the Sacred Secret of the Christian Church. However, there are other sacred secrets as well. For example, Jesus told his disciples sacred secrets about the kingdom of heaven (Matt. 13:11; Mark 4:11; Luke 8:10).

"Sacred Secret," Not Just "Secret"

Why is it a "sacred secret" and not just a "secret"? The Greek language uses *musterion* for secrets in the sacred or religious sphere but uses another word, *kruptos*, for secrets that are in the secular realm. Examples of *kruptos* include: Jesus said to give alms in **secret** (Matt. 6:4-KJV); he taught that every **secret** thing will be brought to light (Mark 4:22-KJV); he went to Jerusalem in **secret** (John 7:10-KJV); God will judge men's **secrets** (Rom. 2:16); and, prophecy reveals the **secrets** of the heart (1 Cor. 14:24 and 25).[12]

Anyone reading the Greek New Testament knows whether God is speaking of a secular secret (*kruptos*) or a sacred secret (*musterion*). A good English version will make that difference too. If both *kruptos* and *musterion* are translated as "secret," the difference between the Greek words is lost to English readers, and if translators use "secret" for *kruptos* and "mystery" for *musterion*, the English Bible is made to say something that it just does not say, that is, the things of God are mysterious.[13]

Is there a way to translate *kruptos* and *musterion* such that the meaning of the Greek words is communicated clearly into English? Yes, there is. There is no place in the New Testament where *musterion* cannot be fittingly translated as "sacred secret," which is exactly what Rotherham's Emphasized Bible (RHM) does. If we translate *kruptos* as "secret," and *musterion* as "sacred secret," the meaning of the Greek is communicated clearly, and we English-speaking people are in a better position to know and understand what God says in His Word.

---

12. Not only does the noun *kruptos* appear in the New Testament, the verb *krupto* appears many times as well, often translated as "hid" or "hidden." Examples include: a city on a hill cannot be **hidden** (Matt. 5:14); the wicked servant **hid** his talent in the ground (Matt. 25:25); a Christian's new life is **hidden** with Christ in God (Col. 3:3); and, Moses' parents **hid** him after he was born (Heb. 11:23).

13. Translating *musterion* as "mystery" has caused many problems in the Church. For one thing, people who are convinced that the things of God are mysterious quit trying to search the Scriptures, and do not bother to pray for answers to their questions—why should they if the subject is a "mystery" and no answers are available? Also, many false and illogical doctrines have been foisted upon Christians, who are told not to try to understand them because they are "mysteries."

Why Hide the Sacred Secret?

Once we understand that this administration was a "sacred secret," certain questions immediately come to mind: "From whom was it hidden?" "Why did God hide it?" "When and how was it revealed?" "How can I learn about it?" These are logical questions and they are all answered in the Church Epistles, the letters from the Lord to his Church. We have seen that God has revealed the Sacred Secret to us (Rom. 16:25 and 26; 1 Cor. 2:7–10; Eph. 3:3–5; Col. 1:26 and 27). God kept the Sacred Secret hidden during the Old Testament and Gospels, first revealing it to Paul and then, in the Church Epistles, to the Christians and the world.

> **Ephesians 3:2 and 3**
> (2) Surely you have heard about the administration of God's grace that was given to me [Paul] for you,
> (3) that is, the mystery [Sacred Secret] made known to me by revelation, as I have already written briefly.

Paul wrote to the Church in Ephesus that he got his understanding of the Sacred Secret by revelation, and he said the same thing to the Galatians.

> **Galatians 1:11 and 12**
> (11) I want you to know, brothers, that the gospel I preached is not something that man made up.
> (12) I did not receive it from any man, nor was I taught it; rather, I received it by revelation from Jesus Christ.

The Administration of the Secret was not revealed to men before the Lord revealed it to the Apostle Paul. If it had been, there would have been no reason for Jesus to reveal it to Paul by revelation and no reason for Paul to make the point that he got his knowledge directly from Christ. Had the information been revealed before the Lord gave it in the seven Church Epistles, then someone could have taught it to Paul, or he could have learned it from reading the Old Testament. Instead, Paul learned it directly from Christ because it was a secret until then. The Sacred Secret was unknown before the resurrection of Christ, so Christians must carefully read and re-read that Scripture written to the Christian Church

(Acts–Jude) if they are going to truly understand the spiritual riches God has conferred specifically upon Christians.

The book of Corinthians gives even more understanding why God hid the administration of Grace and did not reveal it until after Christ's crucifixion. The Administration of the Sacred Secret is so wonderful, and what Christians have in Christ is so glorious and powerful, that had the Devil and his demons known it, they would not have crucified the Lord Jesus.

> **1 Corinthians 2:7 and 8**
> (7) No, we speak of God's secret [*musterion*] wisdom, a wisdom that has been hidden and that God destined for our glory before time began.
> (8) None of the rulers of this age understood it, for if they had, they would not have crucified the Lord of glory.[14]

Christians have permanent salvation and the fullness of holy spirit within them, which Colossians refers to as "…Christ in you, the hope of glory" (Col. 1:27). Satan would rather have had Jesus Christ remain alive

---

14. The "rulers of this age" are the Devil and his demons. Scholars and Bible teachers are divided over this point, many saying that they are earthly rulers such as Herod, Pilate, and the Jewish leaders, and many others asserting they are demons, not people. The reason for the division is that the context is misunderstood, and the vocabulary is ambiguous because it is general in nature and in one form or another is used of both earthly rulers and demonic rulers.

In context, what the rulers did not know was the Sacred Secret (cp. v. 7, *musterion*). Neither earthly rulers nor demonic powers could have known it because it was hidden in God, as we have seen from many verses. In order to properly understand who the "rulers" are, the question we must answer is, "Who would not have crucified Christ **if** they had known the Sacred Secret?" Could it be that if the earthly rulers had known the Sacred Secret, including that mankind would have permanent salvation, the fullness of holy spirit, two more manifestations of holy spirit (speaking in tongues and interpretation of tongues), and more, would they have so wanted to keep those blessings from mankind that they would not have crucified Christ? No, that cannot be what the verse is saying. In contrast, who loses if Christians are spiritually powerful? The Devil does. It is the Devil, who *if* he had known that every Christian would have all those blessings, including the power to cast out demons, would not have crucified Jesus. It is the Devil who would have rather dealt with one man, Jesus, than with an army of God on earth, multitudes of Christians, each secure in their salvation and empowered by holy spirit.

Only by understanding that if Satan had known the Sacred Secret he would not have crucified the Lord can we understand the true reason for God keeping the Sacred Secret a secret and fully appreciate the enormity and power of what we have been given.

than deal with thousands of Christians, each of whom has the fullness of Christ within. However, the Devil did not find out about the Christian Church until **after** he had crucified the Lord, and then it was too late.

As we begin to study the particulars of this administration, we must constantly keep in mind that what we have in Christ was a secret not revealed to anyone until after the resurrection of Christ. Not understanding that, many Christians teach that the Old Testament or Gospels foretold the things that we have today, such as secure salvation. Not so. If God says that the things revealed to and for us did not even enter into the heart of man until after Jesus was crucified, then that must be the case, even if there are similarities between what we have today and what was foretold for Israel's future and the Millennial Kingdom. Throughout history, people knew there were future administrations coming that would have new rules and blessings, but they did not know about the Administration of the Sacred Secret, which God kept hidden.

In spite of the verses teaching that the Administration of the Sacred Secret was hidden in God and unknown until He revealed it after Pentecost, most Christians interpret certain verses in the Gospels as if it were already known at that time. This produces two unfortunate results. First, the wonderful uniqueness of the Christian Church is lost, and the things that God has done only for the Church become hazy and confused. Second, the true meaning of some verses in the Gospels is lost. For example, if someone says that John 3:3 (NRSV), "Very, truly, I tell you, no one can see the kingdom of God without being born from above," applies to the Christian New Birth, he totally misses the fact that Christ was actually speaking of the First Resurrection, which occurs at the start of his Millennial Kingdom.[15]

The need to hide this administration from the Adversary can be seen by noting that no other administration besides the "administration of the sacred secret" is said to be "secret." God revealed information about other administrations coming in the future to the people who lived before them. For example, the Old Testament and Gospels foretold the coming

---

15. For the answers to those questions, and an exposition of this critical account, go to the following Internet link to our website for the teaching titled: "The Only Irish Rabbi Jesus Ever Met." http://www.youtube.com/justtruthit#p/u/88/TsPPedESPuQ

of the Tribulation that will precede Christ's descent to earth with his armies, at which time he will fight the Battle of Armageddon and conquer the earth. The Old Testament and Gospels also have prophecies of the glorious kingdom on earth, which we now know will last 1,000 years. We also know that there will be a Final Paradise that will last forever. In contrast to future administrations that were known or implied in the Old Testament and Gospels, the Administration of the Sacred Secret was kept secret because, as Corinthians tells us, had the Devil known about it, he would not have crucified the Lord of glory.

The Purpose of the Sacred Secret

Although God may have a number of reasons for doing all the wonderful things that He has done in the Administration of the Sacred Secret, two reasons are written clearly in His Word. Ephesians says that God's purpose in making plain the Sacred Secret was in order to make His wisdom known by means of the Church to all the principalities and powers, which refers to all God's spiritual rulers, and especially the Devil and his demons.

> **Ephesians 3:10**
> His intent was that now, through the church, the manifold wisdom of God should be made known to the rulers and authorities in the heavenly realms,

This verse is so weighty that it is proper to take a moment and ponder it. God's purpose in revealing the Sacred Secret was that He could reveal His wisdom to the rulers and authorities in the heavenly realms through the Church, that is, through us.[16] What a tremendous responsibility we have! If we do not obey God, or rise up in our faith, or take advantage of the power of holy spirit that He has given us, the manifold wisdom of God will not be fully displayed. However, when we walk in the power of holy spirit, being confident of the things God has given us in this

---

16. The rulers and authorities in the heavenly realms includes both angelic rulers and demonic rulers. The Devil is called "…the ruler of the kingdom of the air…" (Eph. 2:2) and is not cast completely out of heaven until just before Armageddon (Rev. 12:7–13). That war is not the same as the casting down portrayed in Revelation 12:4, which occurred when Satan rebelled against God (cp. Isa. 14:12ff).

wonderful Administration of Grace, then His manifold wisdom is fully displayed. We must realize that in no other administration did God say that He displayed His wisdom through people. God never says, for example, that Israel made known His wisdom. In His grace, God has done something for the Church that makes us unique, and we owe it to our heavenly Father to be sure of our salvation and walk in the spiritual power we have been given.

Another reason for the Administration of the Sacred Secret was so that God could glorify us, His children.

> **1 Corinthians 2:7**
> No, we speak of God's secret wisdom, a wisdom that has been hidden and that God **destined for our glory** before time began.

Some people find it uncomfortable that the Christian Church was destined by God to have special glory, so let's be clear about it: God has given the Church special blessings that He did not give to men in earlier generations and He did it to show His wisdom and also for our glory. Do we deserve this special glory? No. It is strictly by grace, and is one reason why one of the two names for this administration is "… the administration of the grace of God…" (Eph. 3:2-DHB). When we understand the Father-child relationship that we Christians have in this wonderful Administration of Grace, it is easier to see why God would glorify us. It is natural for parents to be proud of their children and to want to give them special blessings. It was God's good pleasure to give us the glory we now have in the Administration of the Sacred Secret, and now it should be our pleasure to study it and live accordingly before Him.

The Glorious Administration of the Sacred Secret

God has glorified the believers in the Administration of the Sacred Secret above the believers in previous administrations. Where would we look in the Bible to learn about the glory we have been given and the specific details and blessings of the Administration of the Sacred Secret? Not in the Old Testament, because it was written before Jesus was crucified. Not in the Gospels, because almost all the events of the Gospels occurred before Jesus was crucified. We find these wonderful and vital truths in Acts through Jude, which are the writings to the Christian Church.[17]

It would be convenient if all the unique and wonderful things God has done for Christians were written in a list, but that is generally not how God reveals information. He wants us to take the time to read, study, and pray in order to learn about the blessings He has given us. God desires us to spend time with Him via His book. Then, as we read and compare Scripture with Scripture, the spiritual blessings He has given us become clearer and clearer. God loved us enough to do these things for us, and now it is our turn to love Him enough to read the Bible carefully and discover what He has done. "Okay," you ask, "What are we looking for?" We are looking for things unique to the Christian Church that were not revealed in the Old Testament or in the Gospels until after Jesus died.

During the administrations prior to the Church Age, God gave many blessings to mankind, but we today have even more. The Administration of Grace is compared to the Law Administration in 2 Corinthians 3. What does God say about the Administration of the Law that came immediately before the Administration of Grace? He says it was "glorious," but then He calls it "...the ministration [ministry] of death..." (2 Cor. 3:7-KJV). Furthermore, He calls it "...the ministration [ministry] of condemnation..." just two verses later. Then, in 2 Corinthians 3:10 (KJV), Scripture tells us that the Law had "no glory" in comparison to the glory that we have today. Anyone who reads 2 Corinthians 3:6–10 will see that God has elevated the Administration of Grace far above the Law Administration.

The Father-child Relationship in the Administration of the Sacred Secret

There is hardly an area of a Christian's life that is not influenced by the Sacred Secret. It deals with our relationship to God, salvation, the gift

17. The book of Revelation is about a period of time after the Rapture and is not written to the Christian Church. See E. W. Bullinger, *Commentary on Revelation* (Kregel Publications, Grand Rapids, MI, reprinted 1984), p. 3.

of holy spirit in us, our relation to others who are saved, and our hope. It would take a small book to set forth completely even the one truth that salvation in the Administration of the Sacred Secret is permanent. Nevertheless, each Christian should understand "the big picture" of the Sacred Secret in order to clearly see what God has done for our glory, appreciate the grace we have been given, and, for the purposes of this book, gain a better understanding of the gift of holy spirit we have been given and why it is unique to the Christian Church.

The essence, or the "chewy caramel center," of the Sacred Secret that makes it so unique and wonderful is that God has chosen to change the relationship He had with people from a Lord-servant relationship to a Father-child relationship and to bring people into His family by *birth*. The New Birth that each Christian has is not a metaphor; it is a literal birth. God contributes spiritual seed (1 Pet. 1:23), and the Christian is "born again." The change to a Father-child relationship has sweeping implications, affecting how God relates to Christians and how they relate to Him. Christians are born into the family of God, partake of His divine nature, and are His children by birth, which sets the standard for how God's love is shown to Christians; it is unconditional and irrevocable.

> **The New Birth**
> **that each Christian has**
> **is not a metaphor;**
> **it is a literal birth.**

God is love and has always loved, but true love is dealing with people according to the relationship that exists between the two parties. Before the Administration of the Sacred Secret, God dealt with mankind as a Lord over those he rules. Israel was God's servant (Isa. 41:8) and God called His faithful believers "servants."[18] He gave people commands to follow and made covenants with them. In a covenant, both parties agree to do something and true love is "tough love" when one of the parties fails to

---

18. In contrast to Israel, which God calls a "servant," never once is the Christian Church called God's servant. Examples include: Abraham (Gen. 26:24), Moses (Num. 12:7), Caleb (Num. 14:24), David (2 Sam. 7:5), Hezekiah (2 Chron. 32:16), Job (Job 1:8), and Zerubbabel (Hag. 2:23). In those examples, it is God who calls the believer a servant. Christians serve God and thus call themselves servants (Rom. 1:1; James 1:1), but there is no verse in all the writing to the Christian Church where God calls any Christian a servant in the same manner as He says, for example, "Moses, my servant…" (Josh. 1:2).

keep his commitment. Thus, the pattern we see in the Old Testament is that when His people obeyed, He blessed them, and when they turned from Him, He turned from them. When Israel, God's chosen people, turned away from Him, He turned from them, finally so completely that in Hosea, He told them they were no longer His people (Hosea 1:9). This truth was spoken another way in Isaiah 50:1 and Jeremiah 3:8, using the analogy of a marriage: God gave Israel a bill of divorce and sent her away.

In contrast to the Lord-servant relationship that God had with people in the Old Testament, the relationship He has with Christians is a family relationship. God has never made a covenant with the Christian Church. Christians are ministers (servants, administrators) of the New Covenant (2 Cor. 3:6) only in that we partake of some of its blessings and will be ministers of it when it is in effect in Christ's kingdom. Nevertheless, the New Covenant was foretold to, and made with, Israel (Heb. 8:8–10; Jer. 31:31–34). Jesus ratified it in his blood before the Sacred Secret was ever revealed. The covenant blessings that were promised in the Old Testament, such as perfect health, deserts blooming, no hunger, and no war, are not yet realized, but will be in the Millennial Kingdom.

No specific covenant was ever made between God and the Church. Instead, God gives birth to Christians, who are born into His family. This is why family terminology is used liberally in the Church Epistles. God calls Himself "Father" more than 70 times from Acts to Jude; He calls individual Christians "children," and "sons;" "brothers" of Jesus; "heirs of God;" recipients of His "seed;" partakers of His divine "nature;" "born" and "adopted" into His family; able to call Him "Abba;" and the list goes on.

One reason that "Father" does not seem unique to the epistles to the Church (Acts–Jude) is that Jesus instructed his Apostles to pray using "Father" in the Gospels, before the Administration of the Sacred Secret. However, in the Eastern culture, "Father" was a term that was used in a variety of ways. Father was used:

- In the literal and common way it is used today (Gen. 22:7).
- Of a grandfather (Gen. 28:13. Hebrew has no word "grandfather").
- Of a male ancestor (Josh. 24:3).
- Of the originator of something. Thus Jabel was the "father" of tent dwellers (Gen. 4:20), Jubal was the "father" of those who play the

harp and flute (Gen. 4:21), and Abraham was the "…the father of all who believe…" (Rom. 4:11).

- Of someone who provided protection and help (Job 29:16).
- Of someone who could counsel and give advice. Joseph was made a "father" to Pharaoh (Gen. 45:8); Micah asked the wandering Levite to be a "father" to him, but the Danites wanted him to be a "father" to them (Judg. 17:10 and 18:19).
- Of someone worthy of honor and respect. Elisha called Elijah "father" (2 Kings 2:12), Naaman's servants called him "father" (2 Kings 5:13); the king of Israel called Elisha "father" (2 Kings 6:21).

The point is that the term "father" in the Eastern culture did not necessarily refer to birth. In the Old Testament, people thought of God as a Lord to be feared and obeyed. Jesus changed people's perception of God from that distant relationship to a more intimate one. However, Jesus never taught that one day God would be a Father in the literal sense. It was not known until the Sacred Secret was revealed that God, in the Administration of Grace, actually gives birth to people by contributing spiritual seed and that people have God's very nature born inside them and become part of His family. Those things are part of the Sacred Secret.

The family relationship is totally different from the covenant relationship. In a covenant relationship, if one party breaks the covenant, he forfeits its blessings, but in a family, no matter how horribly a child behaves, he or she is still a member of the family. It is because God changed the way He dealt with people from a Lord-servant relationship to a Father-child relationship that the "rules" concerning salvation changed. Salvation has always been an act of grace because no one can save himself. It has always been God who will give everlasting life. But, before the Administration of the Sacred Secret, salvation came by faith demonstrated as obedience, or by doing godly works. This is made quite clear in the Old Testament:

Deuteronomy 6:25
And if we are careful to obey all this law before the LORD our God, as he has commanded us, that will be our righteousness."

It is also why throughout the Old Testament there is constant reference to "the wicked," those who do not do godly works, and "the righteous," those who do godly works (Psalm 1 is a good example of this). Romans and Ephesians show us that God changed what He requires of us to be saved, and today we have salvation through Jesus Christ. It is appropriate that now, since the death of Christ, God would make salvation available by the recognition of the death of His Son, the Christ, as the sacrifice for sin, rather than by out doing good works.

> **Romans 3:21 and 22a**
> (21) But now a righteousness from God, apart from law, has been made known, to which the Law and the Prophets testify.
> (22a) This righteousness from God comes through faith in Jesus Christ to all who believe…

> **Ephesians 2:8 and 9**
> (8) For it is by grace you have been saved, through faith—and this not from yourselves, it is the gift of God—
> (9) not by works, so that no one can boast.

If, in the Administration of Grace, a person cannot be saved by *doing* good works, then, he cannot become unsaved by *not doing* them. If a Christian believes that someone who commits adultery is unsaved, for example, then the way to be saved would be both to believe in Jesus and do the good work of not committing adultery. This is salvation by works; what a person does determines whether or not he is saved. That is precisely what Ephesians says is not the case in this administration. Our salvation, as Romans says, is "apart from law," that is apart from the kind of works that the Law required. The verses above are just a couple that show God has made salvation available through faith in Jesus Christ without works. He has made the way of salvation easy and the instructions clear:

> **Romans 10:9**
> That if you confess with your mouth, "Jesus is Lord," and believe in your heart that God raised him from the dead, you will be saved.

In the Administration of Grace salvation is easy, and it is easy for us because it cost God and Jesus so much. Arguably the most important "rule change" in the Administration of Grace, made possible because of the Father-child relationship, is that salvation is now *permanent*. No Christian can lose his salvation. This is a huge change from the Old Testament and Gospel periods when a person could lose his salvation. Therefore, we should expect that in His Word God has clearly told us that salvation is permanent, something He has in fact done. Of course, to see it one has to pay careful attention to the vocabulary of the writings to the Christian Church (Acts–Jude) in comparison with the writings of the Old Testament and Gospels.

The Permanence of Christian Salvation

It is in comparing what is written to each administration that the permanence of salvation in the Administration of Grace shows up clearly. First, there is the *family* vocabulary. As we have already pointed out, God is called the Father of each believer and we are said to be His children. We understand the permanence of birth when it comes to our own children, because once they are born, they are our children no matter what they do or what happens to them. No child can be "un-born." The same is true for God's family and the New Birth. In contrast, before the Age of Grace, a person's salvation was not secure; he could lose it if he turned against God.[19]

A. Birth

In the Administration of the Sacred Secret, God uses three different Greek words for "born" to show that each Christian is born into His family and that his birth is permanent. One of them is *anagennao*, which is built from the prefix *ana*, "again," and the root *gennao*, "to be born." *Anagennao* literally means "born again," and it is used specifically of Christians (1 Pet. 1:3 and 23). Another word that reveals the Christian's birth experience is *paliggenesia*, which appears in Titus 3:5 as "rebirth." This word is from *palin*, "again, anew" and *genesis*, "origin, beginning, birth." It literally

---

19. This will also be true in the Tribulation period, as is plain from the letters in the early chapters of the book of Revelation (Rev. 2:1–3:22).

means a "new origin" or "rebirth." A third word is in James 1:18, which reads that God "...chose to give us birth through the word...." The Greek word translated "birth" is *apokueo* and means "to bring forth from the womb, to give birth to."

The three separate and distinct words for "birth" used in reference to the individual's salvation by New Birth are used only in letters written to the Christian Church. These words are not used of an individual New Birth before the Day of Pentecost, nor are they used in the book of Revelation, which concerns those on earth after the Rapture. Adding to the evidence are 1 John 2:29, 4:7, and other Scriptures stating that Christians are "born" [*gennao*] of God. These verses use the standard word for birth that is used throughout the New Testament for the birth of human babies, but only in the letters to the Church is *gennao* used of the spiritual birth of an individual.[20] There would be no point in God telling us that Christians were "born," "born again," of "new origin," and "given birth to," if in fact we were not born and the idea of birth and the permanence of it was not real for Christians. In fact, if Christians could be "un-born," unsaved, then one could argue that God was misleading us by using the word "birth." Once something is born, it cannot be unborn. That is absolutely a fact of nature and is the major reason that God uses so many words for birth for the Christian which are not used for believers in the Old Testament who could lose their salvation.

---

20. John 1:13 has occasionally been used to try to show that the New Birth was available before the Day of Pentecost. However, there is good evidence that the opening of the verse is singular and refers to Jesus Christ. There are very competent scholars who, for textual, contextual, and logical reasons, make the case that the opening words refer to Christ, not believers. Using the KJV, which much more literally follows the Greek text, the proper reading should be, "(John 1:12b) who believe on his name, (John 1:13) who [Jesus, referring back to "his name"] was "...born, not of blood, nor of the will of the flesh, nor of the will of man, but of God." This verse is not referring to the New Birth that Christians have, it is referring to the birth of Jesus Christ, and verse 14 continues the theme and says that the *logos* "became flesh." For more information, see R. C. H. Lenski, *The Interpretation of St. John's Gospel* (Augsburg Publishing House, Minneapolis, MN, 1961), pp. 63–70, and Bullinger, *op. cit.*, Companion Bible, marginal note on John 1:13.

B. Adoption

Another word that indicates the permanence of Christian salvation, and one that occurs only in the Church Epistles, is *huiothesia*, which means "adoption." Vine notes that *huiothesia* means, "...the place and condition of a son given to one to whom it does not naturally belong."[21] "Adoption" occurs in Romans 8:15 and 23, 9:4; Galatians 4:5; and Ephesians 1:5 (all KJV).[22] Birth seems so much more desirable than adoption that it is fair to ask why God would even use "adoption." The answer is that in the Roman world a naturally born baby could be disowned from the family, but an adopted child could not. Since many early believers

> **"Adoption" was one of God's ways to let the Church know that children brought into His family could not be taken from it.**

were Roman citizens, using the word "adoption" was one of God's ways to let the Church know that children brought into His family could not be taken from it.[23]

God worked very hard to communicate the permanence of salvation, so in books that have a distinctively Jewish flavor such as Peter, James, and Titus, God uses words for "birth," while in books that were addressed to people who had a Gentile background, such as Romans, Ephesians, and Galatians, God uses the word "adoption." The same truth is communicated by each word: salvation is permanent. The permanence of salvation is a major part of the Sacred Secret and no verse in the Old Testament even hints that one day God would make salvation permanent.

Some people believe that a Christian can make the freewill decision to repent of his Christian faith and become unsaved, but this is not the case. There are some decisions one makes that change him in a permanent way and choosing salvation is one of them. When a person becomes a Christian, his very nature is changed permanently and he cannot reverse

---

21. Vine, *op. cit, Lexicon*, p. 24.

22. Some versions translate *huiosthesia* as "sonship," but "adoption" is correct. However, when one has been adopted, he is considered a son.

23. For a more complete treatment of adoption in the Roman world, and to see that it established a permanent relationship, see Charles Welch, *Just and the Justifier* (The Berean Publishing Trust, London), pp. 208–213.

that by another freewill decision. We accept this thinking when it comes to our flesh. If a person makes the freewill decision to blind himself, he cannot then make the freewill decision to regain his sight. The change is permanent. The New Birth permanently changes us and cannot be undone by a simple freewill decision.

C. Imperishable Seed

The "birth" in a Christian's New Birth is not just a metaphor but a spiritual reality that involves spiritual "seed."

> **1 Peter 1:23**
> For you have been born again, **not of perishable seed, but of imperishable**, through the living and enduring word of God.

Christians have been born of the "seed" of God which is imperishable. Nothing like this verse occurs in the Old Testament or Gospels. Furthermore, as with any birth, the seed of the father has the nature of the father, which then becomes the nature of the child.[24] Our new nature is spiritual because our Father is God, who is spirit (John 4:24). Therefore, we are "…partakers of the divine nature…" (2 Pet. 1:4-KJV). No Jew or Gentile before the start of the Christian Church was ever said to be a partaker of the nature of God, not even those such as Moses, Deborah, or David who had holy spirit upon them.

D. Holy Ones

Christians are literally born into God's family by spiritual seed, becoming children of God. We have God's nature born in us, so we are, like our Father, "holy" by nature. This is why Christians are "holy ones," which many versions call "saints."

---

24. In a human birth, both the father's seed and the mother's egg contribute to the nature of the child, but in the New Birth we only need our spiritual Father, God, to contribute seed.

Romans 1:7a (KJV)
To all that be in Rome, beloved of God, called *to be* **saints**…

1 Corinthians 1:2a (KJV)
Unto the church of God which is at Corinth…called *to be* **saints**…

Ephesians 1:1a (KJV)
Paul,…to the **saints** which are at Ephesus…

Unfortunately, in modern English the word "saints" has come to mean people who are especially good, or especially godly. However, the Greek word means "holy ones," and every Christian is holy, not because he lives a good life, but because he has the holy nature of God born in him. That is why the Church Epistles start out, "To the holy ones," even though some Christians in the Church do not behave in a godly manner. It is important to note that no one in the Old Testament or Gospels was said to be holy unless they lived a holy life. This is because no one had a holy nature until God had children by birth, who would then have His holy nature. Christians today have the responsibility to let their holy inner nature show forth by living a holy life. However, if they do not, they are still the children of God and still holy.

E. Sealed

God is holy and God is spirit, so, the nature of God that is born within us is holy spirit. The birth is permanent, so, another way God tells us of the permanence of our salvation is by saying we are "sealed" with holy spirit.

Ephesians 1:13 (ESV)[25]
In him you also, when you heard the word of truth, the gospel of your salvation, and believed in him, were **sealed** with the promised Holy Spirit [holy spirit],

---

25. We use the ESV here because it properly uses "sealed" as a verb, which it is in the Greek text.

The uniqueness of this verse can be seen by trying to find a comparable verse anywhere in the Old Testament or Gospels. None exist because, before the Administration of Grace, people were not "sealed" with holy spirit. Instead of being part of their nature, it was conditionally upon them and could be taken away if they disobeyed God. In contrast, God seals Christians with holy spirit, a clear indication that their salvation is permanent. What would be the point of using the word "sealed" if in fact what we were sealed with could leave us? We seal a jar so that what is in it stays in, and God seals us for the same purpose. We are not in danger of our holy spirit leaving us. It is sealed in us.

F. Guaranteed

The holy spirit nature of God that is sealed in us is a guarantee of our everlasting life.

> **2 Corinthians 5:5**
> Now it is God who has made us for this very purpose and has given us the Spirit [spirit] as a deposit, guaranteeing what is to come.

The words "deposit, guaranteeing" (NIV), "guarantee" (ESV, RSV, NRSV), "pledge" (NASB), or "earnest" (KJV) are the translations of the Greek word *arrabon*, which originally was a Phoenician word used in their trading. It was a downpayment or pledge of the full amount that was to follow. In our case, the holy spirit that we have now is the downpayment of all that "is to come" in the future, including our new bodies that will be fashioned like Christ's glorious body. There are no verses in the Old Testament or Gospels saying that holy spirit guaranteed salvation because it did not until the Church Age. If a person who lived during the Old Testament had holy spirit, but became hardhearted against God, he, like King Saul, could lose it. Thus, in the Old Testament the presence of holy spirit did not guarantee anything. Today, because holy spirit is the very nature of God born inside us, and because birth is permanent, the presence of holy spirit in a Christian is indeed a "guarantee" that he will be with the Lord forever.

G. Unable to be Separated from God's Love

We are God's children and we are guaranteed to be taken up to be with the Lord at the Rapture. No wonder Romans assures us that nothing will separate us from the love of Christ.

> **Romans 8:35–39**
> (35) Who shall separate us from the love of Christ? Shall trouble or hardship or persecution or famine or nakedness or danger or sword?
> (36) As it is written: "For your sake we face death all day long; we are considered as sheep to be slaughtered."
> (37) No, in all these things we are more than conquerors through him who loved us.
> (38) For I am convinced that neither death nor life, neither angels nor demons, neither the present nor the future, nor any powers,
> (39) neither height nor depth, nor anything else in all creation, will be able to separate us from the love of God that is in Christ Jesus our Lord.

Are there any such verses in the Old Testament or Gospels that say that a believer will never be able to be separated from God's love? No, there are not. In fact, that very point is made right in verse 36 which quotes Psalm 44:22 showing that God's people could be separated from His love and support during Old Testament times. Other Old Testament verses confirm this as well. In the Old Testament Lord-servant relationships, God's righteousness required Him to turn from His people when they turned from Him, but that same righteousness now requires Him to honor His Father-child relationship with each Christian. We are God's family in a literal and unique way and nothing will ever be able to separate Christians from the love of God. Hallelujah!

If a Christian were able to lose his salvation, he might die unsaved. If that were to happen, he would definitely be separated from the love of God because he would be burned up in the Lake of Fire.[26] The only

---

26. It is commonly taught that people who die unsaved burn forever. This is not correct. The Lake of Fire is the "second death" (Rev. 20:14). It would not be called "death" if in

credible way Scripture could say that nothing, not even "death" (v. 38), can separate the Christian from the love of God is if there is no way a Christian can become unsaved.

H. Citizens of Heaven

We are members by birth of God's heavenly family, so we are rightly said to have our "citizenship in heaven."

> **Philippians 3:20a**
> But our citizenship is in heaven…

The only reason we are said to be citizens of heaven is that our salvation is secure in Christ. We were born into God's family and cannot be unborn. No one in the Old Testament or Gospels was ever said to be a citizen of heaven because, before the Administration of Grace, salvation was not secure. In fact, our heavenly position is so secure that Ephesians tells us that we are actually seated in heaven with Christ.

> **Ephesians 2:6**
> And God raised us up with Christ and seated us with him
> in the heavenly realms in Christ Jesus,

We are physically on earth now but our future seat in heaven is so secure that God speaks of it, by way of the idiom of the prophetic perfect, as an accomplished reality. In order for a Christian to become unsaved, he would have to be yanked out of heaven; then, why say he was going to be there in the first place.

I. New Creations

Every Christian has a new and divine nature, so he is called a "new creation."

---

fact the people thrown into it did not die. For more on the final end of the unsaved, see our book, *op. cit., Is There Death After Life*, p. 47–51. See also, Edward Fudge, *The Fire that Consumes* (iUniverse Publishing Company, Bloomington, IN, 2000).

2 Corinthians 5:17
Therefore, if anyone is in Christ, he is a new creation; the old has gone, the new has come!

The NIV is exactly right in saying Christians become "a new creation." The Greek word *ktisis* means "creation." There are some versions that say we become a "new creature" instead of a new creation. It is true that because we are new creations we are new creatures, but, we must understand that the reason we are new is that God has created in us something that is brand new. The word "new" is *kainos*, which means new in quality.[27] Colossians makes a different point but one that involves the same concept of a new creation.

Colossians 3:10
and have put on the new self, which is being renewed in knowledge in the image of its Creator.

The word "new" in this verse is *neos*, which means new in time.[28] When a Christian is born again, at that very moment he is "new." The new, spiritual creation within him is new in time because it is newer than his old self and it is also new in quality. Whereas the old man was dead in sin (Eph. 2:2), the new creation inside us is totally new in quality. As Colossians says, each Christian should "put on" the new self, i.e., live outwardly what God has created inwardly.

When an unsaved person is saved, he is a new creation, freshly "born" into God's family. It is clear that a person's New Birth is a one-time event and not a "process" or something that happens over time. Unlike other administrations in which salvation was dependent on how one lived his whole life, in the Administration of Grace, salvation is a one-time event that cannot be "undone." When a person believes, he is "created" both new in time and in quality. Nothing like this was ever said of believers before the Christian Church began on Pentecost. Being a new creation is part of the "grace" of the Administration of Grace.

---

27. Richard Trench, *Synonyms of the New Testament* (Baker Book House, Grand Rapids, MI, 1989), p. 233.
28. *Ibid.*, p. 233.

At this point, we should stop and reflect on what we know about believers in the Old Testament and in the Gospels. They are never called new creations; they are never said to be born again (in fact, no Old Testament individual is ever called "born" of God); they are never said to be citizens of heaven; they are never said to have incorruptible seed from God; they are never said to have a holy nature, they are never said to be sealed with holy spirit, nor is holy spirit upon them said to be a guarantee of their everlasting life. In fact, it is specifically because these things are not mentioned in the Old Testament and Gospels that some Bible students have a hard time believing God actually did them for Christians.

> **People who try to integrate the Bible into a "whole" rather than pay attention to the specific rules God gave to each administration will find verses they cannot reconcile with their position.**

Many Bible students think that God always deals with people the same way and that He will deal with us the way He dealt with Moses, Miriam, Ruth, or David. However, that is not the case. God makes the rules and what He decided to do for the Christian Church was not "business as usual." God has done something for Christians that was never done before the Church Age, and it is something He kept as a Sacred Secret until after Jesus was crucified.

Once we understand that permanent salvation is due to spiritual birth by receiving the seed and nature of God, and is something special that God has done for the Christian Church, we can better understand why Christians have debated for years whether or not salvation is permanent. There are verses that seem to support both positions. This is due to the fact that salvation was not permanent before the Age of Grace and verses from the Old Testament and Gospels show that. On the other hand, verses from the Church Epistles show that salvation is permanent. People who try to integrate the Bible into a "whole" rather than pay attention to the specific rules God gave to each administration will find verses they cannot reconcile with their position. Why are there verses in the Old Testament and Gospels that clearly indicate a person can lose his salvation and verses in the Epistles that clearly state a Christian's salvation is secure? The answer is that God's rules regarding salvation have changed. Once we understand that Scripture must be examined with the individual administrations or dispensations in mind, the entire subject of salvation fits together.[29]

The Christian and the Gift of Holy Spirit

We have seen in Chapter 6 that God has given His gift of holy spirit to the Church in a way that is totally different than He has ever given it before. In fact, it is so totally different that Scripture, referring to the period before the Day of Pentecost, says, "...for as yet there was no Spirit [spirit]..." (John 7:39-NRSV).[30] Nevertheless, we will summarize a few points. Each and every believer is sealed with God's gift of holy spirit when he gets saved (Eph. 1:13). The gift of holy spirit is imperishable seed (1 Pet. 1:23), the very nature of God. This is born inside each believer, which is why Christians are said to be "born again" of the very nature of God, which becomes our new and spiritual nature. Every Christian is "filled" with holy spirit, "anointed" (completely covered) in holy spirit, and baptized (fully immersed) in holy spirit. To emphasize the fact that we cannot lose the new nature sealed within us, God calls it a "guarantee" of our future hope (2 Cor. 1:22, 5:5; Eph. 1:14-RSV).

Before his ascension, Christ told the Apostles that when they received holy spirit, they would receive "power" (Acts 1:8). The vast amount of spiritual power that each Christian has is summed up by God calling our holy spirit "...Christ in you, the hope of glory" (Col. 1:27b). Although we

---

29. There are a few "difficult" verses in Scripture written to the Church that some scholars have used to show that Christians can lose their salvation. Studying them reveals that in fact they are consistent with the truth that salvation is permanent, but it is not the purpose of this work to explain the few difficult verses in the Church Epistles. Nevertheless, a common rebuttal to the permanence of salvation is, "Well, if that were true, then Christians could do anything they want and still be saved." While that may seem like a good argument, it is based on human feelings and not biblical evidence. Are we to be offended because God is good? The evidence in the text is quite clear that a Christian cannot lose his salvation. Nevertheless, there are good reasons a Christian should not sin even though his salvation is assured. The Bible says that those who practice sin become slaves to sin, which is not a desirable thing. Also, sin affects one's future rewards. The fact that the Christian's salvation is assured allows each of us to let go of anxiety and concern about the future and concentrate fully on pleasing the Lord whether we succeed or fail in our endeavors.

30. For a more detailed explanation of John 7:39, see Appendix C, "The Promised Holy Spirit."

do not literally have Christ inside us, because the Lord Jesus is in heaven at the right hand of God, what we have is so powerful that it is called "Christ" in us because it enables us to be like Jesus. If all Christians had was "Moses" in them, or "Samuel" in them, or "Deborah" in them that would be pretty good because those people walked in the power of God. However, God says that we have "Christ" in us, the power to do what Christ did and to become like Christ in our lives.

Christians also have two new ways to outwardly manifest holy spirit that did not exist in the Old Testament or Gospels. We can speak in tongues and interpret tongues (1 Cor. 12:10, 14:2–5), which are manifestations not practiced or foretold in the Bible until after the resurrection of Christ. Although each Christian receives the gift of holy spirit the moment he is born again, he may not manifest it outwardly (such as by speaking in tongues). Just because a person does not manifest the holy spirit does not mean he does not have it.

When holy spirit is born in us it becomes part of our very nature and influences us like our fleshly nature influences us. In fact, because our fleshly nature and our spiritual nature both exert an influence on us, they are said to be "in conflict" (Gal. 5:17). They pull us in different directions. The "helper" (John 14:26-ESV) helps us walk with God in a way unavailable in the Old Testament.

The Body of Christ

Another aspect of the Administration of the Sacred Secret deals with the reality that God has made all Christians together into "one body," the Body of Christ. There are many facets to this and, if we are going to appreciate all that God has given to us, we need to examine them.

First of all, God did away with the Jew-Gentile distinction and has made every Christian (whether they were formerly Jews or formerly Gentiles) equal in Christ. Throughout the Old Testament, God made the point that He considered the Jews "His people" and separate from the nations. Jews were Jews whether they believed God or not, and they were separate from Gentiles, even those Gentiles who believed. By the time of Christ, Gentiles who believed were called proselytes, and sometimes "God-fearers."[31] Due to the long-standing separation between Jews and Gentiles, God knew it would take very clear revelation to convince people that He has changed the way He deals with both of them. Ephesians 2:11–22 and 3:6 are part of that revelation. There is no prophecy in the Old Testament or the Gospels foretelling that God would ever make Jews and Gentiles equal in Christ and part of one Body—their unity is part of the Sacred Secret.

Second, Jews and Gentiles will once again be separate after the Rapture of the Christian Church in the time period covered in the book of Revelation (cp. Rev. 7:4 and 9, 11:1 and 2). But, in this one administration, the Administration of the Sacred Secret, when born-again Jews and Gentiles make up the one "Body of Christ," they are not separate. "There is neither Jew nor Greek, slave nor free, male nor female, for you are all one in Christ Jesus" (Gal. 3:28). What Christ did for the Jew and Gentile was "… to create in himself one new man out of the two, thus making peace" (Eph. 2:15b).

> **God did away with the Jew-Gentile distinction, and has made every Christian equal in Christ.**

As we see from Galatians 3:28, what God did by making the Jews and Gentiles equal, He also did for males and females, and for slaves and freemen. The fact that each Christian is a part of the Body of Christ also elevates each one to a position of importance. This point is also made in 1 Corinthians 12:11–27.

Third, the "one body" of Christ is a spiritual entity that exists only in the Church Age. The idea of "one body" communicates some wonderful truths. First, there is a connectedness in the body that did not exist in the Old Testament. Just as the parts of a physical body are directly connected to, and communicate fluidly with, the head, the gift of holy spirit sealed inside each believer allows him to have intimate communication with God and Christ. Also, just as the parts of our fleshly bodies are inseparably

---

31. Acts 13:16 reads, "…Men of Israel and you who fear God…" (NASB). Although most versions say something similar to this, perhaps a better term is "God-fearers," and it referred to the Gentiles who believed but who the Jews still considered separate from themselves, which is why when Paul taught in the Synagogues he addressed them separately. F. F. Bruce, *The New International Commentary on the New Testament: The Book of Acts* (William B. Eerdmans Publishing Company, Grand Rapids, MI, 1988), p. 203.

connected, so is our spiritual body. We are in no danger of being "amputated" from the Body and losing our salvation or the love of God.

Identification with Christ

One of the unique blessings of the administration of the Sacred Secret is that each Christian is identified with Christ. Each Christian is part of the Body of Christ, so, from God's perspective, when Christ went through something, we Christians went through it also. For example, Jesus Christ died on the Cross, so, in the eyes of God, when a person becomes a Christian and part of the Body of Christ, it is as if he also was crucified. Thus, we were "crucified with" Christ (Rom. 6:6); we died with Christ (Rom. 6:8); we were buried with Christ (Rom. 6:4); we were raised from the dead with Christ (Eph. 2:6); we even ascended with him and are seated with him in heaven (Eph. 2:6), which is exactly where we will be after the Rapture.

Only by studying the language of identification can one see how new and different it is from the language of the Old Testament and Gospels. Jesus never told the Apostles, "After I am crucified, because you believe in me you will be crucified with me." However, from God's perspective, when a Christian is born again, he or she was crucified, died, was buried, was resurrected, and was given a place in heaven with Christ. No wonder we cannot lose our salvation. How could a Christian become uncrucified, undead, unburied, unraised, and unseated?

The Rapture

At the close of the Administration of the Sacred Secret, Christians are taken into heaven, an event known as the "Rapture" (1 Thess. 4:13–18). We will stay with him there until we return to earth with him to fight and win the Battle of Armageddon (Rev. 19:11–21). Neither the Old Testament nor the Gospels tell believers that they will one day be in heaven. It says that they will get up from the grave and live on the earth (Ezek. 37:12–14). Even after Christ died and was raised, the disciples, who did not yet know the Sacred Secret, asked if he was going to restore the Kingdom to Israel

(Acts 1:6). They did not ask about going to heaven because such an idea was not part of their theology or thinking.[32]

The Rapture of the Church is part of the Sacred Secret, so, no Old Testament prophet spoke of it, nor did Jesus mention it in his teachings. This has caused some theologians to say there is no such thing as the Rapture. The reason Jesus never taught about it is that it was part of the Sacred Secret, and we have seen that the Sacred Secret, including the Rapture, was hidden in God until after the crucifixion. Therefore it makes perfect sense that the only place in the Bible where the Rapture appears is in the writings to the Christian Church, such as 1 Thessalonians.

> **The Rapture of the Church is part of the Sacred Secret, so no Old Testament prophet spoke of it.**

New Bodies Like Christ's Glorious Body

The last aspect of the Administration of the Sacred Secret that we will cover in this appendix is the new body that each Christian will receive at the Rapture. It was not a secret that, in the First Resurrection, Old Testament believers would be given healthy bodies (Isa. 29:18, 33:24, 35:5 and 6, etc.). Part of the revelation of the Administration of the Sacred Secret, however, is that at the Rapture, Christians will get bodies that will be like Christ's glorious body (Phil. 3:21). Now that is something to look forward to! It would be one thing for us to be raised in bodies like we have now, except healthy. But, we should be excited about knowing our bodies will become like Christ's glorious body.

Christians now live in bodies that are perishable, but we will receive bodies that are imperishable (1 Cor. 15:42). Our fleshly body may die in dishonor, but we will be raised in glory. It may die in weakness, but it will be raised in power (1 Cor. 15:43). We currently have a natural body, but we will have a spiritual body (1 Cor. 15:44). This is an amazing revelation that gives every Christian something exciting to look forward to in the future.

---

32. To understand that before the Rapture (for Christians) or the restoration of the Kingdom (for Old Testament and Gospel believers), the dead are dead and not alive in heaven, see our book, *op. cit. Is There Death After Life?*

This life can be very difficult indeed and it can be especially hard if we are dealing with physical disabilities, ailments, and/or the breakdown of our bodies as we age. How empowering to know that when Christ comes for us we will not just have healthy bodies, but bodies like his glorious body.

With all the wonderful things we have been given as Christians, it is no wonder that God calls this Administration the Administration of Grace. Truly, we have been given grace heaped upon grace. No wonder God commands us to be thankful (Col. 3:15). We should be **very** thankful for all He has done for us. No wonder He says that the Sacred Secret is for our glory. No wonder God says that the Old Testament revelation, which was certainly glorious, has "no glory" in comparison with what we have today. God has done so much for us, it behooves all of us to read and study the writings to the Christian Church (Acts—Jude) to continue to learn about all these things God has done for us. We will not find the great truths of the Sacred Secret anywhere else but there.

Appendix B

Usages of "Spirit" in the New Testament

In any given language, many words have at least two meanings, and some have many more than two. The Greek word *pneuma*, which in the New Testament is most often translated as "Spirit" or "spirit," has many meanings. Sometimes this presents challenges to translators as they try to bring the sense into English. The chart on the following page shows uses of *pneuma* in four different versions of the Bible and reveals not only different meanings of *pneuma*, but how translators differ in how they deal with it.[1]

The difference in the lists on the next page highlights the difficulty in properly translating *pneuma* because it has so many meanings. It also highlights the absolute necessity to understand the context of each use of *pneuma*. If we do not understand what God is saying in the context, then it is very easy to mistranslate. The various ways *pneuma* can be translated into English is due in part to the fact that in the Greek New Testament *pneuma* appears in many forms. E. W. Bullinger wrote about the different ways in which the Greek word *pneuma*, spirit, is used (not what *pneuma* means but simply the way the word itself is employed in the Greek text).

---

1. The numbers in each column do not come to the same total for several reasons. Sometimes the Greek text from which one version was translated does not agree with the Greek text another version was based on. For example, the Greek text of Philippians 4:23 from which the KJV was translated from does not have *pneuma*, while the Greek text the NIV was translated from does. The Stephanus Greek text of 1550, which is close to what the KJV was translated from, has *pneuma* 385 times. However, the modern Greek text, which is closer to what the NIV and NRSV were translated from, has *pneuma* 379 times. However, sometimes the translators simply ignored the word *pneuma* and did not translate it (cp. Acts 19:21-NIV). Also, the translators sometimes added "spirit" when *pneuma* was not in the Greek text at all (1 Pet. 4:14-NRSV; 1 Cor. 2:14, first occurrence, NIV).

Ways *Pneuma* Is Translated In Four Versions

	KJV	NIV	ASV	NRSV
Spirit	138	246	231	236
Spirits	4	0	4	0
Spirit's	0	0	0	1
spirit	123	92	112	105
spirit's	28	33	28	37
Ghost	89	0	0	0
ghost	2	2	0	2
life	1	0	0	0
wind	1	1	1	1
winds	0	1	1	1
breath	0	3	3	3
breathed	0	0	0	1
spiritually	1	0	0	1
spiritual	1	2	1	2
attitude	0	1	0	0
heart	0	1	0	0
mind	0	1	0	2
prophecy	0	1	0	0
great	0	1	0	0
greatly	0	1	0	0
deeply	0	0	0	1
burning	0	0	0	1

Let us next note the various ways in which the Greek word *pneuma*, is employed: i.e., the way in which it is used (apart from its meanings, or the sense which is given to it: i.e., its usage):

1. It is used alone, in two ways
   A. without the article: simply *pneuma*
   B. with the article: the *pneuma*
2. It is employed with *hagion* ("holy") in four ways:
   A. *pneuma hagion* (holy spirit) Matt. 1:18, and in 49 other places.

    B. *hagion pneuma* (spirit holy) 1 Cor. 6:19, etc.

    C. the *hagion pneuma*, Matt. 28:19, etc.

    D. the *pneuma* the *hagion*, Matt. 12:32, etc.

3. It is used with *pronouns: e.g.,* the *pneuma* of me: i.e., my *pneuma,* Matt. 12:18, etc.

4. It is used with *prepositions,* which affect its sense:

    A. (*en pneumati*), by or through the Spirit: denoting agency.

    B. Adverbially, as meaning spiritually and sometimes (like *en dolo*), craftily, 2 Cor. 12:16): thus turning the phrase into an *adverb.*

5. It is employed in combination with the Divine Names in seven different forms; of which four have the article, and three are without: e.g., *pneuma Theou* [spirit of God]; *pneuma Christou* [spirit of Christ], etc.

6. It is employed with ten other nouns in the genitive case, which (by [the Figure of Speech] *Enallage*) qualify the meaning of *pneuma.* These again are used with and without the article: e.g., a *pneuma* of sonship (Rom. 8:15), i.e., a sonship *pneuma.*

7. It is employed with a second noun with which it is joined by a conjunction *(Hendiadys).* Thus used it becomes a superlative adjective.

Here [above] are seven different ways in which the word *pneuma* is employed. Each class is distinct, to say nothing of the minor variations. Now, the question is, are we to make no difference in our reading and understanding of these various uses? Can it be that God employs the word *pneuma* in all these different ways, and yet has no object in so doing and has only one meaning for them all? Surely, no one will contend that this is the case.[2]

Bullinger is surely correct that since God has chosen to use *pneuma* in so many different constructions, He must be trying to communicate many different meanings and emphasize different points. The realization of this truth has been hindered by the doctrine of the Trinity because Trinitarians tend to see *pneuma* as referring to "God the Holy Spirit" in a majority of the verses, even if the context militates against that interpretation.

These are the various meanings of *pneuma.*

---

2. Bullinger, *op. cit., Word Studies on the Holy Spirit,* pp. 11 and 12 (his outline style has been reworked for clarity).

(1) *Pneuma* is used of an immaterial "substance." John 4:24 says, "God is spirit...."

(2) *Pneuma* is used of God, the Creator of the universe and Father of the Lord Jesus Christ. Matthew 1:18 says that Mary was pregnant through "the Holy Spirit" [*pneuma*]. Many other verses clearly teach that Christ was the Son of God the Father, here called the "Holy Spirit" (because God is holy and God is spirit). In Acts 5:3, Peter told Ananias, "...you have lied to the Holy Spirit...," whom he identified in verse 4 as "God" via a parallelism.

(3) *Pneuma* is used of Jesus Christ, the Son of God, in his resurrected body. Jesus was not a spirit being, like an angel (Luke 24:39), but his body was empowered by spirit in such a way that 1 Corinthians 15:45 says that he became a "life-giving spirit" [*pneuma*]. After his resurrection, Jesus is occasionally referred to as "the Spirit." "Now the Lord is the Spirit...the Lord, who is the Spirit" (2 Cor. 3:17 and 18). Christ is also referred to as "the Spirit" in Revelation 2:7, 11, 17, 29, 3:6, 13 and 22, as is clear from the context, where Jesus is the one doing the talking. Other noteworthy verses are Romans 8:16 (the first "Spirit" in the verse), Revelation 14:13 and 22:17.

(4) *Pneuma* is used of the gift of God that was given to certain believers before the Day of Pentecost. Before Pentecost, when God gave His gift of holy spirit to people, He: (a) gave it to only some people, (b) gave different measures to different people, (c) could take it away from people, just as He did with King Saul and with Samson. As Scripture testifies, Jesus Christ had holy spirit put upon him: "...I will put my Spirit [spirit; *pneuma*] on him..." (Matt. 12:18). The gift of holy spirit came upon Jesus at his baptism in Jordan, and instead of being only a measure of spirit like that upon so many in the Old Testament, Scripture states that Jesus was given "the Spirit [spirit; *pneuma*] without measure" (John 3:34-NRSV). Thus, in Luke 4:18-NRSV, Jesus stated, "the Spirit [spirit] of the Lord is upon me...." Some other New Testament believers who had holy spirit upon them before the Day of Pentecost were Elizabeth (Luke 1:41), Zacharias (Luke 1:67), and Simeon (Luke 2:25).

(5) *Pneuma* is used of God's gift of spirit (usually called "holy spirit"), which has been given in birth to believers since the Day of Pentecost.

Peter was filled with holy spirit (Acts 4:8). Paul, amazed that the Galatian believers would try to go back to the Law, wrote, "...Did you receive the Spirit [spirit; *pneuma*] by observing the law...?" (Gal. 3:2). When the Gentiles believed, they also received the gift of holy spirit (Acts 10:44 and 45). All of these uses refer to holy spirit, the promised gift of God that was given by Jesus Christ (Acts 2:33) to the Apostles on the Day of Pentecost and is now born inside each Christian.

(6) *Pneuma* is used of angels, who are spirit beings. Hebrews 1:14 says, "Are not all angels ministering spirits [*pneumata*, the plural of *pneuma*]...." See also Hebrews 1:7, where *pneumata* is translated "spirits" in many versions, and "winds" in the NIV.

(7) *Pneuma* is used of evil spirits, i.e., demons, many times in the Word of God. Matthew 10:1 says "He called his twelve disciples to him and gave them authority to drive out evil spirits [*pneumata*] and to heal every disease and sickness."

(8) *Pneuma* is used of spirit beings that are not specifically delineated as either angels or demons in the Word of God. Acts 23:9 says "...some of the teachers of the law who were Pharisees stood up and argued vigorously. 'We find nothing wrong with this man,' they said. "What if a spirit [*pneuma*] or an angel has spoken to him?" Revelation 1:4, 3:1, 4:5, and 5:6 are other examples of this.

(9) *Pneuma* is used of the natural life of the body, which is sometimes called "soul" life (e.g., Heb. 4:12. The Greek for "soul" is *psuche*).[3] As Christ was dying on the Cross, he "...gave up his spirit" [*pneuma*] (Matt. 27:50). What he gave up was his life and the phrase used in Matthew, that he "...gave up his spirit," means that he died. The gift of holy spirit that God placed usually upon people before Pentecost and which has been born inside people since Pentecost is not "vital," in the medical sense. People can live without it. A person could lose it and not die, as we learn from Saul in the Old Testament, and millions of people are unsaved and do not have holy spirit. Thus, as it is used in Matthew 27:50, *pneuma* represents the life of the body. The same use of "spirit" is found in Luke 23:46, when Christ said "...Father, into your hands I commit my spirit...." In Luke 8:55,

---

3. Most of the time *psuche* is used, it refers to the person, the individual, not just the life force of the body.

Jesus raised a little girl from the dead, and the Bible says that "Her spirit [*pneuma*] returned, and at once she stood up...." Again, because holy spirit does not give the human body physical life, this use of *pneuma* refers to the physical life of her body. The same is true of James 2:26, which says that "...the body without the spirit [*pneuma*, here referring to the "life"] is dead...."

(10) *Pneuma* is used of the individual and his attitudes, emotions, etc.

A. *Pneuma* is used of the individual self. Matthew 26:41 says, "...The spirit [*pneuma*] is willing, but the body is weak." Here Christ was referring to the "spirit" as the individual self, not the gift of holy spirit.

B. *Pneuma* refers to personal emotion, attitude, thought, desire, or will. 2 Corinthians 7:13 says, "...we were especially delighted to see how happy Titus was, because his spirit [*pneuma*] has been refreshed by all of you." The holy spirit born within a believer does not need refreshment. Thus, "spirit" here refers to his personal and emotional life, or possibly is used by the figure of speech *synecdoche* for his entire self (see #11 below). Referring to attitude, Matthew 5:3 says, "Blessed are the poor in spirit [*pneuma*]...." Obviously, "poor in spirit" does not refer to the amount of holy spirit one has received from God, but rather refers to an attitude of meekness in the mind. Galatians 6:1 says, "Brothers, if someone is caught in a sin, you who are spiritual should restore him gently (literally "in a spirit [*pneuma*, i.e., *attitude*] of meekness...). The NIV translators recognized that holy spirit was not being referred to, and used the phrase, "restore him gently," to refer to a humble attitude of mind.

C. *Pneuma* can also be used to intensify emotion. Mark 8:12a (KJV) says, "And he sighed deeply in his spirit [*pneuma*], and saith, Why doth this generation seek after a sign?" Interestingly, the NIV translators recognized that holy spirit, the gift of God in Jesus, did not sigh, but rather it was an action of the mind, from the heart of Jesus' emotions, so they translated the verse "He sighed deeply [*pneuma*] and said...." "Sighed deeply" is exactly what Jesus did, represented in the Greek text as "sighed in his spirit."

(11) *Pneuma* is used as a part of a person put in place of the whole person, via the figure of speech *Synecdoche. The American Heritage Dictionary* defines *synecdoche* as:

> A figure of speech in which a part is used for the whole *(as hand* for *sailor),* the whole for a part (as *the law* for *police officer),* the specific for the general (as *cutthroat* for *assassin),* the general for the specific (as *thief* for *pickpocket),* or the material for the thing from which it is made (as *steel* for *sword).*

> In *Figures of Speech Used in the Bible* (Baker Book House, Grand Rapids, MI, reprinted 1968, pp. 613–656), E. W. Bullinger gives many excellent examples of *synecdoche* in the Bible. Under the category, "The Part for the Whole," Bullinger has 17 pages of examples. Among them are the following: "That no flesh [i.e., person] should glory in his presence" (1 Cor. 1:29-KJV); "...let us lay wait for blood [i.e., a person to kill]..." (Prov. 1:11-KJV); "... blessed are your eyes [i.e., you, not just your eyes]..." (Matt. 13:16-KJV); "... the froward mouth [i.e., froward speaking person] do I hate" (Prov. 8:13-KJV); "Their feet [i.e., they] are swift to shed blood" (Rom. 3:15-KJV); "...thy seed shall possess the gate [not just the gate, the whole city] of his enemies" (Gen. 22:17-KJV).

> Similarly, there are clear examples where *pneuma* (spirit) is used for the whole person. In Luke 1:47, Mary says, "...my spirit [not just her spirit, but her entire being] rejoices in God my Savior." In 2 Timothy 4:22, Paul wrote, "The Lord be with your spirit [obviously not just Timothy's spirit, but with Timothy as an entire person]...." This same expression also occurs in Philemon, verse 25.

(12) *Pneuma* is used by the figure of speech *metonymy* for a related noun. *Metonymy* is defined in *The American Heritage Dictionary* as:

> A figure of speech in which one word or phrase is substituted for another with which it is closely associated, as in the use of *Washington* for the *United States government* or of the *sword* for *military power.*

We use *metonymy* in our speech when we say things such as "The White House said today... [i.e., a person in the White House"] or "Watch your mouth [i.e., be careful what you say]." Bullinger has 71 pages (pp. 538–608) of examples of *metonymy* in Scripture. A good example of *metonymy* is found in John 6:63, when Christ said, "...The words I have spoken to you are spirit...." Of course, the words themselves were not spirit, they were words, but they produced spiritual life in all those who believed.

The above categories are not exhaustive in their references, nor do we claim to have noted every distinction or even every category of usage of the word *pneuma*. The above list should, however, demonstrate that when one is reading the Bible, he must pay careful attention when the word "spirit" is used. A large amount of doctrinal error could quickly be corrected if Christians did not think of every use of "the Holy Spirit" as a reference to the third person of the "Trinity," but instead carefully read the context of the verse to see exactly what God, the Author, was trying to communicate. It would be much easier for the reader to do that if translators had not been so quick to add the article "the" before "holy spirit" where it does not belong, or to capitalize "spirit" almost everywhere it occurs. By careful reading, the student of the Bible will usually be able to determine what God means when He uses the word "spirit."

"The Promised Holy Spirit"
Holy Spirit in the Millennial Kingdom

We have seen that during the time covered by the Old Testament and Gospels, God gave holy spirit in a very limited way: it was upon only certain selected people, He gave it conditionally, and by measure. However, God promised much better things for Israel's future. He promised that in the Millennial Kingdom He would "pour out" holy spirit in abundance to everyone who believed. Furthermore, what God promised to Israel, He has given by grace to the Christian Church, which explains why holy spirit in Christians is called "the promised Holy Spirit [holy spirit]" (Eph. 1:13), and the "firstfruits of the Spirit [spirit]" (Rom. 8:23).

The subject of the Millennial Kingdom is not often taught and not well understood, so, before we can discuss holy spirit in the Millennial Kingdom, we must discuss the Millennial Kingdom itself. The Millennial Kingdom is the 1,000 year kingdom that Christ will set up on earth after he returns to earth and fights the Battle of Armageddon. Most Christians know that some day there will be a time of terrible Tribulation on earth. This was foretold in the Old Testament, taught by Jesus, and is described in the book of Revelation. There will be wars, famines, plagues, earthquakes, and massive destruction, and billions of people will die.[1] This time of Tribulation will end when Jesus Christ comes down from heaven and fights the Battle of Armageddon (Rev. 19:11–21), a battle of which most Christians, and many unbelievers have heard, that will end the world as we know it.

After Armageddon, Jesus does not go back up to heaven. He sets up a kingdom on earth. This will be a time of unparalleled blessing and prosperity.[2] The entire world will be laid waste by the Tribulation and Armageddon, so, the earth will have to be restored. In fact, it will be

---

1. Revelation 6:8, which is early in the Tribulation period, says that even by then a fourth of the earth's population will have been killed, which at current population numbers means more than 2 billion people will be dead.

2. The more a person knows about the Millennial Kingdom, the easier it will be for him to understand the promise God made concerning holy spirit in the Kingdom.

restored to such a pristine state that it is said to be created anew (Isa. 65:17, 66:22). Christ will reign from Jerusalem as King and High Priest (Ps. 110; Isa. 9:6 and 7; Zech. 6:12 and 13[3]), the deserts will bloom (Isa. 35:1, 6 and 7), and there will be abundant food (Isa. 25:6, 30:23–26). No one living in Israel will be sick (Isa. 33:24, 35:5 and 6). Even animal nature will be changed so that carnivorous animals return to eating vegetables as they did in the Garden of Eden (Isa. 11:7, 65:25; cp. Gen. 1:30).

This Kingdom will last 1,000 years (Rev. 20:4, 5 and 7), which is why it is known theologically as Christ's Millennial Kingdom (from *mil*, 1,000, and *annus*, a year). In Nebuchadnezzar's dream, Christ's Kingdom is the rock that destroys the kingdoms of the earth and then fills the entire earth (Dan. 2:34, 35, 44 and 45). It was this Kingdom the disciples were referring to when, after the Resurrection they asked Jesus, "…Lord, are you at this time going to restore the kingdom to Israel?" (Acts 1:6b). Christ's Kingdom is on earth, so Christ taught that the meek, those meek enough to accept salvation, will inherit the earth (Matt. 5:5), and why the Old Testament taught that also (Ps. 37:9; Ezek. 37:12).

The Millennial Kingdom will be composed of people with new bodies who have died and been resurrected, as well as people with mortal bodies who survive the Battle of Armageddon (Matt. 25:31–34). In many cases, the promises and prophecies about the Millennial Kingdom are general, without reference to which of those two categories of people are being discussed. When it comes to holy spirit being permanently in people, however, (Point 4 below), it seems that the promises are to people who are raised from the dead, and not necessarily to those who are still in their natural bodies.

It is of this Millennial Kingdom that the prophets of old spoke, saying God would give holy spirit in a different, fuller, more powerful way. Furthermore, the holy spirit Christians have today is the firstfruits of the gift of holy spirit that God has promised to give to believers in the Millennial Kingdom. Therefore, the things about holy spirit that were foretold for the Millennial Kingdom apply to Christians also, even

---

3. The phrase "…the man whose name is the Branch…" tells us that this refers to the Messiah, who is called the Branch elsewhere in Scripture (Isa. 4:2, 11:1; Jer. 23:5, 33:15; Zech. 3:8).

though holy spirit was not specifically foretold for Christians. However, Christians have holy spirit with manifestations that were not promised in the Old Testament prophecies, and these are speaking in tongues and the interpretation of tongues. Acts and the Church Epistles make the point that the gift of holy spirit that Christians have today is "the **promised** holy spirit."

> **Acts 2:33**
> Exalted to the right hand of God, he has received from the Father the **promised** Holy Spirit [holy spirit] and has poured out what you now see and hear.

> **Ephesians 1:13**
> And you also were included in Christ when you heard the word of truth, the gospel of your salvation. Having believed, you were marked in him with a seal, the **promised** Holy Spirit [holy spirit],

It is clear that holy spirit had been **promised** by God, and that Christians now have it. Furthermore, Jesus spoke to his disciples about the **promised** holy spirit in Luke 24:49 and Acts 1:4. In the Old Testament God **promised** to give holy spirit to Israel, not the Church. No one knew there was going to be a Christian Church because it was part of the Sacred Secret which God hid in Himself.[4] God **promised** that holy spirit would be poured out in the kingdom of Christ, but because He has given it to Christians, Scripture calls what we have the "firstfruits of the Spirit [spirit]" (Rom. 8:23).

> **Romans 8:23**
> Not only so, but we ourselves, who have the **firstfruits of the Spirit**, groan inwardly as we wait eagerly for our adoption as sons, the redemption of our bodies.[5]

---

4. See Appendix A, "The Administration of the Sacred Secret."

5. This verse says we are waiting for our adoption because it will not be fully realized until the Rapture.

God calls what we have **"firstfruits"** because we have now what He promised for the Millennial believers. If His promise to pour out holy spirit on believers was made to the Church, then we would not have the **"firstfruits"** of the spirit, we would have the fulfillment of the promise. Germane to this study are some of the blessings God foretold about holy spirit in the Millennial Kingdom, in particular four major differences between holy spirit in the Old Testament and in the Millennial Kingdom.

In the Old Testament and Gospels:

- Only a **few** believers had holy spirit, but in the Millennial Kingdom it will be in **all** believers.
- God gave holy spirit in a **limited** way, by measure, but in the Millennial Kingdom it will be poured out in **abundance**.
- God gave holy spirit **conditionally** and the recipient could lose it. In the Millennial Kingdom, holy spirit will be given **permanently**.
- It is never stated that holy spirit would influence a person to live a godly life. However, Scripture promises that in the Millennial Kingdom, holy spirit will **influence** people toward godliness.

1) In the Old Testament and Gospels, only a few believers had holy spirit, but in the Millennial Kingdom it will be in all believers.

We have seen that in the Old Testament God put holy spirit upon relatively few believers. However, He promised that when He gives holy spirit in the Millennial Kingdom, it will not be in only a few believers, but in all.

> **Joel 2:28 and 29**
> (28) And afterward, I will pour out my Spirit [spirit] **on all people.** Your sons and daughters will prophesy, your old men will dream dreams, your young men will see visions.
> (29) Even on my servants, both men and women, I will pour out my Spirit [spirit] in those days.

That men, women, sons, and daughters would all receive holy spirit was a huge difference from the way things had been throughout the Old Testament. The word "afterward" in verse 28 refers to after the Tribulation and Armageddon, i.e., in the Millennial Kingdom. It is important to realize that Joel is not referring to the Day of Pentecost and the fact that Christians have holy spirit. We live in the Administration of Grace, which is a time period unknown to the people of the Old Testament and, indeed, to Satan himself (1 Cor. 2:7–9). Joel was speaking about Israel, as J. Vernon McGee wrote:

> He [Joel] is speaking of the kingdom which is coming on the earth, and the pouring out of the Spirit [spirit] has reference to the Millennium. Of course none of the prophets spoke of the church age; all of them spoke of the last days in reference to the nation of Israel.[6]

Jesus confirmed that when God poured out holy spirit, it would be to people who believed in him.

John 7:38 (KJV)
He that believeth on me, as the scripture hath said, out of his belly shall flow rivers of living water.

These verses let us know that when Joel said that spirit would be poured out on "all flesh," he was referring to the believers, not everyone alive, no matter what they believed.

2) In the Old Testament and Gospels, God gave holy spirit in a limited way, by measure, but in the Millennial Kingdom it will be poured out in abundance.

God promised that in the Millennial Kingdom He would **"pour out"** holy spirit upon people, i.e., they will have an abundance of holy spirit. This abundance was not how God had given holy spirit during the Old Testament and Gospel periods. During those times, when God placed holy spirit upon people, He did so by "measure," in other words, in a limited way, as we have seen earlier in the book, especially Chapter 6, "The Gift of Holy Spirit Today."

In contrast to the limited measure of holy spirit given in the Old Testament and Gospels, God promised that He would give holy spirit in abundance in the Millennial Kingdom. We read that Joel said, "…I will

---

6. McGee, *op. cit.*, *Thru the Bible with J. Vernon McGee*, Vol. III, Proverbs–Malachi, p. 673.

pour out my Spirit [spirit] on all people..." (Joel 2:28). The words **"pour out"** are significant.

> "...to pour out signifies communication in rich abundance, like a rainfall or waterfall. 'There is no doubt that the prophet promises something greater here than the fathers has experienced under the law...the prophet promises here not what the faithful had formerly experienced, but something greater.'[7]

God did promise something greater for Israel in the upcoming Millennial Kingdom than He had given in the Old Testament. Furthermore, there are other verses besides the one in Joel that promised that spirit would be **poured out** (Isa. 32:15 and 44:3, for example). One thing we should note about the promised holy spirit is that it would be given in great abundance, which, of course, it will be in the Millennial Kingdom. We should point out, however, that even though God promised He would give people an abundance of holy spirit, He did not specifically promise that they would be filled, even though that is clearly implied. In contrast, it is clear in Scripture written to the Church that every Christian is **filled** with holy spirit.

3) In the Old Testament and Gospels, God gave holy spirit conditionally, and the recipient could lose it. In the Millennial Kingdom, holy spirit will be given permanently.

Throughout the Old Testament and Gospel periods, the gift of holy spirit was upon people conditionally and God could, therefore, take it back. In contrast to the way God gave holy spirit in the Old Testament, in the Millennial Kingdom, He will give it permanently to those believers who have been raised from the dead, brought into the Kingdom, and settled in the land.

> **Ezekiel 37:12 and 14**
> (12) Therefore prophesy and say to them: 'This is what the Sovereign LORD says: O my people, I am going to open your graves and bring you up from them; I will bring you back to the land of Israel.

---

7. C. F. Keil and F. Delitzsch, *Commentary on the Old Testament: Minor Prophets* (William B. Eerdmans Publishing Company, Grand Rapids, MI, reprinted 1975), Vol. 10, p. 210.

(14) I will put my Spirit [spirit] in you and you will live, and I will settle you in your own land. Then you will know that I the LORD have spoken, and I have done it, declares the LORD.'"

These verses make it clear that when God raises Old Testament believers from the dead, He will put His spirit, holy spirit, in them forever, as the following verse also shows:

Isaiah 59:21 (KJV)[8]
As for me, this *is* my covenant with them, saith the LORD; My spirit that *is* upon thee, and my words which I have put in thy mouth, shall not depart out of thy mouth, nor out of the mouth of thy seed, nor out of the mouth of thy seed's seed, saith the LORD, from henceforth and for ever.

The New Covenant that God will make with Israel contains many irrevocable promises. For example, He said of resurrected Israel believers that He would "no longer" hide His face from them (Ezek. 39:29). He told them He will give them a "new heart," taking away their heart of stone and giving them a heart of flesh (Ezek. 36:26), and this is a clear reference to the fact that God will write His law on the hearts of His people so that they will all know Him (Jer. 31:33 and 34). Such promises, and those in the following verses, were to be the true hope of Israel.

Ezekiel 11:19 and 20
(19) I will give them an undivided heart and put a new spirit in them; I will remove from them their heart of stone and give them a heart of flesh.
(20) Then they will follow my decrees and be careful to keep my laws. They will be my people, and I will be their God.

God will put His holy spirit in resurrected believers, a "new" spirit, and they will then follow His decrees. They will be His people, and He will be their God. They will not have to fear losing the spirit or losing

---

8. We chose the KJV because it correctly uses a lower case "s" for spirit and uses the relative pronoun "that," instead of "who" to refer to it.

God's favor as they could during Old Testament times. God's people will stand firm in the kingdom of God, which will be "an everlasting kingdom" (Dan. 7:27b).

4) In the Old Testament and Gospels it is never stated that holy spirit would influence a person to live a godly life. However, Scripture promises that in the Millennial Kingdom, holy spirit will influence people toward godliness.

One of the most exciting things about the promised holy spirit was that it will help people live godly lives. There is no evidence in the Old Testament or Gospels that a purpose, or characteristic of the gift of holy spirit that they had at that time, was that it produced a positive transforming influence on people, helping them become more godly. Certainly people such as Moses or Elijah, who walked in great spiritual power, were aware of God more acutely and thus would have worked hard to live godly lives, but there is no statement in the Old Testament or Gospels that one of the purposes of the gift of holy spirit that God gave in those times was to help transform people toward godliness. We have already seen in Chapter 6 that the promised holy spirit is specifically stated to help people live godly lives.

> **John 16:13**
> But when he [it], the Spirit [spirit] of truth, comes, he [it] will guide you into all truth. He [It] will not speak on his [its] own; he [it] will speak only what he [it] hears, and he [it] will tell you what is yet to come.

We also saw that the promised holy spirit is called the "helper."

> **John 15:26 (Author's translation)**
> But when the helper comes, which I will send to you from the Father, *even* the spirit of truth, which comes from the Father, it will bear witness of me,

The Old Testament foretold the direct communication God will have with resurrected, spirit-filled believers in the Millennial Kingdom:

Ezekiel 39:29
I will no longer hide my face from them, for I will pour out my Spirit [spirit] on the house of Israel, declares the Sovereign LORD."

In Ezekiel, God promised that when holy spirit is poured out on resurrected people in the Millennial Kingdom, they will be able to talk with Him directly and intimately and not be hidden from His "face" any more. Having holy spirit does not remove free will or force a person to obey God, and we all know that Old Testament believers who had holy spirit, and Christians (who all have holy spirit), disobey the commandments and sin. Nevertheless, holy spirit, as it is given in the Administration of Grace to Christians, and will be given to believers in the Millennial Kingdom, does have a very powerful influence on the person.

Ezekiel 36:27 (RSV) says the holy spirit will "...cause you to walk in my statutes and be careful to observe my ordinances." Joel 2:28 says people will dream dreams, see visions, and prophesy, which of course would have a powerful impact on them. Ezekiel 39:29 points to the intimacy of communication between God and people with the promised holy spirit by saying that He will no longer hide His face from them. John 16:13 states that holy spirit will guide people into truth, and Jesus even called it "the helper." Other verses, such as the following, also testify to the godly influence of holy spirit.

Isaiah 44:3b–5
(3b) ...I will pour out my Spirit [spirit] on your offspring, and my blessing on your descendants.
(4) They will spring up like grass in a meadow, like poplar trees by flowing streams.
(5) One will say, 'I belong to the LORD'; another will call himself by the name of Jacob; still another will write on his hand, 'The LORD's,' and will take the name Israel.

This kind of positive spiritual influence did not occur in the Old Testament believers who had holy spirit upon them, but it will for believers in the future. Furthermore, we contend that the gift of holy spirit we

Christians have born inside us will exert this kind of influence if we are open to the will of the Lord and do not quench the spirit because of fear, selfishness, sin, etc.

When one sees the positive and godly influence that holy spirit in each believer will have in the Millennial Kingdom, it is easy to see why it will be a time of unparalleled peace, prosperity, and joy. Of course there are many other reasons for this, including the fact that Jesus will be ruling from Jerusalem as King of the world, the Devil will be chained and unable to influence people, there will be plenty to eat, and no sickness or war. However, the most wonderful aspect of life in the Millennial Kingdom is that those who have been raised to newness of life will be whole and have perfect fellowship with God and the Lord Jesus.

Appendix D

Reasons "Holy Spirit" is One of the Names of God or the Gift of God

In every verse of Scripture in which *pneuma hagion*, holy spirit, is used, it can refer either to (a) one of the names of God, which emphasizes His power in operation, or (b) the gift of God. Therefore, there is no compelling reason to take the words *pneuma hagion* as referring to a being known as "the Holy Spirit" who is part of a Triune Godhead, separate but equal with the Father and the Son. In fact, we see many reasons to believe that such a being does not exist. This appendix presents some of the more salient reasons why we believe there is no "Person" known as "the Holy Spirit."[1]

The Bible never specifically says there is a "Trinity" or that "the Holy Spirit" is a "Person in the Godhead." We assert that is because the Bible teaches there is the Father, Son, and holy spirit (the gift of God), but they are not all "God," neither are they "co-equal" or "co-eternal" as the doctrine of the Trinity states. In contrast, Trinitarians argue that there was no need for Scripture to say, "There is a Trinity," because everyone knew it. Historically, what we today know as the doctrine of the Trinity was not clearly codified until the 4th century A.D.

Given the differences in opinion, it seems clear that any case for or against the existence of a being known as "the Holy Spirit" has to be built from the entire scope of Scripture, using the best tools of exegesis and logic, and working very hard to stay away from false assumptions and circular arguments. We have tried to do that with the reasons below, which set forth evidence showing that there is no "Person," the Holy Spirit, and

---

1. These reasons are drawn from our own study of Scripture and from the work of James H. Broughton and Peter J. Southgate, *The Trinity: True or False* ("The Dawn" Book Supply, Nottingham, England 1995), from the work by Anthony Buzzard and Charles Hunting, *The Doctrine of the Trinity; Christianity's Self-Inflicted Wound* (International Scholars Publications, New York, 1998), from Charles Morgridge's book done in 1837, *The True Believer's Defense*, from Fredric A. Farley's book (1873) *The Scripture Doctrine of the Father, Son and Holy Ghost*, and from *The Racovian Catechism* (1605). Furthermore, we believe that Scripture is clear that Jesus is the Son of God, not God, which we discuss in our book, *op. cit., One God & One Lord: Reconsidering the Cornerstone of the Christian Faith.*

thus indicating that *pneuma hagion* is used either as a name for God, the Father, or as the gift of God which He gives to empower believers.

(1) The "breath" of God and the "spirit" of God are synonymous terms, a point that is easily seen in the original text, but not always so obviously translated (Job 4:9, 27:3; Ps. 33:6, 104:29 and 30; John 3:8; 2 Thess. 2:8;). The breath of God is not a distinct person from God any more than the breath of a human could be a person distinct from that person.

(2) The "spirit of God" is synonymous with the hand and the finger of God, which can be seen from the fact that, referring to the same thing, they are used interchangeably (Job 26:13-KJV; Ps. 8:3; Matt. 12:28; Luke 11:20). This is strong evidence that "the Holy Spirit" is the name of God when His power is in operation. If God and "the Holy Spirit" were two co-equal "Persons," it would not make sense to understand "the Holy Spirit" as the "hand" of God. As a man's hand and finger are subordinate and submissive to the will of a man, so the spirit of God is subordinate to the will of God. As what is done by the hand of a man is done by the man himself, so what is done by the spirit of God is done by God Himself.

(3) In Matthew 11:27 (KJV) Jesus says that "...no one knows the Son, but the Father; neither knoweth any one the Father, save the Son...." If the doctrine of the Trinity were correct, and "the Holy Spirit" is a "Person" in the Godhead, then He too would have known the Father and the Son, and Jesus' statement would not have been true.

(4) Jesus said in Matthew 24:36 that no one knew the hour of his Second Coming except the Father. How could "the Holy Spirit" not know this if he were part of the Godhead, and if he did know, why did Christ not mention him? The best explanation for this is that there is no such distinct being as "the Holy Spirit."

(5) When Jesus returns, he comes in his own glory, the glory of the Father, and the glory of the "holy angels." There is no mention of any glory of "the Holy Spirit" (Luke 9:26). The most reasonable explanation for this is that there is no distinct being as "the Holy Spirit."

(6) The "soul" or the "spirit" of man is often personified, as is the spirit of God. "Why art thou cast down, O my soul?..." (Ps. 42:5). "...I will say to my soul, 'Soul, thou hast much goods laid up...'" (Luke 12:19-KJV). "The Spirit [spirit] is willing..." (Matt. 26:41). The spirit of Titus was refreshed

(2 Cor. 7:13). Yet no one would say that the "spirit of man" is a separate person from the man himself. Similarly, the spirit of God is not a distinct person from God. The spirit of man bears the same relation to man as the spirit of God bears to God (1 Cor. 2:11). As the spirit of man is not another person distinct from himself, but is his human consciousness or mind by which he is able to be self-aware and contemplate things peculiar to himself, so the spirit of God is not another person distinct from God. It is that consciousness and intelligence that is essential and peculiar to Him, whereby He manifests and reveals Himself to man. As the spirit of man is a way of referring to the man himself (the essence of a man is his mind), so the "spirit of God" refers to God Himself. The parallel usage of mind and spirit is seen in the Apostle Paul's citation of Isaiah 40:13, "Who has directed the Spirit [spirit] of the LORD, or as his counselor has instructed him?" (NRSV) and in Romans 11:34 and 1 Corinthians 2:16 where "spirit" is rendered "mind."

(7) The spirit God gives is said to be divisible and distributable. God took of the spirit that was upon Moses and placed it upon the 70 elders of Israel (Num. 11:17–25). Joel 2:28, quoted by Peter on Pentecost (Acts 2:18-KJV), says that God "…will pour out in those days of my Spirit [spirit]…." Understood literally, the Greek says "some of," or "part of" my spirit. The footnote in Weymouth's translation reads "literally 'of' or 'from' my spirit—a share or portion." Though we cannot conceive of how a **person** might be so divided, we can understand that the spirit of God (the spirit that comes from God), as the nature and power of God, can be distributed among many.

(8) The "holy spirit" is clearly said to be given by God to men. A divine "person" cannot be given or bestowed by another divine person, because to be given is to be under the authority of another. If "the Holy Spirit" were co-equal with the Father, "He" would not be under His authority.

(9) The spirit **of** God is, by definition, derived **from** God. That is why 1 Thessalonians 4:8 says that holy spirit is God's: "…God, who gives you **his** Holy Spirit" (1 Thess. 4:8b). If "the Holy Spirit" were a "co- equal," "co-eternal" part of a triune Godhead, this verse makes no sense. It could not refer to "the Holy Spirit" as being God's.

(10) "The Holy Spirit" is equivalent to "…the power of the Most High…," as Luke 1:35 clearly indicates by the use of parallelism (cp. Luke 24:49; Acts 1:8, 10:38; Rom. 15:13, 18 and 19; 1 Cor. 2:4 and 5). The context is the conception of Jesus Christ. Matthew 1:18 also records that Mary "…was found to be with child through the Holy Spirit." Yet all through the New Testament are references to the fact that **God** is the Father of our Lord Jesus Christ. The reason that "the Holy Spirit" is said to father the Lord, but God is the Father of the Lord, is that "the Holy Spirit" is the name used of God that emphasizes His active power.

(11) John 7:39 says that until Jesus was glorified, there was no holy spirit.[2] Furthermore, in Acts 1:4 and 5 Jesus tells his disciples to wait for "the gift my Father promised…," which would come "in a few days." If the Holy Spirit were a person, and present in the Old Testament, how then is it possible for "Him" to be spoken of as not yet being in existence? This problem is solved when we understand that the spirit of God that we receive is not a separate person, but rather the gift of God to empower His people, and that what we have today was not in existence during the Old Testament or Gospel periods.

(12) The Holy Spirit is never worshiped as the Father and the Son are, nor does any verse of Scripture command such worship.

(13) In the opening of their New Testament epistles, every one of the writers identifies himself with God the Father and the Lord Jesus Christ, but not one does so with "the Holy Spirit" (Rom. 1:7; 1 Cor. 1:3; Gal. 1:3).

(14) In the Church Epistles (Romans through Thessalonians), the Apostle Paul sends personal greetings from "God the Father and the Lord Jesus Christ." If "the Holy Spirit" were an integral and personal part of a triune Godhead, then surely he would have sent personal greetings as well. The fact that nowhere does "the Holy Spirit" send greetings to the Church is good evidence that he does not exist as a distinct being.

(15) When Paul does include additional persons in his greetings, salutations and adjurations, he names the elect angels, not "the Holy Spirit" (1 Tim. 5:21; cp. Luke 9:26 and Rev. 3:5).

(16) 1 John 1:3 says that "…our fellowship is with the Father and with his Son, Jesus Christ." Surely if "the Holy Spirit" were a Person in the

---

2. That John 7:39 says holy spirit did not exist is explained in Chapter 6.

Triune Godhead, we would have fellowship with him also. The fact that 1 John 1:3 does not mention fellowship with "the Holy Spirit" is good evidence that there is no such being.[3]

(17) In the Holy City of Revelation 21 and 22, both God and Jesus Christ are prominently featured. Each is said to be sitting on his throne (Rev. 22:1). If "the Holy Spirit" is a "co-eternal" member of a triune Godhead, it is strange indeed that he seems to have no seat of authority on the final throne. This is good evidence that there is One God, the Father, and One Lord, Jesus Christ, but not a separate person, "the Holy Spirit."

(18) When Jesus prayed, he prayed to the Father (John 17:1). Furthermore, he taught his disciples to pray to the Father (Matt. 6:9). After Jesus' resurrection, people prayed to him also (1 Cor. 1:2 and 3; 2 Cor. 12:8), but no prayer is ever offered to "the Holy Spirit."

(19) When Jesus prayed to the Father, he called Him "...the Lord of heaven and earth..." (Matt. 11:25). The Father would not be "the Lord" (singular) if "the Holy Spirit" were also a co-regent with the Father. The most logical reason why Jesus did not mention "the Holy Spirit" being lord with the Father is that there is no such being.

(20) When Jesus prayed to the Father in John 17, he called Him "the only true God" (John 17:3). The fact that Jesus does not mention "the Holy Spirit" as part of the true God is good evidence that such a being does not exist.

(21) Scripture says that a person who is antichrist "...denies the Father and the Son" (1 John 2:22b). Surely if there were a Trinity of "co-equal," "co-eternal" Persons making up the One God, then an antichrist would be said to deny the Trinity, or the Father and the Son and the Holy Spirit.

(22) Jesus taught his disciples that "the Father loves the Son and has placed everything in his hands" (John 3:35). If "the Holy Spirit" exists as an equal part of God, Jesus should have said that the Father and "the Holy Spirit" love the Son. In fact, "the Holy Spirit" is never said to love the Son.

---

3. In the NIV, Philippians 2:1 refers to "fellowship with the Spirit." A better translation of Philippians 2:1 is the KJV, which renders the phrase "fellowship of the Spirit [spirit]," pointing to the fellowship among believers who share a common spirit and who ought therefore to be able to get along with each other.

(23) Jesus made a distinction between himself and "the Holy Spirit," saying that if someone spoke against him it could be forgiven, but that blasphemy against "the Holy Spirit" would never be forgiven (Matt. 12:32). However, he never mentions "God" or "the Father." This is very good evidence that "the Holy Spirit" is another name for God, because it is unlikely that Jesus would omit the Father in that context.

(24) Scripture teaches that "…whoever continues in the teaching has both the Father and the Son" (2 John 1:9b). It seems evident that if there were a "Holy Spirit" who was "co-equal" and "co-eternal" with the Father and Son, he would be mentioned here. Conversely, Scripture teaches: "No one who denies the Son has the Father; whoever acknowledges the Son has the Father also" (1 John 2:23). The fact that only the Father and Son are mentioned is evidence that there is no other being, "the Holy Spirit."

(25) Jesus taught: "…I tell you the truth, the Son can do nothing by himself; he can do only what he sees his Father doing, because whatever the Father does the Son also does" (John 5:19b). If "the Holy Spirit" were a "co-equal" being with the Father, involved in reigning over the universe, then surely Jesus would do what he saw both the Father and "the Holy Spirit" doing. The fact that Jesus never said he followed the example of "the Holy Spirit" is good evidence that such an independent being does not exist.

(26) Jesus said to the crowds, "Do not work for the food which perishes, but for the food which endures to eternal life, which the Son of Man shall give to you, for on Him the Father, *even* God, has set His seal" (John 6:27-NASB). The first thing we learn from this verse is that Jesus called the Father "God." He apparently did not think of God as a Triune being of which he himself was a part. Furthermore, if "God" were composed of both the Father and "the Holy Spirit," then Jesus would have been sealed by them both, but "the Holy Spirit" is never mentioned.

(27) Exodus 23:20 mentions the angel of God's presence that would go before Israel in the wilderness. God has permitted angels to represent Him by speaking as if they were God Himself, and even to use His personal name, Yahweh. A few examples of this principle are Manoah and his wife (Judg. 13:21 and 22), Jacob wrestling (Gen. 32:1 and 30; Hosea 12:3–5), Moses (Exod. 3:2, 6 and 16), and Gideon (Judg. 6:12, 13, 16, and 22).

What is sometimes attributed to Jesus or to "the Holy Spirit" in the Old Testament is better explained by this principle of God manifesting Himself by means of an angelic messenger who speaks for Him in the first person ("I, the Lord," etc.) and manifests His glory.

(28) Though the Hebrew word for "spirit" (*ruach*) can refer to angels or evil spirits, which are persons or entities with a personality, the Hebrew usage of "the spirit of God" never refers to a person separate from, but a part of, God. Neither does the phrase, "the spirits of God," occur in a way that cannot be explained by God having angels (spirits) at His command rather than separate spiritual entities within a multipersonal God. For example, Revelation 1:4 refers to the "seven spirits" before the throne of God. However, there is no reason not to take the verse literally and believe that these are seven actual spirits who serve God and the Lord rather than a unique and confusing way to refer to "the Holy Spirit" or a triune Godhead.

(29) Trinitarian scholars admit that the concept of the Trinity cannot be substantiated in the Old Testament. In particular, "the Holy Spirit" as any kind of independent or distinct entity has no place in Old Testament revelation. Therefore, they say the concept must be derived from the New Testament. However, the New Testament gives no specific and certain teaching that there is a Trinity with one of the three "Persons" being "the Holy Spirit" who is "co-equal" with the Father and the Son. Surely if the doctrine of the Trinity were the foundation of biblical truth and the true nature of God, then it would be clearly set forth somewhere in the Bible. The fact that it is not is very good evidence that there is no Trinity, and hence no "Person" known as "the Holy Spirit."

(30) People have argued that the "spirit of truth" in John 14:17 is a person. If this is true, then "the spirit of error" in 1 John 4:6 (KJV) would also have to be a person, since the two are directly contrasted. The better explanation is that each "spirit" represents an influence or power under which a person acts, but neither is a person in itself.

(31) The "Spirit [spirit] of your Father," is synonymous with "the Holy Spirit," and is said to speak in our stead on certain occasions when we might be brought before men for possible persecution or trial (Matt.10:19 and 20; Mark 13:11; Luke 12:12). On the same topic, Luke 21:15 says

that Christ will give us "…a mouth and wisdom, which all your [our] adversaries shall not be able to gainsay or resist." Rather than saying that a person called "the Holy Spirit" will speak through us, these verses teach that we will be inspired by the supernatural power of God and Christ to speak as they give us guidance.

(32) The spirit of God is referred to as "the helper" (sometimes known as "the Comforter" or "the Encourager") in John 14:16, 26, 15:26, and 16:7. "Helper" is a masculine noun, so masculine pronouns are used with it. However, it is clear from Christ's teaching that the helper is not a person. John 14:26 calls it "the holy spirit," and its attributes match those of the gift of holy spirit. It was "with" the Apostles, but would be "in" them (John 14:17), which is what happened when holy spirit went from being with or "upon" people in the Old Testament and Gospels to being "in" people in the Church and the Millennial Kingdom. The helper (the holy spirit) is sent by the Father (John 14:26) and Jesus (John 16:7), and it does not speak on its own, but it speaks "only what he [it] hears" (John 16:13). Nevertheless, there are distinct overtones of the figure of speech *personification* in John, which occurs when the qualities of a person are attributed to things that have no personality or consciousness.[4] "Wisdom" is personified in Proverbs 8 and 9, for example. In Isaiah 14:8 (KJV) the trees are said to "rejoice" and speak. The gift of holy spirit is the nature of God, and as such it works in us, in conflict with our sin nature, to form us into the image of Christ. So, personifying it and saying that it guides, teaches, speaks, etc. is highly appropriate.

(33 Jesus said that the "helper" would fill the void created by his going to the Father (John 14:12). Yet, by this spirit, he was the one who would still be present: "…I will come to you" (John 14:18); "I am in you" (John 14:20); and I will "show myself" (John 14:21). By this spirit, his work with them would continue: it "will teach you" (John 14:26); it "will remind you of everything I have said…" (John 14:26); it "will testify about me" (John 15:26); it "will guide you into all truth…" (John 16:13); it "… will bring glory to me by taking what is mine and making it known to you" (John 16:14). It seems clear that the "helper" is not someone other than Jesus but rather a way that Jesus himself can be present. It makes

---

4. Bullinger, *op. cit., Figures of Speech*, pp. 861–869.

sense that "the holy spirit" is the gift of God that allows Jesus to be present with us and in us.

(34) All of these statements point to the role of the gift of holy spirit in continuing the work that Jesus started and even empowering his followers for greater works. This spirit is not independent and self-existent but is "the mind of Christ" within the believer, guiding, teaching, reminding, and pointing the believer to follow his Lord and Savior. This spirit is not "co-equal" when by its very design it is subservient to God and Christ. It carries the personal presence of God and Christ into the life of every believer.

(35) If the spirit of God were a unique and separate person, and if having "spirit" were prerequisite to having a unique and separate personality, then the person called "the Spirit of God" would have to have his own "spirit" peculiar to himself and distinct from the Father and Son. Otherwise, he could not be said to have a separate "personality." If "God" were three equal persons, the third person can no more be "the spirit" of the first person than the first person can be "the spirit" of the third person. We can avoid this awkward rationale by recognizing that "the spirit of God" does not have a separate personality, but is the power, influence, sufficiency, fullness, or some extension of the Father, who is the real and unitary person called "the One True God."

(36) Many words associated with God's spirit give it the attributes of a liquid. Such language is consistent with the spirit being God's presence and power. We are baptized (literally "dipped") with and in it like water (Matt. 3:11; Acts 1:5). We are all made to "drink" from the same spirit, as from a well or fountain (1 Cor. 12:13). It is written on our hearts like ink (2 Cor. 3:3). We are "anointed" with it, like oil (Acts 10:38; 2 Cor. 1:21; 1 John 2:27). We are "sealed" with it as with melted wax (Eph. 1:13). It is "poured out" on us (Acts 10:45; Rom. 5:5). It is "measured" as if it had volume (2 Kings 2:9; John 3:34-KJV). We are to be "filled" with it (Acts 2:4; Eph. 5:18). This "filling" is to capacity at the New Birth and to overflowing as we act according to its influence. Even the use of spirit as "wind" implies a liquidity, for air masses behave as a fluid, flowing from areas of higher to lower pressure. All this figurative language is designed

to point us to the truth that the spirit of God is the invisible power and influence of God.

(37) In Acts 5:3, Peter says Ananias lied to "the Holy Spirit," and in verse 4 Peter says he lied to "God." This is an example of a very Semitic way of expression. It is common in Eastern and thus biblical writing to create a parallelism of equivalent terms. Thus, what Peter said is not evidence that Ananias lied to two separate persons. If that were the case, why would verse 4 not say that Peter lied to "the Father" instead of to "God"?[5]

(38) The term "Holy Spirit" (properly "holy spirit") is used synonymously and interchangeably with "the spirit of Jesus" (Acts 16:7); "the spirit of the Lord" (Luke 4:18, etc.); "the spirit of his son" (Gal. 4:6); and "…the spirit of Jesus Christ…" (Phil. 1:19). In this usage, "the spirit" is the active power of Jesus Christ, who fills believers with holy spirit and then, through it, guides them to do the will of God. He is, after all, the expert in how humans can be brought to obey the will of God without coercion or intimidation. The following are examples of the interrelationship and interdependence between Jesus Christ and the spirit.

> (A) Acts 13:2 (ASV) says, "…The Holy Spirit said, Separate me Barnabas and Saul for the work whereunto I have called them.'" Later, in Acts 16:6, amidst the work Paul was called to, "the Holy Spirit" kept Paul and his companions from preaching in Asia. Verse 7 says that the "spirit of Jesus" would not allow them to enter Bithynia.

> (B) 2 Corinthians 3:17 and 18 says that the Lord (Jesus) is "the Spirit." This is an appropriate reference to Jesus now that he is in his new, spiritual body. He has been invested with all spiritual authority and power to effectively carry out his responsibility as the Head of his Body. By his "spirit," he is able to guide and direct his many servants.

> (C) Galatians 5:22 and 23 list the "fruit of the spirit" (the nature of Jesus Christ); John 15:5 says, "…If a man remains in me and I in him, he will bear much fruit…."

---

5. For more on this verse see our book: *op. cit., One God & One Lord*, Appendix A.

(D) We are sanctified by the spirit (2 Thess. 2:13); we are sanctified in Christ Jesus (1 Cor. 1:2), whom God made to be sanctification for us.

(E) The gift of holy spirit is the helper (*parakletos*); we have an advocate (*parakletos*) with the Father, Jesus Christ the righteous (1 John 2:1-KJV).

(F) We are strengthened by the spirit in the inner man (Eph. 3:16); Christ dwells in our hearts (Eph. 3:17).

(G) We have access to the Father by the spirit (Eph. 2:18); in Christ and through faith in him we have confidence and access to God (Eph. 3:11 and 12).

(H) The spirit apportions to each one individually as he wills (1 Cor. 12:11); The Lord Jesus pours out the spirit (Acts 2:33) and gave some to be apostles, some to be prophets, etc. (Eph. 4:11).

(I) The spirit intercedes for us (Rom. 8:26); Christ Jesus intercedes for us (Rom. 8:34).

(J) The Spirit says to the churches… (Rev. 2:7); the revelation of Jesus Christ…to show to his servants (Rev. 1:1).

(39) Many Trinitarians assert that "the Holy Spirit" comes and permanently dwells within a believer when he accepts Jesus Christ as his Savior. But many also teach that "the Holy Spirit" comes upon a believer **after** he is born again. They also pray for "the Holy Spirit" to attend their meetings, and welcome "Him" to come as "He" desires. This puts them in the difficult position of having to explain how a Christian can have the "person" of "the Holy Spirit" simultaneously dwelling in him while at the same time coming and going from Christian meetings.

The simple answer to this dilemma is that there are two usages of "the spirit" that must be distinguished. One is "the gift of God's nature that is permanently received when a person is born again." The other is "the power and influence of God" as He manifests His presence in His Creation (Gen. 1:1) and among His people (2 Chron. 5:14). In contrast to the gift, this can wax and wane according to the faith of those present and the will of God in the situation. The gift of God's nature, holy spirit, is not always being energized into manifestation. God, "the Holy Spirit" (the Giver), energizes the spirit within believers as they act in faith (Acts 2:4).

(40) The gospel of Matthew has been said to show the Trinity. It says, "... baptizing them in the name of the Father, and of the Son and of the Holy Ghost" (Matt. 28:19-KJV). However, this verse is quoted in a different form by the early Church Fathers, notably Eusebius (340 A.D.), who quotes the verse at least 18 times as follows: "... baptizing them in my name." This agrees with the testimony of the book of Acts and Paul's Epistles, which associate only the name of Jesus Christ with baptism. Even if this verse reads as found in modern versions today, it does not mention the Trinity or say that the three are one God, or even that "the Holy Spirit" is a separate "person" from God. All it says is there is the Father, the Son, and the holy spirit, which we agree is correct. There is no reason to believe that "the holy spirit" refers to a "Person." If the phrase is indeed in the original text, it refers to the gift of God.

(41) God is said to have a throne (1 Kings 22:19; Dan. 7:9), and inhabit heaven as His dwelling place (1 Kings 8:30, 39, 43, 49), yet "heaven and the highest heaven cannot contain" Him (1 Kings 8:27). So how can He have a throne and a dwelling place and yet be uncontainable? Psalm 139:7 indicates that God's **spirit** and His **presence** can be equivalent terms. God is therefore omnipresent by His "spirit," which is not a separate "person." This presence can also be extended by His personal ministers and agents, whether angels, Christ, or believers. None of these is a separate person who is also "God," but rather they are empowered agents who are equipped to do the will of God.

Appendix E

"Slain in the Spirit"

The experience called "slain in the Spirit" usually occurs in churches when the minister or speaker has an altar call and puts his hand on the forehead of the person who has come forward for ministering, who then falls over. Sometimes the minister does not even have to touch people, but only gestures toward them and they fall down. When they fall, the people may be unconscious, semi-conscious, or fully conscious. Occasionally, even people in the pews or the audience, fall over when the minister gestures or waves his arm at them.

The whole experience of slain in the Spirit is hotly debated, with some people claiming it is a powerful move of God, while others saying it is from the Devil. We believe that slain in the Spirit, as it is usually seen in churches and on television, occurs as the result of one, or a combination of, peoples' free will action, emotional response, and/or demonic manifestations. That is not to say that God does not move powerfully in people's lives in unusual ways, but when He does, He never contradicts His Word, which contains all things pertaining to "life and godliness."

The most important thing that Christians must keep in mind when studying spiritual *matters* is that the Word of God is always our only rule of faith and practice. God does not want us to be ignorant about spiritual *matters* (1 Cor. 12:1) because they hold such opportunity for both deliverance and bondage. For too many Christians, "spiritual experiences" and "sincerity" are given priority over the written Word of God as the criteria to determine doctrinal truth and practice.[1] Furthermore, all too often Christians use their experiences to validate the Word of God rather than allowing the written Word to be the ultimate "discerner" (Heb. 4:12-

---

1. A major reason for this is that most people do not read and study the Bible. They may own one, but do not read it regularly. Furthermore, when they do read it, they do not understand much of what they read. So it is natural for them to give more credence to what they experience than to the Word. The solution to this is for Christians to read the Word of God regularly and ask questions about what they do not understand until they learn it.

KJV) of the things that pertain to life and godliness (2 Pet. 1:3). This leaves them open to counterfeit spiritual experiences. "Counterfeit?" you ask. Yes, the Devil is a spirit being who is adept at creating spiritual experiences for worshipers of all faiths. The Bible calls these "… counterfeit miracles, signs and wonders" (2 Thess. 2:9). It is vital for Christians to learn to be discerning in worship lest they displease the God and Lord they seek to honor and deceive themselves.

The conflict between the truth of Scripture (which may or may not have specific emotional appeal) and religious or spiritual experiences (which are by nature exciting and impressive) has been going on for centuries. For example, when Jesus sent out his disciples, they "returned with joy" because of what they had experienced, and said, "…Lord, even the demons submit to us…" (Luke 10:17). Jesus then reminded them, "… do not rejoice that the spirits submit to you, but rejoice that your names are written in heaven" (Luke 10:20). The same tension exists today.

Certainly, genuine spiritual phenomena are to be expected in the life of a Christian, but we must diligently examine these occurrences. The Bible gives many examples of false prophets who deceived people by demonstrations of spiritual power. The magicians of Egypt turned sticks into snakes, but their power was not from the true God. Thank God that He gave us His Word so that we have a standard by which to discern His will. It is only by carefully examining one's experiences in light of the principles of the Word of God that the power or force behind the experience can be determined.

A cardinal rule is that we do not abandon what we understand from Scripture when faced with an experience that we do not fully understand. So, regarding the subject in question, being slain in the Spirit, what do we know from God's Word? There are six major biblical truths that pertain to the practice of ministers "slaying" people in the spirit.

First, we know that free will is a precious gift from our Creator, and that He is very slow to do anything that might diminish our ability to choose what we say and do. God is the perfect gentleman, and is very respectful of people's right to choose to believe, love, and obey Him. Love is not true love without the freedom not to respond to that love, and God graciously gives us that freedom. We are not puppets. The countless imperative verbs in Scripture, and the number of times He asks us to choose, clearly indicate that the choice is up to us whether or not to obey God's loving directives.[2]

However, God's love is also quite parental, and every parent knows that at times it is loving to provide discipline and correction of one's child to keep him or her on a safe and healthy path. This involves a variety of temporary infringements on the child's freedom (grounding, time out, etc.) to the end that he can better handle responsibility and freedom in the future. As parenting involves preparing children for the realities of adulthood, the purpose of God's "parental" love is to bring us into spiritual maturity and greater understanding

> **God's love is also quite parental, and every parent knows that at times it is loving to provide discipline and correction of one's child to keep him or her on a safe and healthy path.**

of His purposes so that we might know Him better and more effectually serve others on His behalf.

There are records in the Bible where God directly or indirectly (i.e., through an angel) interferes with a person's free will. This happens, however, only under specific conditions:

- God already has a relationship with the person whose commitment to Him is apparent.
- God's purpose in the situation is clear.
- The person in question is standing against that purpose, whether ignorantly or deliberately.
- The condition of discipline or restraint is temporary.
- There is great profit evidenced either in the person's ministry or by making him an example to others that God is not to be trifled with.

An example of this is when the priest Zechariah, the father of John the Baptist, was told he would not be able to speak for a season (Luke 1:5–23, 59–79). This occurred because of his lack of faith in the angel's announcement that he and Elizabeth would have a child who would

---

2. We have the freedom of will to obey God or not, which is why He takes so much time instructing us what to do and is disappointed when we do not obey. Also, many verses testify to the fact that we make choices whether or not to be godly (cp. Deut. 30:19; Judg. 5:8; 1 Sam. 8:18; Ps. 119:30; Prov. 1:29; Isa. 1:29, 56:4; Phil. 1:22).

be a mighty prophet and prepare the way for the Savior. His muteness was not painful, and because he was a priest, it kept him from being able to minister in the Temple, which gave him time to prepare with his wife for the birth of their child. Furthermore, when this season of being mute was over, he prophesied powerfully about his son's ministry. This record meets all five of the above conditions.

Another example is Paul being blinded by the glory of the Lord (Acts 9:3–9). Paul was deeply committed to being in God's will but was ignorantly resisting Him and God needed to get his full attention. As with Zechariah, Paul's brief period of blindness was redemptive. It was not painful and it gave him time to repent of his past actions and reassess his thinking about Scripture and the Messiah.

Zechariah and Paul were deeply committed to doing God's will, but in ignorance were actually standing against His righteous purposes. Their actions provoked God's redemptive rebuke, also known as "… the discipline of the Lord…" (Heb. 12:5–10-RSV). What happened to Paul and Zechariah was temporary and redemptive. It was not a Satanic attack, nor was it painful or permanent.

We must understand that when someone who loves God opposes Him out of ignorance, the Devil is more than happy to take advantage of the situation. There are occasions when God will chastise a believer who is willfully disobeying Him, but He never does so by harming him. Any tragedy that befalls a believer in such a situation is due to the Devil taking advantage of the situation. A good example of this would be the Christians who misunderstand Mark 16:18 and pick up poisonous snakes in their church service. Their intention is good, but they are nonetheless acting out of ignorance and many of them have been bitten, some fatally. That is not "…the discipline of the Lord…," because God does not kill anyone in order to correct them.[3] That is disobedience out of ignorance, which, in some cases, can have deadly consequences.

---

3. God is not the cause of sickness and death today. That is not to say that He has not nor will not judge the wicked, and kill them, because He has, for example, in the Flood of Noah. Also, He is willing to defend His people, as when He closed the waters of the Sea over Pharaoh and his army. Never does He kill His own people. For a detailed study of this important subject, see our book, op. cit., Don't Blame God!

Second, we know that it is the Devil who wants to control people by infiltrating their minds, demonizing them, and thus making them do things contrary to God's will and purposes (Acts 10:38, etc.). We use the word "demonize," not "possess." The Greek is *daimonizomai*, which means to be afflicted by a demon. The word "possess" is misleading and too restrictive. First, a person can be afflicted by a demon in many ways. A person in a haunted house who is scared because of noises, apparitions, moving objects, etc., is "demonized" in the biblical sense of the word. He is afflicted by a demon, but not "possessed" in the way the word is generally used. Second, the demon, even if inside the person, does not own him, so "possess" is misleading. The demon simply takes residence in the person and then does his evil work.

> **The Devil is interested only in stealing, killing, and destroying God's people, and, if he can, he will cause people to do things that they do not want to do, or to do things that make Christianity look bad.**

Both Christians and non-Christians can be demonized. The Devil is interested only in stealing, killing, and destroying God's people, and, if he can, he will cause people to do things that they do not want to do, things that make Christianity look bad. In 1 Corinthians 14, Paul addresses the issue of the corporate witness of the Church in worship.

1 Corinthians 14:23 (RSV)
If, therefore, the whole church assembles and all speak in tongues, and outsiders or unbelievers enter, will they not say that you are mad [demonized]?[4]

In this verse, the Lord, via Paul, sternly sets forth that there should be no speaking in tongues without interpretation in the congregation because some might come into the assembly and think the believers were taken over by demons. This is a huge point. The Lord does not want to open the door for anyone to even **think** that Christians are demonized. The

---

4. We explain why we say "mad" really refers to being "demonized" in footnote 4, on 1 Corinthians 14:23 in Chapter 10, "Speaking in Tongues."

fact that many congregations today disobey this directive does not mean they are demonized, but an observer may think they are.

If the Lord was so careful to keep his people from being accused of being demonized in the first century, are we to believe that he now "slays" people and causes them to behave even more bizarrely than if everyone in the congregation were to speak in tongues at the same time? We think not. There is no question that not only outsiders, but also Christians themselves, are very divided about whether being slain in the Spirit is of God, the Devil, or of one's own action. This division and accusation is exactly what God was trying to avoid in the first century, so we find it hard to believe that He would now introduce such a controversial and divisive act of power without Scriptures to clearly support it, and there are none. The manifestation of speaking in tongues is controversial, but Scripture is very clear about it.[5] Given the aforementioned inconsistency between God's Word and the strange behavior of being slain in the Spirit as it is seen in most churches, we do not believe it is God's initiative.

Third, we know that the true God is a God of decency and order, and not the author of confusion (1 Cor. 14:33 and 40). Some worship services become so "out of control" with so-called "spiritual manifestations" that no teaching of the Word of God is possible. We do not see how this is edifying the Church, which the Apostle Paul makes the central goal of what is allowable in public worship. Is it really "decent and in order" to have people lying all over the floor in church, even if the women in dresses are covered with towels? Is there any clear purpose or profit to such a scene? In a pragmatic sense, despite the fact that many groups have "catchers" behind people to break their fall, the possibility of physical injury is certainly present, and has occurred on occasion. Would it ever be the will of God to hurt a believer coming to participate in worship? We think not.

Fourth, we know that when our heavenly Father does something, there is always purpose and profit in it (1 Cor. 12:7, 14:6). Some people report healings, visions, deliverance from demons, and other profitable aspects of

---

5. The Devil has been so successful in sowing division into the Christian Church that there are few biblical doctrines that are not controversial. However, there is a difference between a doctrine that is set forth in Scripture but interpreted differently by Christians, and a doctrine that is not based on any Scripture at all.

the experience of "being under the power" (as some call it). In those cases, although we would be slow to condemn the experience as ungodly, we are cautious, recognizing that demons can give people positive experiences to win them over, such as when a false prophet gives true information to get the person to believe and thus be "set up" for the future.[6] The overall profit to the Body of Christ must be considered as well.

Some people report that they were unconscious and not aware of any profit other than the experience itself. In these cases, we strongly suspect the influence of counterfeit, demonic power. There are only nine ways listed in 1 Corinthians 12:8–10 that the holy spirit is to be manifested in the Church, and all are profitable or "for the general good." These are a message of wisdom, a message of knowledge, faith, gifts of healings, miracles, prophecy, discerning of spirits, speaking in tongues, and interpretation of tongues. Being slain in the Spirit is unlike any of those nine manifestations, and does not merit being referred to as a "manifestation" of the true spirit of God. At best, being "slain" might qualify as an occasional spiritual phenomenon, but certainly not something that has clear biblical warrant or precedent. If it is a God-given phenomenon, it will have evident profit for the person who has the experience, and also profit the Church at large.

We are aware that the people ministering slain in the Spirit to congregations speak of it as "new wine," a new move of God, but we do not think so. Throughout history God has moved in ways that coincide with His Word, which He thought final enough to say that no one should add to it (Rev. 22:18). We think the points we made above about the general principles by which God works with people and in history show that what we said in the opening paragraphs (that slain in the Spirit is due to one or more of people's free will action, emotional response, and/or demonic manifestations) is valid.

Fifth, we know that in nearly every biblical record where someone fell down in the presence of God, the Lord, or an angel, he fell on his face (a sign of respect in the Eastern culture), was not unconscious (he could still hear the angel), and was told to get up before the angel would give

6. Deuteronomy 13:1–5 speaks of those who prophecy that something will come to pass, and it does, and who then they use their credibility to try to lead people away from the true God.

him the message (Dan. 10:8–11). According to the biblical evidence, God seems considerably more interested in getting people to stand up and receive His Word and His blessings than He is in knocking them down and rendering them semi-conscious or unable to easily communicate.[7]

Sixth, there is no biblical evidence of a minister of the Lord Jesus Christ knocking people down "under the power." When Peter ministered to the people in Cornelius' household (Acts 10:34–46), they received the holy spirit and manifested speaking in tongues while he was in the process of speaking to them. He did not lay a hand on them or even gesture toward them. One can look in vain for any biblical example of what has become all too common in evangelical circles these days, where ministers lay hands on people and expect them to fall down.

> **There is no biblical evidence of a minister of the Lord Jesus Christ knocking people down under the power of the Lord.**

A good question to ask, then, is whether a person who "fell under the power" did so by his own choice or whether he was acted upon by a force outside of his own free will. Our experience is that the majority of believers who fall down like this do so by their own volition because they have been taught this is the thing to do and that it is a legitimate "manifestation of the spirit." This is especially the case when it is some well-known Christian personality who lays his or her hands on them. It seems they do not want to be one of the "unspiritual" ones who does not receive the Lord's "blessing." We have often wondered why being knocked to the ground is considered a blessing? Would an unbeliever think that being knocked unconscious by God was honoring his choice to believe?

Keeping in mind the six criteria we have cited above, what about those who definitely **were** acted upon by a force that rendered them unconscious. Was it God Almighty who knocked them over? Not unless He says so in

---

7. It is certainly worth noting that people who are slain in the Spirit fall backwards. In the Bible, falling or going backwards was a sign of God's displeasure or judgment, or the person's disobedience or shame. No one who was being blessed by God fell backward. There are numerous examples of falling or going backward, which can be clearly seen in the King James Version: Genesis 49:17; 1 Samuel 4:18; Psalm 40:14, 70:2; Isaiah 1:4, 28:13, 44:25, 59:14; Jeremiah 7:24, 15:6; Lamentations 1:8; John 18:6.

His Word, and we do not find this in the pages of Scripture. However, demons are ready, willing, and able to take over a part of the minds of those who open themselves up to let "the spirit" have its way. But is this spirit the holy spirit of the Lord or a demonic spirit? The ability to focus "kundalini energy" is one form of Eastern religious worship, and members of a variety of non-Christian religions who practice forms of witchcraft do experience blacking out, being knocked over, etc. This should at least give Christians pause to reflect upon what the Bible says on this subject before submitting to the ministry of someone who "slays" people in the Spirit.

It remains an important question whether or not a person's will was usurped. Did he fall down, or was he knocked down? We have heard rather bizarre testimonies of people who were "knocked flat" or even "thrown across the room," supposedly by "the power of God." At best, this is highly suspect. It is therefore our general conclusion that if and when a person is overpowered by a force outside his free will, and is thereby knocked to the ground, that force is not from the true God, but from Satan. We will hold this view until it can be demonstrated to us that there was long-term godly fruit as a direct result of such an experience. We have seen many instances of God healing people without them falling down upon the floor.

We know there are people who testify that the Lord healed them during such an experience. That is certainly possible, because we know that healing is the will of God, and that He and the Lord Jesus are always doing all they can to bring healing to pass for anyone they can. However, biblically, and generally in our experience, such healing occurs in response to active faith in the individual who is seeking healing, and not a function of getting slain in the Spirit by a minister. Praise God for anyone who is healed, but we assert that it was not "falling under the power" that healed them. It was God's love and grace in response to their faith.

Jesus emphasized the role of individual faith when he said, "...your faith has healed you" (Matt. 9:22; Luke 18:42). The context of those healings shows they could not be done without the power of God in evidence, but by emphasizing the role of faith, Jesus was teaching them that healing and miracles are not just sovereign acts of God. Rather, they are done in conjunction with one's faith and trust in God's power as it resides in those who manifest that power. Paul's handkerchiefs (Acts 19:12) and Jesus' spit (Mark 8:23) brought healing because people had faith in the power of God conveyed through these godly men.

The fact that some people are healed when they are slain in the Spirit does not necessarily indicate that the "slain" part of the experience was of God. Although we like to be able to neatly categorize spiritual experiences into "good" and "evil," there can be both in any given experience. In that sense, spiritual experiences are like people. There can be both bad and good in the same package. God is always at work to bless people, and if someone has faith that he will be healed if a certain minister touches him, then God honors this faith even if the minister is not acting for God at the time. We see that with Eli in the book of Samuel. He himself was actively disobeying God, and was so full of wrong judgments that he thought Hannah, who was praying, was drunk. Yet he blessed her, which changed her whole attitude and she became pregnant with Samuel (1 Sam. 1:12–20).

The Devil is a liar and very crafty, and he will do anything to discredit God. That includes making true statements to get people's attention, and then introducing error later on. Psychics give much factual information, and the woman with the demon in Acts 16 rightly spoke the truth about Paul and his companions when she said, "…These men are servants of the Most High God, who are telling you the way to be saved" (Acts 16:17b). If demons did only evil, or gave only false information, they would quickly be discovered, and would not be able to sow confusion among believers. Some people get help from psychics, tarot card readers, "white witches," etc., and then wonder why God forbids those practices. God forbids them because the demons do good only to get an opportunity to do evil. We have personally ministered to people who had been slain in the Spirit and had a wonderful experience. However, after going back several times they began to have disturbing things happen in their lives, and ended up having to seek spiritual deliverance. We have never experienced that with anyone who was prayed for or ministered to by a Christian healer who did not practice slain in the Spirit or the other "new outpourings" such as "holy laughter," etc.

Another thing the Devil is adept at is leading people from truth into error. He knows he cannot now effectively refute speaking in tongues, prophecy, etc., because there is too much biblical evidence for those manifestations and too many people speaking in tongues and prophesying. So what can he do to lead people away from God? Introduce unbiblical manifestations that confuse and divide them. People who seek power and experience will go along with these new manifestations of power, while people who search for Scriptural support will hold back and the congregation will be divided—a main aim of the Devil.

One reason we have heard why people think that being slain in the Spirit is from God is that sometimes people pray, "Lord, if this is not from you, do not let it happen to me." Then they go up to the front of the church, and when "slain" by the minister, they believe that the experience must have been from God. This is not proper thinking. God often cannot protect someone from a harmful experience he enters into ignorantly but willingly. This is a huge point and has been confirmed many times. The "snake handlers" who are bitten and die are a good example. Another is missionaries who travel overseas and eat unfamiliar food, ignorant of what it will do to them. Many of them get indigestion (or worse) even though they have prayed for the food. God expects us to use wisdom, and not willingly enter into something that may be harmful.

We need to say more about "miracles" and "phenomena."[8] There are occasions when God goes "above and beyond" the general pattern of reciprocal relationship that He has established with human beings. In these cases, He acts independently of our cooperation, and does what can be called either miracles or phenomena. Miracles are rare and unusual supernatural acts of God that are creative and responsive to particular situations, and sometimes involve God superseding natural laws or the natural course of events. They are inextricably linked to His own purposes, are an important part of His relationship with people, and will never be

---

8. The dictionary definition of a phenomenon (plural = phenomena) is: "An occurrence or circumstance that is perceptible by the five senses; an unusual or significant event or occurrence." For the purposes of clarity as we study the Bible, when the Lord gives information in a rare, unusual, unpredictable way, we say that is a phenomenon. Thus, phenomena are a subset of miracles. Miracles are supernatural acts of God but their purpose is not necessarily to communicate information. When the sun stood still for Joshua, it was a miracle but not a phenomenon. When God wrote on the wall of Belshazzar's palace, it was a miracle that was also a phenomenon.

at odds with the written Word. In fact, they significantly support what He has revealed about His character and His methods.

Miracles and phenomena can be perceived by unbelievers, whether or not they understand what is going on, and thus they are not visions or subjective experiences. With the exception of the manifestation of miracles, they are not promised to God's people, nor can they be expected or demanded. They demonstrate His love and support of His people, and they also glorify Him and attract people to Him. In many cases they are a response to faith and to people's need. Nevertheless, they are not the standard of truth, or even a sign that someone is walking in truth or faith. John the Baptist, as great as he was, did no miracles (John 10:41). Though we cannot totally comprehend the whole of God's purposes in manifesting miracles, we can discern that at various times phenomena show forth His judgment, mercy, protection, glory, and approval. In short, God always has a good reason for displaying His power.

Some examples of miracles and phenomena are: the Flood of Noah; the scattering of languages at the Tower of Babel; fire and brimstone raining upon Sodom and Gomorrah; the pillar of fire at night and the cloud by day that led Israel through the wilderness; the finger of God writing the Law onto tablets of stone; fire falling from heaven to light the sacrifices; the earth swallowing up Dothan; Balaam's donkey talking to him; the writing that appeared on the wall at Belshazzar's feast; Zachariah's muteness; the darkness upon the earth the afternoon of Christ's crucifixion; the earthquake that rolled back the stone on his sepulcher; the cloven tongues of fire and sound of the mighty wind on Pentecost; the house shaking (Acts 4:31); the brilliant light and Paul's subsequent blindness; the Philippian prison earthquake; the appearance of angels throughout the Word; and perhaps the miracle, which is still to come, that is the melting of the present heaven and earth with fervent heat.

We bring up miracles and phenomena because God will be God and move upon the earth for the benefit of His people as He sees fit. The power and variety of these biblically recorded miracles and phenomena lead us to be cautious and discerning as we evaluate slain in the Spirit and other experiences that the Bible does not specifically sanction, for though we have seen that God is infinitely creative and often unpredictable, it is clear that each of the biblical miracles and phenomena had a purpose and a profit. Let us emphasize once again that God's ways will be in concert with His character of love and justice as revealed in His written Word. He will not do evil that good may come (Rom. 3:8), or "push people around" so that they might believe.

In regard to this issue of being slain in the Spirit, we must distinguish between the genuine power of God in action and the emotional or physical reaction that a person may have in response to it. God's power is awesome and ultimate, and in His righteous and holy presence, the sinful man of flesh may: "fall on his face" (Gen. 17:3), "fall on his knees" (2 Kings 1:13), become as one whom wine has overcome (Jer. 23:9), become "overwhelmed" (Dan. 10:7), "turned...pale" (Dan. 10:8), "tremble" (Dan. 10:11), "shook" (Matt. 28:4), "become like dead men" (Matt. 28:4), "become dumb" (Luke 1:20), and "fall to the ground" (Acts 9:4). If a person faints while being ministered to, we should say that he fainted. We should not say he was slain in the Spirit and attribute to God what is actually the frailty of the flesh.

We must also recognize that sometimes when the power of God touches a person, his behavior may be the result of a demon being expelled from him. Clearly, this is a time for the manifestation of the spirit called "discerning of spirits," because one would not want to attribute the activity of demons to God. When demons are stirred up in a person during worship, or while he is listening to the teaching of the Word, or by spiritual warfare, the appropriate response is to take authority over the demon and cast it out by the power of the Lord Jesus Christ. Unfortunately, many Christians are ignorant of demons and their activities, and naively think that all unusual manifestations are the work of God. This naiveté has even extended to such extremes as saying that people writhing around on stage like serpents are doing so because of "the Holy Spirit."

Other behaviors that have been baptized as evidences of "the Holy Spirit" are barking like dogs, clucking like chickens, roaring like lions, laughing uncontrollably for hours, etc. In such situations, spiritually mature believers should consider the possibility that the person is either under the power of a demon or in the process of being delivered from demonic strongholds. In such cases, the individuals should be taken aside and led into deliverance from the demons that have manifested themselves. It is tragic that many of God's people are so ignorant of spiritual *matters* that they mistake demonic manifestations for those prompted by the holy spirit of God.

A major part of the spiritual battle raging between God and the Devil is the battle of words. Given the "bottom line" that God is love, the very terminology, slain in the Spirit, is offensive to many Christians, because "to slay" means "to murder," and, of course, murder is something God specifically condemns in the Ten Commandments ("You shall not murder" is the accurate translation in Exod. 20:13). The phrase, slain in the Spirit, casually used by many sincere Christians, subtly implants in people's minds the idea that God can and will act upon His people in such a way as to incapacitate them. Not so.

In fact, the Pentecostal circles in which the phenomenon of slain in the Spirit was first manifested were marked by a strong aversion to leadership of a worship service by ministers. Complete "submission to the Spirit" was encouraged and this fostered a climate that discouraged spiritual discernment. Though the upside of this was the renewal of the godly manifestation of speaking in tongues in the Christian Church, ungodly manifestations were also let in, like being slain in the Spirit. Our challenge is to not throw out the baby with the bathwater spiritually, but to allow the Word of God, the "sword of the spirit," to be our faithful guide in all spiritual matters.

In closing, we must emphasize the importance of going to the written Word of God as the only rule of faith and practice in everything, and especially spiritual *matters*. We certainly do not want to be guilty of labeling as satanic something that God is doing in a person's life. At the same time, we do not want to be guilty of discouraging discernment among God's people and thus leaving them vulnerable to satanic counterfeits. Let us neither put God in any box of our own making nor attribute to Him things for which He does not claim responsibility. Let us beseech Him to continue to expand our understanding of His glory and power and to grant us discernment to perceive the counterfeit spirit power manifested by His archenemy, the Devil. God's power will be manifest among those who seek to glorify, honor, and serve Him and who walk in obedience to Him and His written Word.

Bibliography

Anstey, Martin. *How to Master the Bible*. Pickering & Inglis, London.

Arndt, William, and Wilbur F. Gingrich. *A Greek-English Lexicon of the New Testament and Other Early Christian Literature*. University of Chicago Press, Chicago, 1979.

Barrett, C. K. *Black's New Testament Commentary: The First Epistle to the Corinthians*. Hendrickson Publishers, Peabody, MA, 1968.

Bromiley, Geoffrey, editor. *The International Standard Bible Encyclopedia*. William B. Eerdmans Publishing Company, Grand Rapids, 1982.

Broughton, James H. and Peter J. Southgate. *The Trinity: True or False*. "The Dawn" Book Supply, Nottingham, England 1995.

Bruce, F. F. *The New International Commentary on the New Testament: The Book of Acts*. William B. Eerdmans Publishing Company, Grand Rapids, MI, 1988.

Bullinger, E. W. *Commentary on Revelation*. Kregel Publications, Grand Rapids, MI, reprinted 1984.

Bullinger, E. W. The Companion Bible. Zondervan Bible Publishers, Grand Rapids, MI, reprinted 1974.

Bullinger, E. W. *Figures of Speech Used in the Bible*. Baker Book House, Grand Rapids, MI, reprinted 1968.

Bullinger, E. W. *Word Studies on the Holy Spirit*. Kregel Publications, Grand Rapids, MI, 1979.

Butler Trent, editor. *Holman Bible Dictionary*. Holman Bible Publishers, Nashville, TN, 1991.

Buzzard, Anthony, and Charles Hunting. *The Doctrine of the Trinity; Christianity's Self-Inflicted Wound*. International Scholars Publications, New York, 1998.

Collins, Raymond. *Sacra Pagina: First Corinthians*. The Liturgical Press, Collegeville, MN, 1999.

Edersheim, Alfred. *Bible History: Old Testament*. William B. Eerdmans Publishing Company, Grand Rapids, MI, reprinted 1975.

Elwell, Walter. *Evangelical Dictionary of Theology*. Baker Book House, Grand Rapids, MI, 1984.

Farley, Fredrick A. *The Scripture Doctrine of the Father, Son, and Holy Ghost.* Boston, 1873. Reprinted by Spirit & Truth Fellowship International, Martinsville, IN, 1994.

Findlay, G. G. *The Expositor's Greek Testament.* Wm. B. Eerdman's Publishing Company, Grand Rapids, MI, reprinted 1990.

Free, Joseph. *Archaeology and Bible History.* Zondervan Publishing House, Grand Rapids, MI, 1982.

Fudge, Edward. *The Fire that Consumes.* iUniverse Publishing Company, Bloomington, IN, 2000.

Graeser, Mark, John A. Lynn, and John Schoenheit. *Don't Blame God!* The Living Truth Fellowship, Indianapolis IN, 2011.

Graeser, Mark, John A. Lynn, and John Schoenheit. *Is There Death After Life?* The Living Truth Fellowship, Indianapolis IN, 2011.

Graeser, Mark, John A. Lynn, and John Schoenheit. *One God & One Lord: Reconsidering the Cornerstone of the Christian Faith.* The Living Truth Fellowship, Indianapolis IN, 2011.

Hastings, James. *A Dictionary of the Bible.* Hendrickson Publishers, Peabody, MA, originally published by T. & T. Clark, Edinburgh, 1898, reprinted in 1988.

Keil, C. F. and F. Delitzsch. *Commentary on the Old Testament: Minor Prophets.* William B. Eerdmans Publishing Company, Grand Rapids, MI, reprinted 1975.

Liardon, Roberts. *God's Generals.* Whitaker House, New Kensington, PA, 1996.

Liddell, Henry and Robert Scott. *A Greek-English Lexicon.* Oxford University Press, NY, 1992.

Lenski, R. C. H. *The Interpretation of I and II Corinthians.* Augsburg Publishing House, Minneapolis, MN, 1963.

Lenski, R. C. H. *The Interpretation of St. John's Gospel.* Augsburg Publishing House, Minneapolis, MN, 1961.

Lenski, R. C. H. *The Interpretation of St. Paul's Epistle to the Romans.* Augsburg Publishing House, Minneapolis, MN, reprinted 1961.

Lynn, John A. *What is True Baptism?* The Living Truth Fellowship, Indianapolis IN, 2010.

Marshall, Howard, editor. *New Bible Dictionary.* Intervarsity Press, Downers Grove, IL, 1997.

Mazar, Benjamin. *The Mountain of the Lord*. Doubleday and Company, Inc., New York, 1975.

McGee, J. Vernon. *Thru the Bible with J. Vernon McGee*. Thomas Nelson Publishers, Nashville, TN, 1982.

Metzger, Bruce. *A Textual Commentary on the Greek New Testament*. United Bible Societies, Germany, 1975.

Meyer, Joyce. *How to Hear from God*. Warner Faith, USA, 2003.

Morgridge, Charles. *The True Believer's Defense*. Boston, 1873. Reprinted by Spirit & Truth Fellowship International, Martinsville, IN, 1994.

Plummer, Alfred, and Archibald Robertson. *The International Critical Commentary: 1 Corinthians*. T&T Clark, Edinburg.

Rachovian Catechism, The. Reprinted by Spirit & Truth Fellowship International, Martinsville, IN, 1994.

Robertson, A. T. *Word Pictures in the New Testament*. Baker Book House, Grand Rapids, MI, reprinted 1960.

Smith, William. *Smith's Dictionary of the Bible*. Baker Book House, Grand Rapids, MI, reprinted 1981.

Strong, James. *The New Strong's Expanded Dictionary of Bible Words*. Thomas Nelson Publisher, Nashville, TN, 2001.

Styles, J. E. *The Gift of the Holy Spirit*. Fleming H. Revell Company, Old Tappan, NJ, 1971.

Thayer, Joseph H. *Thayer's Greek-English Lexicon of the New Testament*. Hendrickson Publishers, Inc., Peabody, MA, reprinted 2000.

Tenney, Merrill, editor. *The Zondervan Pictorial Encyclopedia of the Bible*. Regency Reference Library, Grand Rapids, MI, 1976.

Trench, Richard. *Synonyms of the New Testament*. Baker Book House, Grand Rapids, MI, 1989.

Vincent, Marvin. *Vincent's Word Studies in the New Testament*. Hendrickson Publishers, Peabody, MA.

Vine, W. E. *The Expanded Vine's Expository Dictionary of New Testament Words*. Bethany House Publishers, Minneapolis, MN, 1984.

Webster, Noah. *American Dictionary of the English Language*. Foundation for American Christian Education, San Francisco, CA, 1828.

Welch, Charles. *Just and the Justifier*. The Berean Publishing Trust, London.

Welch, Troy. *Bible Doctrine 102: A Syllabus*. Channel Island Bible College and Seminary, Oxnard, CA.

Zodhiates, Spiros, The Complete Word Study Dictionary New Testament. AMG Publishers, Chattanooga, TN, 1992

Scripture Index

Topical Index

Index of English Transliterations of the Hebrew and Greek

Hebrew (with English translations)

adonai: "God, Lord, Almighty," 9

el: "God, Lord, Almighty," 9

elohim: "God, Lord, Almighty," 9

elyon: "God, Lord, Almighty," 9

mal'ak: "messenger," 151

mashach: "to anoint," 70

mashiach: "anointed," 70

ruach: "breath, wind, spirit," 7n. 2, 237

shaddai: "God, Lord, Almighty," 9, 9n. 8

Yahweh: "LORD" 9, 9n. 7, 39, 236

Greek (with English translations)

aggelos: "messenger," 151, 151n. 3

allos: "another," 89–91, 125, 125n. 12, 126

ana: "again," 197

anagennao: "born again," 197

apokueo: "birth," 198

arrabon: "guarantee, guaranteeing, pledge, earnest," 58, 137, 137n. 7, 202

baptismos: "immersions, baptisms," 76

charismata: "gifts," 117, 118

chrio: "to anoint," 70

christos: "anointed one," 70

christou: "Christ," 215

daimonizomai: "demonize," 247

de: "but or now," 118

dechomai: "receive," 51, 51n, 52

dia: "through," 120

diairesis: "distributions," 117n. 4

diakrisis: "discerning," 107

doma: "gifts," 18n. 7

dorea: "gift," 15, 17

dunamai: "to be powerful, to be able," 141

dunamis: "powerfully," 168

ekporeuomai: "to go forth, or out, to depart," 61n. 23

en: "by," 120

energemata: "energizings," 74

energeo: "energizes," 74

epi: "upon," 40

epipipto: "falls upon, happens to, occurs in," 51n

genesis: "origin, beginning, birth," 197

gennao: "born," 197

hagion: "holy," 1, 11, 11n, 13–16, 15n. 2, 15n. 4, 19n. 10, 20, 21, 24, 28n. 8, 31, 32, 34, 35, 214, 215, 231, 232

hagios: "holy/saints," 11, 57

heis: "one," 120

hekastos: "each," 122n. 7

heteros: "different one," 89–91, 125, 125n. 12, 126

hexis: "practice," 176n. 5

hodegeo: "it will guide," 36

huiothesia: "adoption," 199

kainos: "new (new in quality)," 205

kata: "because of," 89n. 3, 115n. 2, 120

kathaper gar: "for just as," or "for even as," or "for as," 123n

koilia: "belly," 68n. 3

kome: "village," 33

kruptos: "secret, secular secret," 186, 186n. 12

ktisis: "creation," 205

lambano: "receive," 51–53, 51n

logos: "word," 34, 95, 198n

louo: "to bathe," 76

luchnos: "lamp," 32

musterion: "Sacred Secret," 134, 182–186, 184n. 9, 184n. 10, 185n, 186n. 13, 188, 188n

neos: "new (new in time)," 205

nipto: "washings," 76

oinos: "wine," 33

paliggenesia: "rebirth," 197

palin: "again, anew," 197

pantokrator: "almighty," 9n. 8

parakletos: "counselor, helper, comforter, advocate, friend," 33, 33n. 5, 35n, 61, 61n. 21, 241

phanerosis: "manifestation," 87

phero: "to bring or to carry," 173, 174

pimplemi: "filled," 82n

pistis: "trust, confidence, assurance," 100

pleroo: "filled," 82n

pletho: "filled," 82n

pluno: "washings," 76

pneo: "to blow or breath," 6

pneuma: "spirit, breath, wind," 1, 6–8, 7n. 2, 11–16, 11n, 15n. 2, 15n. 4, 19n. 10, 20, 21, 24, 28n. 8, 31–35, 34n. 7, 37, 62n. 26, 106n.16, 172n, 213–220, 213n, 231, 232

pneumata: "spirits," 217

pneuma hagion: "holy spirit," 11, 11n, 13–16, 15n. 2, 15n. 4, 19n. 10, 20, 21, 24, 28n. 8, 31, 32, 34, 35, 214, 231, 232

pneumatikos/pneumatikon: "spiritual things or spiritual matters," 111n, 113

polin: "city," 33

psuche: "soul," 217, 217n

rhema: "word," 34

suke: "fig tree," 33

theou: "God," 215

What Is The Living Truth Fellowship?

The Living Truth Fellowship is an international community of Christian believers connected by the love of God, the spirit of God, and a common belief of the truth as it is revealed in the written Word of God. We desire to make known that truth to as many people as possible. As a legal entity, we are a non-profit, tax-exempt United States (Indiana) corporation: The Living Truth Fellowship, Ltd.

The name of our ministry contains an intentional double entendre. The Word of God is the truth (John 17:17), and because it contains the very life of God (Eph. 4:18), it is the living truth (John 6:63; Heb. 4:12). As such, the word "living" is an adjective. But God intends that His truth be practiced, that is, He wants us to make "living" a verb by being living epistles of His truth. In that sense, being "verbal" means more than just speaking the Word; it also means doing it.

Our Father desires that we put His truth in our "inner parts" (Ps. 51:6) so that we might not sin against Him (Ps. 119:11). God looks on the heart of each person, and He does not measure the quality of one's life by how much Bible he knows, but by how much knowledge of the truth he practices in his relationships, that is, how much of the heart of God does he manifest. We can objectively measure the quality of our lives by the quality of our relationships with people (Mark 12:28–31; 1 John 4:20 and 21).

Jesus Christ is our supreme example. In John 17:17, he said: "your word is truth," and he exerted a lifelong effort to learn it precisely. But Jesus also LIVED the truth so flawlessly that he could say, I AM the truth (John 14:6). In other words, he BE true. And those are the two sides of the coin of truth, if you will: doctrinal and practical, propositional and relational. Without both sides, that coin won't spend, that is, people won't "buy" what we have to offer.

Our mission is to provide accurate biblical teaching so as to make known the Lord Jesus Christ, The Living Truth, and thus facilitate a worldwide community of mature Christians committed to following him by living the truth of God's Word and sharing it with others.

We accomplish that mission by way of live teachers, camps and conferences for all ages and categories of people, books, newsletters, audio and video teachings, and internet outreach via our website. Those who choose to partake of and participate in these aspects of our ministry are free to utilize our resources as they see fit, whether by starting their own local fellowship or using our work in an already established group of Christians. Our goal is to provide avenues for individual Christians to exercise their unique callings in the Body of Christ.

The basis of all our belief and practice is the Bible, which is the revealed Word of God, flawless in its original writing by those 40 or so believers who wrote during a period of about 1500 years "...*as they were* moved by the Holy Spirit" (2 Pet. 1:21-NKJV). An honest look at the Bible reveals a coherence that is impossible for those writers to have achieved by collaboration. So-called "errors" or "contradictions" are due to man's subsequent interference in the transmission of the text, or to mistranslations, or to misunderstandings of what is written. We seek truth rather than the religious traditions of men.

Our goal in setting forth the Scriptures is to enable each believer to understand them for himself so he can develop his own convictions, become an effective communicator of God's Word, and fulfill his individual ministry in the Body of Christ. Jesus said that knowing the truth would set one free (John 8:32), and our teachings have practical benefit in terms of one's quality of life—spiritually, mentally, emotionally, and physically.

One of our goals is to teach the Word to "...faithful men who are able to teach others also" (2 Tim. 2:2 - NKJV). We plan to produce seminars and courses of study whereby those who so choose can become able ministers of the Gospel of Jesus Christ. We will ordain to Christian ministry those whom our faith community recognizes as meeting this criterion, whether by training in our ministry or via an ordination they received elsewhere that we recognize.

Further Study Material

Other Books, Booklets, and Audio Teaching Seminars available from:

The Living Truth Fellowship
7399 N. Shadeland Ave., Suite 252
Indianapolis IN 46250
Phone # (317) 721-4046
Email: admin@tltf.org
Website: www.tltf.org
YouTube Channel: www.youtube.com/justtruthit

Books

One God & One Lord: Reconsidering the Cornerstone of the Christian Faith

Is There Death After Life?

Don't Blame God! A Biblical Answer to the Problem of Evil, Sin, and Suffering

Booklets

Beyond a Reasonable Doubt—23 Arguments for the Historical Validity of the Resurrection of Jesus Christ

How to Eliminate Apparent Bible Contradictions

23 Reasons to Believe in a Rapture before the Great Tribulation

25 Reasons Why Salvation is Permanent for Christians

34 Reasons Why the Holy Spirit is Not a Separate "Person" From the Only True God, The Father

47 Reasons Why our Heavenly Father has no Equals or "Co-Equals"

What Is True Baptism?

Audio Teaching Seminars on our website:

Romans (18 hrs)

Jesus Christ, the Diameter of the Ages (6 hrs)

Related Audio Teaching on our website:

<u>King of the Mountain</u> **(Dec 03)**

This teaching shows that Jesus Christ is called "god" in the Bible meaning that he is the first and only man who ever perfectly represented his heavenly Father, the one true God, to mankind. In the Hebrew culture, human beings designated by God to represent him in service to His people were called "gods." Following that thread through Scripture, the incredible precision and integrity of God's Word is evident concerning who Jesus Christ is and what he will be and do when he becomes "King of the Mountain" during his Millennial Kingdom.

CPSIA information can be obtained
at www.ICGtesting.com
Printed in the USA
LVOW09*1447050117

519873LV00012B/183/P